The Key to "Revelation"

VOLUME II

The Key to "Revelation"

VOLUME II

Stephen Kaung

CHRISTIAN FELLOWSHIP PUBLISHERS, INC.
NEW YORK

Christian Fellowship Publishers, Inc.
New York

ISBN: 978-1-68062-083-2

Available from the Publishers at:

11515 Allecingie Parkway
Richmond, Virginia 23235
www.c-f-p.com

Printed in the United States of America

PREFACE (from Volume I)

The book of Revelation is the last of the sixty-six books of the Bible. As such, it is the concluding word of God and therefore occupies a special position. Whereas a blessing is attached to its reading, a curse is pronounced against anyone adding to its text—thus reflecting how very important is this book of God's word.

The content of this present work, which will be two volumes in length, comprises the text of what were two separate series of messages on Revelation spoken by the author in, respectively, the year 2007 and back during the 1950s. After these many years, and inasmuch as we sense the return of the Lord Jesus to be increasingly imminent, we believe that there is a need to make these spoken words available in print in order that many more of God's people may receive the promised blessing.

The reader will therefore find that this two-volume work when fully published will consist of four Parts. The messages of Part One, The Revelation of Jesus Christ, were delivered (and audio-taped for later possible publication) on 12 to 14 July 2007 at the Western Christian Conference held on the campus of Biola University, Los Angeles, California. The messages comprising the other three Parts—The Testimony of Jesus in Relation to: the Church, the World, and the Jews—were spoken over a lengthy period of time during the decade of the 1950s as a series of weekly Bible studies on the book of Revelation. They were shared by the author before a group of Christians who gathered together in Jamaica, Queens, New York City. It should be noted that the text source for these studies was a series of extensive notes which had been written down by a sister in the Lord who had attended these studies and which had then been transcribed in typewritten form by her as well. It should also be noted that in preparing these transcriptions for today's publication, this entire book's text has been extensively edited, and further, that numerous additional Scripture verses—both texts and/or citations thereof—have been inserted here and there where deemed necessary and/or helpful to the reader.

It is our prayer that all who shall read this book will receive God's blessing in their being better prepared for the imminent return to the earth of our blessed Lord Jesus Christ.

CHRISTIAN FELLOWSHIP PUBLISHERS

Contents—Volume II

Unless otherwise indicated,
Scripture quotations are from the
New Translation by J. N. Darby.

Part Three
The Testimony of Jesus:
in Relation to the World

Chapter One

The Testimony towards the World

And I saw on the right hand of him that sat upon the throne a book, written within and on the back, sealed with seven seals. And I saw a strong angel proclaiming with a loud voice, Who is worthy to open the book, and to break its seals? And no one was able in the heaven, or upon the earth, or underneath the earth, to open the book, or to regard it. And I wept much because no one had been found worthy to open the book nor to regard it. And one of the elders says to me, Do not weep. Behold, the lion which is of the tribe of Juda, the root of David, has overcome so as to open the book, and its seven seals.

And I saw in the midst of the throne and of the four living creatures, and in the midst of the elders, a Lamb standing, as slain, having seven horns and seven eyes, which are the seven Spirits of God which are sent into all the earth: and it came and took it out of the right hand of him that sat upon the throne. And when it took the book, the four living creatures and the twenty-four elders fell before the Lamb, having each a harp and golden bowls full of incenses, which are the prayers of the saints. And they sing a new song, saying, Thou art worthy to take the book, and to open its seals; because thou hast been slain, and hast redeemed to God, by thy blood, out of every tribe, and tongue, and people, and nation, and made them

> to our God kings and priests; and they shall reign over the earth.
>
> And I saw, and I heard the voice of many angels around the throne and the living creatures and the elders; and their number was ten thousands of ten thousands and thousands of thousands; saying with a loud voice, Worthy is the Lamb that has been slain, to receive power, and riches, and wisdom, and strength, and honour, and glory, and blessing. And every creature which is in the heaven and upon the earth and under the earth, and those that are upon the sea, and all things in them, heard I saying, To him that sits upon the throne, and to the Lamb, blessing, and honour, and glory, and might, to the ages of ages. And the four living creatures said, Amen; and the elders fell down and did homage.
>
> Revelation 5:1-14

During the past few weeks we have been considering together one important matter: the testimony of Jesus. And our key verse has been, and continues to be, Revelation 19:10—"the spirit of prophecy is the testimony of Jesus." We have been emphasizing again and again that there is nothing more important to God than the testimony of Jesus. This is His chief concern, and it ought to be our main concern as well. The testimony of Jesus is the spirit of prophecy, and that testimony is today deposited especially in the church; or we may put it another way: the church is the vessel of, and instrument for, the testimony of Jesus. And heretofore we have spent considerable time fellowshiping together on the testimony of Jesus in relation to the church or on the church in relation to the testimony of Jesus.

And today it is my sense that we should go further forward and by the grace of God come to see and understand something of the testimony of Jesus in relation to the world or, to phrase it another way, come to see and understand something concerning the testimony of Jesus towards the world.

First of all, however, let me explain what the word world means within the context of what I wish to share in our time together today. By the word world I mean not only this physical earth on which we dwell—the word certainly includes that—but I also mean by the word world all the inhabitants that dwell upon this earth and whose chief inhabitants are man. By this same word world I mean as well to include the cosmos—the world as an organized system. The word world is likewise meant to include not only the earth but also its immediate surroundings. This word world includes all other creatures besides man—those such as the fowls of the air, the fish of the sea, and all the animals living on the earth. It thus means our entire universe; or, if you so wish, you can enlarge the meaning of the word world to encompass all of creation—with of course man constituting the center of God's creation on earth.

Let us therefore understand that when that word world is used in our discussion today it includes everything just now mentioned; but our main attention will of course be centered upon this earth, and especially upon man as being the chief inhabitants of the earth. Let me add further, though, that in order for us to understand the testimony of Jesus in relation to the world, we must go back in history to the very beginning of the world. Please therefore bear with me as we go back in time and attempt to provide ourselves with a right setting before engaging in a discussion on the relevant passage in the book of Revelation that was read out just moments ago and which shall be the focus of our fellowship together for today.

Now if we turn back from the Bible's concluding book—Revelation—to its very first book—Genesis—we will no doubt recall that from this first book's opening verses we learned that at the very beginning God had perfectly created the heavens and the earth. But we also learned that subsequent to God's creation, the earth underwent a catastrophic change. What occurred was that the earth fell into formlessness and desolation, was entirely covered with water, and was engulfed in total darkness everywhere. In brief, the earth was plunged into complete chaos from its earlier perfectly created habitable state.

We do not know how long this chaotic condition lasted, but we thank God that the Bible tells us in those same opening verses that the Spirit of God commenced brooding and moving over the water, and through the warmth and the love and the energy of God's Spirit the earth was restored once again to a habitable state. The chaos was changed back into a cosmos—that is, back into an orderly system; and in six days thereafter God restored the earth as a place that could be inhabited by all kinds of living things and creatures, with the sixth day having been devoted by God to the creation of man. In fact, on that day He created man in His own image and after His likeness. Yes, God used the reddish clay soil of the earth and formed it into the shape of a man that was called man. And God then breathed into the nostrils of man, and this breath of His that entered man became the spirit of man; and because that breath was now in this body of clay, man became a living soul as a result (1:3-28a, 2:7).

God created man in His own image, after His likeness; and immediately after God had created man He blessed him. He said to the man: Be fruitful and multiply and fill the earth and have dominion over the fowls of the air and the fish of the sea and over all the animals and creeping things upon the earth (1:23-24). In other words, God made this earth as a place not only for man to dwell in and enjoy all its richness and fullness but as a place also upon which God put man in order for him to have dominion rule over all the created things on God's behalf. That is to say, man was intended by God to be the prince regent or governor-general of the entire world. That is to say, God placed the world in the hands of man for him to dwell there and subdue and govern all things and bring all things back to God's rightful possession as Creator and for His glory. So let us first of all be reminded of this, that man was created in God's image and was commissioned to govern the earth and this world for His glory.

In this connection, Psalm 8 of David is most appropriate here for us to revisit and review. In this song of his David sang about the following things: "What is man that thou, O Lord, art mindful of him? and the son of man, that thou visitest him? Thou hast made him a little lower than the angels, and hast crowned him with glory and splendor. Thou hast made him to rule over the works of thy hand; thou hast put everything under his feet: sheep and oxen, and also the beasts of the field; the fowl of the heavens, and the fishes of the sea, whatever passeth through the paths of the seas" (vv. 4-8).

Here we are told that God has made man a little lower than, or a little inferior to, the angels. The angels are spiritual beings, but man has a body and a soul and a spirit, according to the very order of creation as explained in Genesis. Man has been made a little lower than angels and yet God has crowned him with glory and honor and has put all things of the earth into his hands. And why? Let us notice that at the very beginning of this same psalm the psalmist declared this: Jehovah, our Lord, how excellent is Thy name in all the earth; and at the very end of his psalm he declared again: Jehovah, our Lord, how excellent is Thy name in all the earth; but in between this twin-declaration David was moved to sing that out of the mouths of babes and sucklings Thou, O Lord, hast established strength because of Thine enemies, to silence the foe and the avenger.

We know that once upon a time long, long ago God had created the heavens and the earth, and that it was totally perfect (for would He make anything imperfect?); and at that time God had placed all the works of His creation into the hands of the angels. He had entrusted them with the rule and government of His entire creation and to be undertaken by them for His glory.

One day, however, the archangel—named Lucifer (meaning "the bright morning star") and described in Scripture as the beauty of all creation—began to have pride in his heart (Isaiah 14:12-14). He wanted to rise up and be equal with God and even overthrow God, and the result was that he was eventually driven out of heaven (Ezekiel 28:16). He fell and ultimately became known as the devil, and who has variously been called Satan, the adversary, and wicked one. It was this fallen archangel, in fact, who was the author of the world's catastrophic alteration from its perfect habitable state of creation to a state of complete uninhabitable desolation and chaos. All fell that was under his control on the earth and the immediate surroundings and parts.

Nevertheless, as we were reminded earlier from Genesis, God restored the earth to a condition of habitation and did not entrust the earth to angels again but thereafter entrusted it to man—to him whom the psalmist had termed as being a little inferior to angels. For God's purpose was now to use the inferior in teaching a lesson to the superior. Let us understand from this that so far as the chronology of events in Creation is concerned, man is the babe and suckling in the order of creation; and yet, out of the mouths of babes and sucklings, sang David the psalmist, there shall come forth praise to God for the adversary's benefit—which is to say, that God will use man the inferior one to defeat the fallen superior one, who is the devil.

Unfortunately, however, here is when the tragedy of world history began. The enemy, having been created one of the archangels with higher intelligence than man, realized that man was destined by God to replace him and to be the instrument in His hand to overthrow his kingdom of darkness; accordingly, the enemy subtly tempted man into disobeying God, and thus man rebelled against God. Having fallen into sin, man now fell into the hand of Satan; and he, along with man as his accomplice, plunged the whole world into another chaotic phase.

Today, Satan the devil is called the ruler, or prince, of this world (John 12:31). In fact, even Jesus while on earth had noted that "the ruler of this world comes, and in me he has nothing" (John 14:30b). Even so, Satan took the world out of the hands of man, having usurped the place of man as the prince regent of God's created world. This, then, constitutes the background and setting for what we are so well aware of as the tragic story of this world. As a matter of fact, this will perhaps answer many questions which may have been in our minds: Why so much sorrow? Why so much violence? Why so much wickedness? Why so much sin? Why this and why that? The overall answer to these and many other similar questions is that the whole world now lies under the domination of the wicked one, and, therefore, what else can anyone expect than what has occurred in this world as a result?

But let us wake up and not be any longer unaware that though Satan is today the god and ruler of this world, he nonetheless came into this rulership not through any legitimate right of benefit but through the subtle, manipulative means of temptation and ultimate usurpation. Because of Adam's failure to defeat the tempter's test, man—and with him, all of creation—states the Bible, is today under corruption and vanity (Ecclesiastes 1:2); and this is not what all of creation has appreciated or liked. But through that one failed man all of creation—the entire universe—has been brought into subjection to vanity and frustration. In fact, the whole creation is now in bondage to decay and corruption; indeed, ever since the failure of that one man Adam the whole creation has lain in a state of abject vanity, purposelessness, disharmonious relationships, and gradual, but total, disintegration; moreover, it is because of man that all of creation fell with man into that further chaotic phase of the world's tragic history. Nevertheless, the whole of creation, including redeemed mankind, has been groaning and groaning as in the pains of childbirth for the coming day of the manifestation of the sons of God, and then all creation shall be delivered from its bondage to corruption and brought into the freedom of the children of God (Romans 8:19-23).

Though that first man of the earth, Adam, fell—and with him God's whole creation, there came a day when God sent from heaven into the world the second man, and the second man is the Lord Jesus (I Corinthians 15:47), who is the incarnation of very God himself; as it is written, the Word became flesh and temporarily tabernacled among man (John 1:14a), for when Jesus, the Son of God, came into this world, He came as a man, just as the book of Hebrews in its chapter 2 makes clear in much detail and quoting from that now familiar Psalm 8 of David's and referencing its verses to the man Jesus himself:

> What is man, that thou, O Lord God, rememberest him or the son of man that thou visitest him? Thou hast made him a little inferior to the angels; thou hast crowned him with glory and honor, and hast subjected all things under his feet. Now in subjecting all things under him, God has left nothing unsubjected; but now we see not yet all things subjected to him; but we see Jesus, who was made a little inferior to angels, on account of the sufferings of death, now crowned with glory and honor; so that by the grace of God he should taste death for everyone; for it was fitting that God, for whom are all things and by whom are all things, in bringing many sons to glory, should make perfect the leader of their salvation through sufferings (see vv. 6b-10).

What God had not obtained in the first man Adam He has now obtained through the second man Jesus. Yes, Jesus is very God, but He is also very man. He is God but He came into our world to be a man, and His name is Jesus. We know that the name Jesus means Savior, and He shall save His people from their sins (Matthew 1:21). It is His earthly name, and that name reveals the fact that He is a man. In one very significant sense Jesus in His earthly life was a man like you and me: He had a physical body with flesh and blood; and yet He is different because though He was tempted in all things, He was without any sin while on earth. The Son of God as the Son of man bore the sweet name of Jesus.

God the Father sent into this world His Son Jesus—the second man—and concerning that man it is said that by God's grace He, Jesus, has tasted death and the suffering of death for everyone. We have not yet seen all things brought into subjection to Jesus, but we have come to see that He—the second man—has tasted the suffering of death for all people and all things. And by that death the second man is in the process of reconciling all things back to God, and we who believe in Him are the firstfruits of His redemption.

Who is this Jesus to the world? To the world He was and still remains just a man from the obscure Judean town of Nazareth. To the world He was a commoner, even a blasphemer claiming He is God. The world would not have Jesus but rejected Him and crucified Him, not knowing that this very man was, and still is, heir to the entire world. The world of men today still rejects Jesus and will not have Him as king over them. And Psalm 2 explains the reason, first rhetorically asking: "Why are the nations in tumultuous agitation and why do the people meditate against the Lord? The kings of the world take their stand and the princes gather together against Jehovah and against His Anointed One." The latter, of course, would be Jesus. The psalm continues, indicating the thoughts and words of those in opposition to Jehovah God and His Anointed: "Let us break their bands asunder and cast away their cords from us." Oh how the world continues to want to throw off any rule or authority of the Lord Jesus and will not have Him over it. But the One enthroned in heaven, writes the psalmist, shall laugh and the Lord shall scoff at them in derision. Then, continues the psalm further, He will speak to them in His anger, and His severe displeasure will terrify them, the Lord Jehovah declaring: "I have anointed my King upon Zion, the hill of My holiness." The psalmist then writes that he will proclaim the decree of Jehovah, who said to His Anointed King: "You are My Son; I this day have begotten You. Ask of Me and I will give You the nations for an inheritance and the ends of the earth for Your possession. You shall rule them with a scepter of iron; You shall dash them to pieces like pottery."

Hence, we can say that the testimony of Jesus in relation to the world is essentially this: the Lord Jesus is Heir to all the world and King over all in it. It does not matter whether you recognize Him as Heir and King or not, whether you confess Him as Lord or not, whether you bow your knee to Him or not; for Scripture declares that a day is coming when every knee shall bow and every tongue confess that Jesus is Lord (Philippians 2:10-11a). You are blessed if today you have already confessed Jesus as your Lord and have willingly bowed your knee to Him. If you have not and you do not intend to, then one day you will be forced to do so, because the decree has already been proclaimed that God's Anointed—even Jesus—is King of kings and Lord of lords (Revelation 17:14b, 19:16; cf. Philippians 2:9-11). Such, then, is the testimony of Jesus in relation to this world.

With all that as background and the establishment of the relevant setting, I would like for us to turn to the book of Revelation. As was discussed earlier, its first three chapters cover the first vision given to John, which was that of the seven golden lampstands and in their midst the glorified Son of man; and we were given to understand that this vision was concerned with the testimony of Jesus in relation to the church. And following that vision there came forth the Son of man's call for overcomers to arise in the church, with the mission of overcomers to be none other than to maintain the testimony of Jesus.

We today come next to the second vision of this book. We read at the beginning of the fourth chapter of Revelation that John heard the same voice as at the first, which now said to him to come up; and John was taken up in the Spirit, and there he saw a door which opened into heaven. And he saw in the heaven of heavens a throne and upon the throne one sitting who had the appearance of jasper and sardonyx. Next, John saw a rainbow around the throne which resembled an emerald, and surrounding the throne he saw twenty-four other thrones with twenty-four elders sitting on the thrones and robed in white and with golden crowns upon their heads. John also saw before the throne seven lamps burning, day and night, which are the seven Spirits of God; and underneath the throne there was what looked like a sea of glass that was clear as crystal. The apostle also beheld four living creatures dashing in and out and around the throne and who were crying aloud: "Holy, holy, holy is the Lord God Almighty, who was, and is, and is to come." And as they were praising and giving thanks and glory to the Enthroned One, those twenty-four elders fell down in worship to the One on the throne who lives forever and ever. Moreover, these elders were seen by John laying their crowns before Him who was seated on the throne and saying: "You are worthy, our Lord and God, to receive glory and honor and power, for You created all things, and by Your will they were created and have their being."

All this, however, was only part of that second vision. The second part is to be found in chapter 5 of Revelation. I do not intend dwelling upon the fourth chapter, even though to me it is very, very interesting; nevertheless, allow me to say just this much today, with perhaps more to be said about it next time we gather. In chapter 4's vision John was shown the glory of God as the Creator of all creation, and he heard what is often referred to as "the Song of Creation." That vision and that song indicate the fact that all things have been created by God and all things were created for His will.

Oh how we ourselves—like John—need to have a vision of the glory of our Creator. We need to realize afresh that all things have been created by God; but more than just that: we also need to realize that all things have been created *for His will.* The question therefore naturally arises: Do all of us present here today know and acknowledge that we have been created by God? And if we do, do we realize that we have been created for His will? We ourselves are not the center of our existence. If we make ourselves the center, we will very soon discover how empty, purposeless and meaningless our life truly is. We have been created for God and for the fulfillment of His will and purpose. First and foremost, we have been created according to the pleasure of His will. Hence, if we make God the center of our life, we will discover how purposeful and meaningful our life is. If, however, we live a life simply for ourselves, we miss the very purpose of our creation. Little wonder, then, that so many people on this earth live a purposeless, meaningless life.

I next wish for us to enter into the second part of Revelation’s second vision. The apostle John reported that he saw a book in the right hand of the Enthroned One. The book which He held in His right hand had writing on both sides, and the book was sealed with seven seals. John next reported that he saw a mighty angel proclaiming something in a loud voice. Why was the angel doing so in a loud voice? Because this voice must be heard throughout the universe—not only in heaven but on earth and even under the earth. Every created thing must hear that voice, which proclaimed this: “Who is worthy to take the book and open its seals?” And John reported and lamented greatly that no one was found worthy: no one in heaven, no one on earth, and no one under the earth: neither man nor angel was found worthy to take the book, open its seven seals, or look inside. When John became aware of this circumstance, he wept much. Indeed, confided the apostle: "I wept and wept because no one was found worthy."

Why is this sealed book so important that all of creation needed to hear the angelic proclamation concerning it? And why is it that when John discovered that no one throughout the world was qualified to receive the book, open its seals, or even look inside it, he wept so very much? With respect to John's reaction, I would observe that no one weeps until and unless a person has been reduced to hopeless desperation. In a given situation or circumstance you come to realize that you cannot do anything about it and yet you want to do something about it but find yourself so frustrated that you can do nothing but weep over the situation. And here we learn that the apostle John wept very much. On the other hand, with respect to this book's importance, I feel led to say this, that it must symbolize or stand for something tremendously important; for if this book were not extremely significant and important, there would have been no need for that mighty angel to challenge the whole universe with his loudly-voiced proclamation nor would there have been any need for John to weep and weep over the inability of anyone in the universe to take the book and to open its seals. What, therefore, is that book?

In giving answer to that question, I wish at first to state that though there is a need for me to explain somewhat, it will not be another exposition. Indeed, my purpose in this series of messages is not to give you an exposition on the book of Revelation but to discover and to demonstrate what I believe is Revelation's governing principle, which is, the testimony of Jesus.

Having said that, I must here acknowledge that we have now arrived at a most crucial point in our discussion today regarding the testimony of Jesus in relation to the world. We see in this vision that the book is in the hands of the Creator of the world, and we are told that a challenge has been issued to that entire world, but nobody was found qualified to answer the challenge, and consequently John wept uncontrollably. We may say that in one sense John represents the church spiritually. This is because spiritually speaking, the church is weeping because she is concerned with this book and what it signifies. If the highly respected apostle John was concerned about this book, should we not be concerned about it as well? What, then, is it? Well, some say it is the book of Revelation itself. Certainly this part of Revelation, covering as it does the seven seals, the seven trumpets, and the seven vials or bowls—is the outcome of that book; for all of that constitutes the central skeleton of the book of Revelation. Personally, however, I believe this book which figures so prominently in Revelation 5 represents much more than that.

Most commentators agree with what I am about to suggest by way of interpretation; and if you do not agree with it, that is perfectly alright. I readily acknowledge that a given interpretation on this or that matter may or may not be what the Bible says. I certainly believe the Bible—all of it—but I do not need to be dogmatic about my interpretation on any given matter; therefore, you are free to have your own interpretations so long as they do not bring dishonor to the Lord. But in order that we may see the aforementioned principle, let me put forward for your consideration what I believe the sealed book in question is in its essence. I lay it before you by way of suggestion, so please do not go out from here and say that brother Kaung said that his interpretation is it. No, I have not said that; I am simply suggesting.

Let me therefore suggest that this book which the apostle saw in the right hand of God the Creator is the title deed to the entire creation of the earth and universe. It is common knowledge that if you buy a house, a field, or some other kind of property, you are given a title to it in the form of a book, a scroll, or some such legal paper document; and that grants you the legal rights to the field or to the house or to whatever it may be which you have purchased or come into possession of. And in olden days, such title document was usually sealed. So in reference to this book of chapter 5, it is the title deed to the entire world. And whoever possesses this book is the owner of what the inside of the book has described. You may attempt at being a squatter and proceed to erect your tent or construct a house or other structure upon a plot of land or utilize the land in some other way; but eventually you will be driven out because you do not possess the title to the land. You may have been a usurper but you were never the owner.

Let us now apply that situation to all the world of God's creation. Has not Satan become the usurper of the earth? He is only a usurper and not the owner. One thing comforts me tremendously when we consider ourselves as redeemed people of God who are part of His creation. And here I am referring to what the Lord Jesus once said: that no one can pluck any of us out of His hand nor out of the Father's hand (John 10:28c-29). No one can, not even Satan. Thank God that we today who believe the Lord are in His hand and there we are safe.

Nevertheless, I am comforted as well that not only I myself am safe in God's hands but that also the whole world is safe, for the title deed to it is in His hands. God is still the owner of the world. By right of creation He is the owner. Hence, whoever may be trying to occupy the earth does not have the legal right to it nor the legal right to this entire universe. All of the world still belongs to God, and one day He will come back in the person of His Son and claim it for himself. Now this I believe is the suggested interpretation and it satisfies me the best.

I return again to the question of why John wept—and why it was that no one was found worthy to take the book and to open its seals. If this book is in fact the title deed to the whole world, then the question of who is worthy to take it is most relevant. Man has tried and tried to be the ruler of the earth without God. So has Satan. Yet no one was found worthy and able. And because of this failure John wept much; for if no one is worthy and no one is able to execute the rights of God over His creation, then what will be the situation in future? The apostle was thrown into deep perplexity and concern as to whether the testimony of Jesus would ever prevail over the earth.

We are living in a world that on the one hand is highly organized and on the other hand is completely chaotic. This is because we live in a world which is under the dominion of the wicked one. We find wickedness, sin, and disharmony in everything most everywhere on this earth. It is most assuredly not a place that, spiritually speaking, we would wish to live in and make it our permanent home. We see many unreasonable—indeed, irrational—things happening all over this world which should not be happening, yet we must acknowledge that such things are occurring all around us. Is there not therefore a cry in our hearts: "Lord, when will You come back and reclaim the world back to the Father? When will Your kingdom come and be established on the earth? Can You, will You, allow this state of affairs to continue indefinitely? Is there not to be a merciful end to this chaotic condition? Must there not be an end to this usurpation by Your archenemy, Satan? When, finally, will Your will be done on earth as it is in heaven?"

This was surely the cry in John's heart; should that not be the cry in our hearts, too? God's word makes clear that we who are His must not be a friend of this world, for if we choose to be friends of the world we become enemies of God (James 4:4). On the one hand we should not be enticed by, and become entangled in, the many things of this earth. Let us not become occupied with, nor set our hearts upon, the things of this world; because if our hearts become entangled in the things of this world, then when the Lord shall come again, we will be so tied down to the earth that we shall be unable to loosen ourselves from its grip and be raptured to heaven. Therefore, on the one hand let us not be worldly-minded: let us live in the world but let us not follow the fashion of the world; instead, let us have the mind and spirit of other-worldliness (cf. Romans 12:2a, b).

On the other hand, shall our interest in the world be limited to only what is related to or concerns ourselves? Is our world only as large as ourselves? We need to realize and acknowledge that even when we are seeking for spirituality, it is nonetheless centered entirely upon ourselves. Is that the extent of your and my world? Quite true, we ought not to be worldly; nevertheless, we must not limit our interest in the world to that which only concerns ourselves, but we must also be concerned for the testimony of Jesus in relation to the rest of the world. We ought to be interested in what the entire world and not merely our little world will become. We should be very much interested in how the kingdom of God can come to this world. In short, we need to be interested in the will of God prevailing over the whole universe.

If the world should continue to be dominated and ruled by the wicked one—if the world should continue in its present trend of plunging deeper and deeper into darkness—can we not, and should we not, be concerned with the concern of God? This is God's world, this is His creation; are we not therefore concerned that His glory be manifested over this earth? We certainly should be. And it was for this reason that John wept and wept. He wept much because his heart was occupied with, and concerned for, the testimony of Jesus in relation to the entire world of God's creation.

If there be but one thing which the Lord would impress upon our hearts as we end our time together today, I pray that it would be this: that we all would have a concern for the testimony of Jesus in relation to this world—that every one of us have an abiding interest in, and concern for, the testimony of Jesus, that it may spread and prevail throughout the world. As to how, we must lead as a church in showing the way.

Chapter Two

The Vision of the Redeemer

And I saw on the right hand of him that sat upon the throne a book, written within and on the back, sealed with seven seals. And I saw a strong angel proclaiming with a loud voice, Who is worthy to open the book, and to break its seals? And no one was able in the heaven, or upon the earth, or underneath the earth, to open the book, or to regard it. And I wept much because no one had been found worthy to open the book nor to regard it. And one of the elders says to me, Do not weep. Behold, the lion which is of the tribe of Juda, the root of David, has overcome so as to open the book, and its seven seals.

And I saw in the midst of the throne and of the four living creatures, and in the midst of the elders, a Lamb standing, as slain, having seven horns and seven eyes, which are the seven Spirits of God which are sent into all the earth: and it came and took it out of the right hand of him that sat upon the throne. And when it took the book, the four living creatures and the twenty-four elders fell before the Lamb, having each a harp and golden bowls full of incenses, which are the prayers of the saints. And they sing a new song, saying, Thou art worthy to take the book, and to open its seals; because thou hast been slain, and hast redeemed to God, by thy blood, out of every tribe, and tongue, and people, and nation, and made them

> to our God kings and priests; and they shall reign over the earth.
>
> And I saw, and I heard the voice of many angels around the throne and the living creatures and the elders; and their number was ten thousands of ten thousands and thousands of thousands; saying with a loud voice, Worthy is the Lamb that has been slain, to receive power, and riches, and wisdom, and strength, and honour, and glory, and blessing. And every creature which is in the heaven and upon the earth and under the earth, and those that are upon the sea, and all things in them, heard I saying, To him that sits upon the throne, and to the Lamb, blessing, and honour, and glory, and might, to the ages of ages. And the four living creatures said, Amen; and the elders fell down and did homage.
>
> Revelation 5:1-14

It has been mentioned previously that the first vision the apostle John saw on the island of Patmos was that of the glorified Son of man standing in the midst of the seven golden lampstands, and that vision speaks to us of the testimony of Jesus in relation to His church. And this vision was the subject of the first three chapters in the book of Revelation. The second vision John saw, however, was recorded in chapters 4 and 5; and I have termed this second vision as the testimony of Jesus in relation to the world.

Now it was noted last time that this second vision has two distinct parts to it. The first part appears in Revelation chapter 4, and there John was given to see the glory of the Creator and to hear "the Song of Creation." And this was briefly discussed in terms of its implications upon our personal walk with the Lord. Though much more could be commented upon regarding this vision's first part, my purpose today is to concentrate further beyond what was said during our last time together on this vision's second part having to do with the glory of the Redeemer and the accompanying Song of Redemption. All this we find recorded in chapter 5 of Revelation.

We will recall from our previous fellowship on Revelation that in this second vision we saw that God the Creator was on the throne and that a rainbow like to an emerald encircled His throne. This reminds us, does it not, of what we are told in the book of Genesis that after the universal flood God made a covenant with Noah, his family, and all living things upon the earth that He would never again destroy the earth by means of a flood; and that further, in order to comfort and reassure the trembling hearts of man as well as show mercy to all birds and animals, God placed a sign upon the clouds to this effect, which was that of a rainbow. This would forever serve as a reminder to God, for He declared: "When I see the rainbow, I will remember my everlasting covenant with man and all the earth" (see 9:8-17). And here in this vision we see God upon His throne and a rainbow surrounding it—thus indicative of the fact that He is a God who remembers His covenant with man and the entire world. Such is the nature and character of the God whom we behold in this remarkable vision: that He remembers His covenant with this world even when He is about to judge that world at the time of the opening of the seven seals which seal the book that He holds in His hand (see later in this series of messages regarding God's judgment).

Now concerning that book which in this second vision the Enthroned One was holding in His right hand, I believe I need to review briefly here what was shared at some length during the previous discussion on the book of Revelation; for it will serve as an essential prelude to what I wish to present for our consideration together today. But as I tried to make clear last time, I wished to suggest what to me is the most satisfying interpretation as regards what this book represents. We are told that the book was written both within and without, and was sealed with seven seals. Now if a book is sealed, then, of course, the seals must be opened in order for what is written there to be seen. And God had the book in His right hand waiting for someone worthy to take it and unseal it. And it was suggested last time that this book represents the title deed to the entire world. God as the Creator of this world is the owner of it and all things in it, including man. And, thus, as Creator and Owner, He rightfully holds the deed to the world in His right hand.

Now the fact that the title deed to the world is shown in the vision to still be in God's hand should be a source of comfort and reassurance to our hearts. For as we witness all the many terrible events happening in the world today that are clearly contrary to the will of God, it may seem to us believers as though God has absented himself from the world, as though He is no longer interested in the world, as though He wants nothing more to do with it and has abandoned the world to the rule of sin, wickedness, and the devil. Is it any wonder, some of us may even have thought, that those who have no faith have declared that God is dead? We can take heart, however, in the fact that, despite all of these terrible and discouraging events in the world, God continues to hold in His hand this book containing the title to the entire world—hence indicating that He has *not* abandoned the world nor yielded up His ownership to it. On the contrary, the world is still His by right of creation; and His throne is upon the earth (this latter statement I shall explain in a later message in this series).

Nevertheless, in the vision the book remained sealed. So, a strong angel stepped forward and loudly proclaimed, asking, Who is worthy to take this book from God's hand, unseal it, and read it? The angel's voice was so strong that it could be heard not only in heaven but also on earth and underneath the earth. In other words, it served as a challenge made to all the created things throughout the world. However, nobody responded to the challenge.

And because of that, the apostle John wept—yet not a little but very much. Why so much weeping on John's part? Because much was, and still is, involved. We know that this world and all created things in it belong to God, but we also know that today the world is under the dominion of the wicked one. It would appear, in fact, that all creation has gone away from God, that men do not want Him but have rebelled against Him—even to the extent that when He sent His Son to this world, they crucified Him. Now how are these two things to be reconciled? On the one hand, the world belongs to God and was created for His purpose and for His glory; and yet, on the other hand, we find that because this earth and the world in general is under the dominance and rule of the wicked one, all created things have seemingly drifted away from God and continue to do so further and further. Consequently, is there any possibility for the two—God and His creation—to be reconciled back together?

In other words, when will be the day that God reclaims the world as His own? When will come the day that God will reconcile the world and all created things back to himself? When will the day arrive when the kingdom of God shall finally be established upon the earth? When shall righteousness be the rule, principle, and law governing this earth? When? For it seems as though God's archenemy—the devil—has such absolute control over man and over all other created things upon this earth, that both morally and spiritually it would appear as though the world shall never return to God nor manifest His glory nor His purpose be fulfilled. If one realizes all of that, then it should come as no surprise that John wept and wept and wept.

From what has been said here we can readily discern that the hope of this world does not lie with people, for no man answered the challenge. No one was worthy or qualified. All hope of reconciliation now seemed impossible for mankind and the rest of creation. At this point, however, one of the twenty-four elders approached John and comforted him by saying: "Do not weep. Behold, the lion which is of the tribe of

Juda, the root of David, has overcome so as to open the book, and its seven seals."

Let us all thank God that there is one—even the lion of the tribe of Judah and the root of David—who has overcome and is able to take the book and open its seals. We of course know well that the lion is the king of all beasts. And lion in Scripture is a symbol of strength and majesty, of power and royalty. We may remember that King Solomon of old had built a throne which had been lined on both sides with twelve lions (I Kings 10:18-20). So lion is a symbolic representation spiritually of power, majesty, authority, and royalty.

"The lion of the tribe of Judah, the root of David." This description of Messiah-Jesus reminds me of the time of Jesus' sojourn on earth when He put one particular question to the Jewish religious leaders of His day. We will recall that the Scribes, Pharisees, Sadducees, Herodians, and lawyers all attempted to entrap the Lord in His words of response to their purposely difficult questions they continually put to Him. Jesus, however, always silenced them with a very good answer. There came a day, though, that He put a follow-up question to them for which they had no answer whatsoever. Now Jesus had at first asked the Pharisees about the Christ as to whose son He is. Every Pharisee of that day, of course, knew that the coming Christ would be the son of David, for this had long been prophesied; and thus they so answered. But Jesus followed up their reply with a further question: How, then, is it that David, in speaking by the Spirit in one of his psalms, calls the Christ "Lord"? For David wrote: "The Lord said to my Lord." If then, added Jesus, David calls the Christ "Lord," how can the Christ be David's son?—thus signifying that the son of David is the Lord of David. How, asked Jesus, is that possible? And none of the Pharisees could answer, and so they were silenced (Matthew 22:41-46, quoting Psalm 110:1).

Yes, the Lord Jesus came out of David (Matthew 1:1, 16; Luke 1;27b, 32b); nevertheless, He is also the root of David.

David was the king of Israel, but Christ is the King of kings and Lord of lords (Revelation 17:14b, 19:16). Thus Jesus is both the son of David and David's Lord. He is symbolized here in the words of this elder as being the Lion of the tribe of Judah. He who was trampled upon by others' feet while on earth is one day to put everyone and everything under His own feet. The Lord Jesus, who was despised in his days of humiliation, is to be the King of majesty over all the world. Christ Jesus has overcome; and, therefore, He can be hailed as the Lion of Judah.

Let us closely notice, however, that when John looked up from his weeping, he did not see a lion but saw a lamb. He saw a lamb as slain standing in the midst of the throne and of the four living creatures and of all the elders. Is that not strange? He heard the word lion but he saw a lamb. He was told by the comforting elder that the Lion of the tribe of Judah and the Root of David had overcome. Naturally speaking, one would expect a lion to overcome, for he is, of course, the king of all beasts; nevertheless, John discovered that the comforting elder's lion is a lamb. What a strange combination!

A lamb, we well know, is the very picture of meekness, lowliness, gentleness, and helplessness; by contrast, a lion symbolizes power, fearlessness, and might. In the Bible a lion is viewed as the animal that devours all things, whereas a lamb is seen as an animal that is to be offered up as a sacrifice. A lion represents strength but a lamb represents weakness. Do we see these two sets of contrasting characteristics? And yet John is presented here with an odd, even perplexing, combination: the Lion is the Lamb and the Lamb is the Lion.

When Jesus came into this world two thousand years ago, John the Baptizer—upon seeing Jesus coming towards him to be baptized—testified, saying: Behold the Lamb of God who takes away the sin of this world—He is the Lamb of God (John 1:29).

Thus, when God sent His Son to this world He came not as a lion but as a lamb. Moreover, Jesus once said that He did not come to judge but to save (John 12:47b). When Jesus came to this earth the first time He came as the Lamb of God who voluntarily offered himself on the altar that for Him was the cross. Why? To be our substitute. He bore on His body our sins so that through His death we might live. Oh, Jesus is the gentle Lamb of God. It seems as though everybody could stomp on Him with impunity. It seems as though He came underneath every weight of pressure and attack imaginable, and He was rejected, neglected, laughed at and mocked; and eventually He was crucified. He was looked upon as nothing. Yes, Jesus as the Lamb of God was so meek, so lowly, so helpless, and so weak; and so He was crucified on the cross. Yes, He came as a lamb to offer himself to God for you and me.

Even so, this Lamb is also a lion. One day Jesus will come again, and when He does so the second time, He shall come as the Lion of the tribe of Judah. When Jesus presents himself to this world the second time, He shall do so as the Lion who shall judge all this world; and whoever resists Him and neglects to obey and honor Him shall be put under judgment. The Son of man is not only the Lamb of God but also the Lion of Judah.

What is the testimony of Jesus towards this world? It is twofold in nature. On the one hand, the testimony concerning Jesus is that He is the Lamb of God. If today you do not behold the Lamb, there is coming a day that you shall behold Him as the Lion. If today you reject Jesus as the Lamb of God who takes away your sins, then one day hereafter you shall bow to Him as the Lion of the tribe of Judah. If today you are not moved by the Lamb of God's great love and yield yourself to Jesus willingly and completely and declare—as did the apostle Thomas—"My Lord and my God" (John 20:28), then the day shall come when your knee shall bow and your tongue shall confess that Jesus is Lord (Philippians 2:10-11a); and you shall do so whether you want to or not, because the Lamb of God shall then be the Lion of God. So what is the testimony of Jesus to us? He is both the Lamb of God and the Lion of Judah. He is both the Savior of this world and the Heir to this world, and therefore the Lion King over us all. A strange combination but that is what Jesus the Son of man is.

Legally the world is God's and the title deed to it all is still in His hand, for God has never given up His ownership. Quite true, the stewardship of this world has changed several times over the course of world history. Initially, after God had created the universe of both heavens and earth in the first place, He had given the management of the world to the archangel Lucifer; but that archangel rebelled against God and became the devil. Then God—after restoring the world to a state of habitation once more—took the stewardship over the world out of the hands of the devil and placed it into the hands of man. But the archenemy of man, the devil, was so devious and so tricky in the Garden of Eden as to have enticed man into giving up his stewardship over the world; so once again the world's management fell into the hands of the devil with a vengeance. And that is what we see today throughout the world. Yes, indeed, the world is under the rule of the wicked one with a vengeance. And that explains why all the many terrible and evil things have been happening, and with increasing frequency and intensity.

Nevertheless, let us realize that the world's stewardship may change hands but the world's ownership never does; it shall remain forever in the hands of God. So that, though you may not be faithful to God in stewardship, even so, you belong to Him legally by right of creation; He owns you, whether you are faithful to Him or not.

But thank God, in that second vision of Revelation, the apostle John observed that this Lamb of whom we have been considering came forward and took out of the hand of the Enthroned One the book containing the title deed to God's created world. This thus signifies that not only legally, but also morally and spiritually, the crucified, risen and ascended Lord Jesus inherits this world from God the Father. As the Son of

God, Jesus has the legal right to this world; and as the Son of man, He has a moral right to the world. Consequently, it can rightfully be said that both the ownership and the stewardship of the world have now come into the hand of Jesus as the Lamb of God. Indeed, He is the man after God's own heart.

Let us now look more closely at this lamb which in the vision John saw standing—and looking as though slain—in the midst of the throne and of the four living creatures and in the midst of all the elders. It needs to be mentioned here that someone has pointed out that the fuller meaning of the word slain employed here signifies that this lamb John saw standing had been *newly* slain—that is to say, had just recently been slain. If this be true, then that description of the lamb probably indicates that the essential substance of this vision—the lamb's receiving and taking inherited title to the world—was historically and chronologically fulfilled at the time of the ascension of the glorified Son of man. Jesus was crucified on the cross, was laid in a tomb for three days, was thereafter raised from the dead and for forty days appeared to His discipled followers, and was finally taken up and received back to the Father; and, historically, as He was ascending up on high, He asked of the Father and was given all the nations as His inheritance and the ends of the earth as His possession; and thus the whole world now belonged to Him (cf. Psalm 2:8).

Why, though, must this lamb have been slain? The Bible tells us that by the blood of Jesus' cross He has reconciled all things back to God His Father (Colossians 1:20). Let us understand here that though all things of this world are legally God's, morally speaking, they have drifted away from Him. There was caused by His enemy a break in the unity of the world to have occurred; indeed, by the nefarious work of God's archenemy, there occurred disruption, disharmony, and disintegration; and hence, in order to bring back to God all things of the world into that perfect unity and harmony once more, the blood of the Lamb of God must be shed. It must be through the shedding of the blood of a sacrificial lamb—even that of the Lamb of God—that all things could be reconciled back to God so that not only would God have a legal claim upon this world—by right of creation—but also He would have a moral claim upon this world by right of redemption. God had not only created the world but now He has also redeemed it. And such is the significance that is conveyed to us by that word slain. We who are God's people shall adore the Lamb of God who has been slain.

Now John saw in the vision that the lamb had seven horns and seven eyes which are the seven Spirits of God sent into all the earth. In the Scriptures horns symbolize power and strength, whereas eyes represent wisdom and intellect. We may recall the apostle Paul, writing his I Corinthian letter, referred to Christ as being the power of God and the wisdom of God (1:24b), and whose power and wisdom are in His hand.

Why does the apostle say these horns and eyes are the *seven* Spirits of God; for we know that so far as the *person* of the Holy Spirit is concerned there is only one Spirit in the Godhead: one Father, one Son, and one Spirit. However, so far as the Holy Spirit's *function* is concerned, His function is sevenfold; and the number seven in the Scriptures represents perfectness or completeness. The Holy Spirit in His function is therefore the energy of God, and hence, we discern here that the Spirit in His function is full of energy, power, and wisdom.

Perhaps some of you would like to know what are the identities of the seven Spirits of God. Probably, the only place in the Bible which comes close to identifying these seven spirits by name would be the passage in Isaiah 11 verse 2. There we are told that the Messiah-King descendant of David—even Jesus—shall be anointed with the Holy Spirit; and we are told further that the Spirit of Jehovah shall rest upon the Anointed One: namely, the spirit of wisdom and understanding, the spirit of counsel and might, the spirit of knowledge and of the fear of Jehovah. Thus here, perhaps, are the identities of the seven

Spirits of God: first the Spirit of Jehovah himself, and then the spirit of wisdom, of understanding, of counsel, of might, of knowledge, and of the fear of the Lord.

However, there is a marvelous element to all this. This requires a little explanation. By having been slain in crucifixion, Jesus as the Lamb of God had thus completed the work of the redemption of man as well as of all the other created things in the world; and having accomplished that immense task, He ascended back up to the heaven of heavens. Possessing those seven horns and seven eyes which are the seven Spirits of God that were to be sent forth into all the earth, Jesus, as the slain but now glorified Lamb of God, after having ascended back to the Enthroned One in the highest heaven, poured forth into all the earth the Spirit of His Father, just as He had said to His disciples He would do (cf. John 14:16-17, 15:26, 16:7b).

What, though, was the purpose in His having sent the Holy Spirit into all the earth? It was—and continues to be—for the purpose of demonstrating the power and the wisdom of God as manifested in the finished redemptive work of Christ. It was—and still is—for the purpose of making the redemption of Christ a personal experience to all those who would receive Him. And that is the marvelous element to which I referred a few moments ago. Yes, Jesus has completed the work of redemption, and now not only all things belong to Him but also He has reconciled all things back to the Father. However, this needs to be personally experienced by all who would believe in Christ; and such can only be accomplished through God's power and wisdom as extended to them by the Holy Spirit. For as Jesus explained to His disciples, when the Holy Spirit comes (and by all means He *has* come), He shall convict the world of sin, righteousness, and judgment: of sin, because men do not believe in Jesus; of righteousness, because He, Jesus, would be returning—and did return—to the Father; and of judgment, because the prince of this world is now judged (John 16:8-11).

We do thank God that the Holy Spirit is upon this earth and that He has been sent forth to all the corners of the earth. We do thank God that through the working of the Holy Spirit we, in our personal experience of Him, may be reconciled to God.

Now let us notice that when the Lamb of God took the book from the hand of the Enthroned One, something immediately happened in heaven: the four living creatures and the 24 elders fell before the Lamb, each of them having a harp and a bowl full of incenses which are the prayers of the saints. And all of them together sang a new song: the Song of Redemption that was full of praise and worship of the glorious Redeemer for having accomplished the work of redemption.

But let us also notice one special detail about this same heavenly scene. For it would appear that only in response to the prayers of the saints down on the earth did Jesus—as the slain, resurrected, and ascended Lamb of God—step forward, take the book from the Enthroned One, and thereby receive into His own hands the title deed to the entire world. The saints on earth had prayed and their prayers had ascended up to the throne of God and had proved effectual.

Yet this was not the only instance of such a phenomenon having occurred. In fact, there is recorded in the book of Revelation instance upon instance of heaven having been prompted to make a move in response to the prayers of the saints on earth. Or this can be stated slightly differently: Before heaven can make a move God will have put a burden of prayer on the heart of the church, that through the prayer of the church heaven shall move. Let us not think that God means for the saints and the church to sit idly by passively waiting for things from heaven to happen. To the contrary, the marvelous facet to the will and purpose of God is this, that after the Lamb of God—slain, buried, and resurrected—had completed the work of redemption, the Ascended and Glorified One will refuse to make a move until those who are the firstfruits of His redemption shall join with Him in His further work.

Yes, Christ our Redeemer has now received into His hands the title deed to this world in response to the prayers of earlier saints. But when is He going to finish opening those seals which have not yet been unsealed? When is He going to reclaim the world as His own in a practical way, when is He going to bring the world back to himself so that the kingdom of God may finally come upon this earth? When and how is the Lord going to do all of that? He will simply wait till the prayers of the church ascend to the throne before heaven will move in regard to this or that to be done.

Now if you wish me to provide an example of this in specific, concrete, historical terms, I shall do so using what is narrated in the book of Acts concerning the day of Pentecost as one instance of this. If, as was suggested earlier today, the time chronologically for when the newly slain Lamb of God received the title deed to the world was during His ascension back to the Father, then the prayers of the saints which prompted heaven to effect this were the prayers of those 120 believers who were gathered together in the Upper Room in Jerusalem on Pentecost Day. They had devoted themselves to prayer for ten days following Jesus' ascension-departure till the day of Pentecost. Were they praying for the outpouring of the Holy Spirit? I do not believe so, for though Jesus had told them to wait in Jerusalem until they should receive as promised the power from on high for going to all the world as His witnesses, and though they did in fact wait for the promised outpouring of the Holy Spirit, there was no mention in the Acts narrative that they prayed for the Spirit's outpouring. Then for what were they praying? Well, let us recall from the Acts account of these post-resurrection events that for 40 days the Lord Jesus had appeared and talked to His disciples concerning the kingdom of God (Acts 1:1-14, 2:1). And I personally believe that during those ten days while they were on their knees praying, their prayer was only one: Lord, You, by the shedding of Your blood, have reconciled this world back to God; now, therefore, claim it!

Claim it, Lord. And thus, the prayer of the church in that Upper Room led the way for heaven to move in beginning to bring the world back again to the purpose of God.

What a privilege, but also, what a responsibility has been given to the church on earth. Can it be that because of the coldness of our hearts, because of the slowness of our understanding, because of the lack of prayer on the part of the church, that the kingdom of God is not yet here? Can it be that because we do not pray as we ought, that because we do not show sympathy with God and His interests as we should, that because our prayers as incense have not ascended up in such volume as they should—therefore, the world is still under the power of the wicked one? Can it be that we are only interested in advancing our personal spirituality? Should we not be more interested in seeing the kingdom of God established? That ought to be the case; and thank God that when Jesus as the Lamb of God was ascending back to heaven's throne and received the title deed to this world, the church on earth had been praying in the Upper Room for that very move of heaven to occur.

Throughout the centuries the church has been and still is praying. It is to be lamented, however, that we who are living a relatively peaceful life are not too much concerned with the interest of Christ upon the earth; but those who are in difficult situations, those who are behind iron bars or undergoing persecution in difficult parts of the world, we can perhaps understand how much they pray for God's kingdom to come. And this should be our prayer as well. All our prayers should be for His return; and if that be true of them, then such prayers shall bring in the power of heaven upon the earth. If the content of our prayers have the Lord's interests at their center, then such prayers should pave the way for the dispelling of the power of the wicked one. Indeed, such prayers shall be the means of bringing the redemption of Christ into the whole world. And the sound of the new song being sung—the Song of Redemption—

shall ultimately be heard everywhere: "Thou art worthy ... because thou hast been slain, and hast redeemed to God, by thy blood, out of every tribe, and tongue, and people, and nation, and made them to our God kings and priests; and they shall reign over [all] the earth."

There is no time left today to go more deeply into this new song—the Song of Redemption—except to comment this much about it. It is a beautiful song, declaring as it does that the precious Lamb of God has redeemed us by His blood out of every tribe, every tongue, every people, and every nation, and has made us kings and priests to God so that we may reign with Christ over all the earth. The will of God shall finally rule and reign over the world.

John reported that after the four living creatures and all the elders had sung the Song of Redemption, he heard all the angelic beings of heaven join together in singing an anthem of praise of their own to the Lamb. But this was then followed immediately, wrote John, by every creature throughout all creation singing a hymn of praise themselves: all creatures in heaven, on earth, under the earth, upon the sea, and in the sea—all joined in and sang, "To Him who sits upon the throne and to the Lamb, Blessing and honor and glory and might to the ages of ages."

Please bear in mind here that this is *all* of creation whom John heard in the vision uttering these words of praise and worship to God the Father and the Lamb. And all of creation includes: (a) all those who will have believed and received the Lamb of God and will most willingly sing that song; and (b) all beings who shall have resisted the Lamb, for one day they shall meet the Lamb who shall now come forth as the Lion and they will be *required* to say to Him: "Glory, honor, power, and dominion be to You!" (cf. again Philippians 2:10-11) All of creation shall have to declare that, willingly or unwillingly.

And in response to all of creation's song of praise to the Enthroned One and to the Lamb, John saw and heard what the four living creatures and the elders said, Amen—"So be it"; and then all the elders fell down and worshiped the Father and the Lamb of God.

Chapter Three

The Song of Redemption

And I saw in the midst of the throne and of the four living creatures, and in the midst of the elders, a Lamb standing, as slain, having seven horns and seven eyes, which are the seven Spirits of God which are sent into all the earth: and it came and took it out of the right hand of him that sat upon the throne. And when it took the book, the four living creatures and the twenty-four elders fell before the Lamb, having each a harp and golden bowls full of incenses, which are the prayers of the saints. And they sing a new song, saying, Thou art worthy to take the book, and to open its seals; because thou hast been slain, and hast redeemed to God, by thy blood, out of every tribe, and tongue, and people, and nation, and made them to our God kings and priests; and they shall reign over the earth.

And I saw, and I heard the voice of many angels around the throne and the living creatures and the elders; and their number was ten thousands of ten thousands and thousands of thousands; saying with a loud voice, Worthy is the Lamb that has been slain, to receive power, and riches, and wisdom, and strength, and honour, and glory, and blessing. And every creature which is in the heaven and upon the earth and under the earth, and those that are upon the sea, and all things in them, heard I saying, To him that sits upon the throne, and to the Lamb, blessing, and honour, and glory, and might, to the ages of ages. And the four living creatures said, Amen; and the elders fell down and did homage.

Revelation 5:6-14

We mentioned during our last time together that the second vision which the apostle John saw on the isle of Patmos was recorded in chapters 4 and 5 of the book of Revelation, and it was in two parts. The first part could be described and entitled as, the Glory of the Creator, for John saw God sitting upon the throne with a rainbow round about Him. And he also saw four different living creatures and twenty-four elders worshiping and praising God. And the words they uttered in praise and worship could be described and entitled as, the Song of Creation: "Thou art worthy, O our Lord and our God, to receive glory and honour and power; for thou hast created all things, and for thy will they were, and they have been created."

Then the apostle beheld the second part of this vision—and it could be described and entitled as, the Glory of the Redeemer. One item in particular John saw, which was in the hand of the Creator God: a sealed book; and he saw and heard a mighty angel proclaiming: "Who is worthy to take the book and to open it and to read it?" And John took sad notice that no one in heaven nor on earth nor under the earth was worthy, and consequently, the apostle wept very much. But at that moment one of the elders comforted him by saying: "Behold, the lion of the tribe of Judah, even the root of David, has overcome, and He is able to take the book and to open it." And John reported that he saw a lamb, as though newly slain, standing in the midst of the throne, and having seven horns and seven eyes which are the seven Spirits of God sent forth into all the earth. And the lamb came forward, took the book from the Enthroned One, and as soon as it had taken the book the living creatures and the elders fell down before that lamb, worshiped, and sang a new song—the Song of Redemption. But then, following our discussion together of all this, much more was said concerning this slain lamb—the Lamb of God—as our Redeemer; and at that point our discussion had to come to a close.

Now as I waited upon the Lord for today's message, I felt that we ought to linger a little longer in further consideration of this Song of Redemption. For we come to realize that seeing the glory of the Redeemer draws out from His people a new song of redemption. If we are given a vision of the glory of our Redeemer, then we will burst out with a new song of redemption. Yet, very often we feel we are lacking in our content as well as in our expression in worship. We do not know how to worship the Lord our Redeemer. We do not have the right words to express our feelings. Now, why? I believe it is because we are deficient in our vision of the Redeemer. If we see more of the glory of Jesus our Redeemer, then it is my sense that we will worship in a better way. So I feel that we should stay focused a little while longer on this theme of redemption.

First of all, then, let us consider what the meaning of redemption is. In the Greek language of the New Testament there are three different words used in Scripture to describe redemption. We are not interested in the Greek words as such, so we will merely identify their various meanings. These three different Greek words convey to us the thought of redemption according to three basic ideas. The first Greek word's idea of redemption conveys the thought of being delivered by means of the payment of a price. The second Greek word's idea to be conveyed concerning redemption is the thought of being purchased out of the slave market. And the final idea conveyed is the thought of being liberated or set free. Hence, these three Greek words for redemption convey the thoughts of deliverance, purchase, and liberation. And in all these thoughts there is the underlying idea of a price, a ransom, or a cost having to be paid in order that a person may be delivered, purchased, or liberated.

In order for us to better understand these three thoughts it may be helpful to illustrate them by pointing out some practical Old Testament examples to be found in the book of Leviticus chapter 25, which is a great chapter on the theme of redemption in practice and not just in teaching. And as background to these practical illustrations of redemption, it should be remembered that God had blessed His people, the Israelites, with possessions of land and fields on which to live.

Now it is stated in that Leviticus chapter that if among the Israelites there is a brother who becomes so poor that he is unable to hold on to his field, he must sell it. But in that case, the nearest among his kinsmen—the one who is closest to him by blood—has the right of redemption, and in fact ought to exercise that right, to step in and purchase that field out of the hand of his debtor and thus redeem it.

This Levitical law was not only true for land and field but was also true with respect to houses. If a brother becomes so poor that he has to sell his house, the same thing happens: his nearest kinsman shall step in and exercise the right of redemption and purchase that house for him.

Yet, again, this was not only true for a house, a piece of land, or a field, but was also true with regard to a person. Should a brother become so poor that he must sell himself as a slave to survive but does not have the means to redeem himself, then his nearest relative has, and must exercise, the right of redemption; and he shall therefore step in and buy and deliver and liberate his brother. These were the cases of redemption which the Levitical law governed with respect to lands, fields, houses, or persons.

In this connection, there is a wonderful story told in that beautiful little Old Testament book of Ruth which concerns itself with this very theme of redemption. You may recall that Elimelech and his family left the land of Israel and sojourned in the unbelieving land of Moab, and there they were disciplined by the Lord because of that: Elimelech passed away, his two sons passed away, and finally Naomi and her daughter-in-law Ruth, just the two of them, were compelled by force of circumstance to return to Naomi's own place at Bethlehem. But these two were so poor that Naomi had to sell the property of her deceased husband Elimelech. However, you may further recall that the nearest kinsman, Boaz, exercised the right of redemption. He purchased the land of Elimelech and, together with the land, he also purchased Ruth to be his wife. She was to be joined together with Boaz into one; and thus we have a beautiful story of redemption.

Now in a spiritual sense, what has happened to mankind is that they sold themselves to sin. And mankind, of course, includes us. Do we think we at one time were free men and women? We were not, because our forefather Adam had sold himself to sin and to the devil. The Bible makes clear that God was not the one who divorced us from himself nor was He the one responsible for us having been sold; on the contrary, it was because of our sin that we found ourselves sold for a profit: "Through [or, because of] your iniquities, ye have been sold" (see Isaiah 50:1). And what do we get for having sold ourselves? In this same Old Testament book of Isaiah, we are given the answer: You have been sold for nothing; therefore, you shall be redeemed without money (52:3).

Do we realize that at one time all of mankind (including every one of us) had sold themselves to sin? Because of Adam, all of us have at one time or another sold ourselves to sin, and after having done so, we became slaves to sin (John 8:34, Romans 7:14). We came under the bondage of sin and the curse of the law (Galatians 3:10).

The psalmist tells us that none can by any means redeem his brother, for is there anyone who can give a ransom to God?—for the cost of redemption of another's life is too costly and thus his life must be given up forever (Psalm 49:7-8). According to our own condition, we had been sold to sin and were lost, not having the power to redeem ourselves, it being too costly. None could pay redemption's price. Therefore, we each were a hopeless case, a soul lost forever.

Let us realize, however, that we sold ourselves illegally, since we had no right to sell ourselves because, having been created by God, we were not our own. Being God's possession by right of creation, we illegally sold ourselves to sin and to the devil. Yet, we not only sold ourselves, we also illegally sold to the devil all the other things in this world. And that was illegal as well because the world had only been entrusted by God to our care and management; the world was not our property. So we have illegally sold away ourselves and the rest of the world to the devil.

Hence, that was our situation. But thank God, we had a very close relative—our nearest kinsman—He who is our God. For the Word became flesh in the person of Jesus the Christ, who came down to this world and took upon himself a body of flesh and blood just like we all have (John 1:14a). Having thus partaken of our flesh and blood, Jesus became a man; and as He was now a man, He became the nearest of our relatives and exercised the right of redemption. Jesus our Kinsman-Redeemer, purchased us, bought us out of the slave market, and set us free. Now that is redemption.

The Lord Jesus paid a terrible price to purchase us out of the slave market and buy us back to God so that we might be set free. Oh, the wonder of redemption! Let us recall the patriarch Job exclaiming: "I know my Redeemer liveth"! (Job 19:25) And let us take note of Jacob, who in his old age could testify concerning the angel of God who had redeemed him from all evil (Genesis 48:16a). He, too, knew his Redeemer. Blessed are we if we can testify that we know our Redeemer lives and has redeemed us from all evil.

Second, what is the object of Christ's redemption? We read in Romans that all who believe are justified freely by God's grace through the redemption which is in or comes by Christ Jesus (3:24). Redemption is in Christ Jesus alone because He alone is the Redeemer of the world. He is in fact the only redeemer throughout all of creation. But in Jesus having paid the price to fulfill the work of a redeemer, how inclusive has been His redemption? The Lord Jesus has redeemed the whole of creation, He having reconciled by His blood all created things back to God (Colossians 1:20); even so, the primary objective in His redemptive work has always been mankind—including you and me. Is that not precious?

In one of His kingdom parables Jesus likened the kingdom of heaven to treasure hidden in a field by a man who had found it there. After hiding it, the man in his joy goes away, sells all he has, returns, and buys the field in order to possess the treasure (Matthew 13:44). It being a parable, it can be said that the field represents the world, the man is the Lord Jesus, and the treasure is the church—which is the real kingdom of the heavens. We can conclude from this parable that though present, the true church—the kingdom of the heavens in reality—is not visible in the world, and no one has the insight, knowledge, and wisdom of ever discerning and finding it. Jesus, however, does have the necessary ability of seeing and finding the treasured church. He then hides the church because He is afraid that those who do not know her value may spoil or destroy her; nevertheless, for the joy of having found the church in the world, the Lord sells everything.

Is it not true that the Lord Jesus gave up everything, even His life's blood? And why? To purchase those who He discerned would make up the church. Jesus purchased and redeemed the world but did so not because of the world itself but because of the treasured church hidden therein.

Therefore, though the extent of Jesus' redemption by His blood covers the whole created world and all things in it, the focus of His redemptive work is the church. And that is why we find expressed in the Song of Redemption that the slain Lamb has redeemed to God by His blood all those who out of every tribe and tongue and people and nation would make up His church. We can therefore say that the church is the focus and object of the work of redemption.

Oh how we do rejoice in the Lord's presence today that He has looked upon us who are so unworthy, so undeserving, so corrupted, and so worthless as having value, and having it to such an extent that He was willing to give up everything to have us as His treasured possession. Normally, people on earth would never give up all they possessed in order to obtain as their own that which is inferior, corrupted, broken and useless; yet that is what the Son of man as the Lamb of God has done. That is His wonderful redemption, that He was willing to be slain so that by His blood He could redeem us to God out of every tribe, tongue, people, and nation.

And third, what is the price—the cost—of redemption? In the apostle Peter's first epistle he explained that we believers were not redeemed by corruptible—that is, perishable—things such as silver or gold, but by the precious blood of Christ, a lamb without blemish or defect (1:18-19). We have been redeemed by the Lord Jesus having paid a terrific price: shedding His precious blood. And why was the shedding of blood necessary? Because life is in the blood (Leviticus 17:14): it requires life to redeem another life. The Lord Jesus has so loved us that He has given His life for us. He shed His blood for us that we might be redeemed, and because of that we need to remember that we were bought at a huge price and that we are no longer our own (I Corinthians 6:19b-20).

And fourth, what is the scope of redemption?—how far-reaching in its effect is Christ's redemption? If we search God's word carefully, we shall discover that the scope of redemption is limitless. Redemption is not solely negative in its effect upon us who believe: being delivered out, purchased from, and liberated from a state or condition of existence. Yes, redemption includes all those negative qualities or characteristics. However, redemption is more than being extricated from something negative but is being brought into, entering upon, and becoming something positive. In other words, redemption brings us into a new and uplifting position before God. Now that is the wonder of redemption. Hence, in our remaining time together today, let us briefly consider the scope and breadth of redemption—both negative and positive.

As to the negative side, first, we are redeemed from sin and guilt. Paul writes: "In Him, that is, in the Son of God's love, we have redemption, the forgiveness of sin" (see Colossians 1:13b-14). Thus, redemption is the forgiveness of our sins. We all have sinned against God, against others, and even against ourselves. But through Christ's redemption every one of our sins is forgiven: Great sins and small sins, many sins and fewer sins. All of them God can forgive. How can God do this? Because the Son of His love has redeemed us: Jesus has paid the price, He has given the ransom money, He has shed His blood for us so that our sins can be forgiven of God.

Yet, not only our sins but also our iniquities and transgressions and guilt are forgiven. This we find asserted in Paul's Ephesian letter: In Him, that is, in the Beloved of God, we have redemption through his blood, the forgiveness of offenses (1:6b-7a). Most certainly we all have sinned; but in having sinned, we all have offended the righteous God by having transgressed His law; and we were all therefore guilty before the court of God. There was a case in heaven against us, but thank God, not only the sins we had committed have all been forgiven but the legal case against us in God's court, in which we had been found guilty of having transgressed His righteous law, has been wiped out through God's forgiveness on the basis of His beloved One's work of redemption.

Hence, we come to realize that the scope of Christ's redemption includes not only the forgiveness of sins but also the forgiveness of offenses, and this we can see very clearly laid out for us in the book of Hebrews chapter 9. There we read that Christ is the mediator of a new covenant so that there can be a basis for the redemption of the transgressions committed under the first covenant (v.15). In other words, we who have been called of God had transgressed His law as represented by the first covenants, but our transgressions against that law have now been forgiven through Christ's death as a ransom paid to redeem us from those transgressions. Thus, our being redeemed from all sins, iniquities, transgressions, and all the guilt arising from those transgressions, constitutes the first—though negative—aspect in the all-embracing scope of our Redeemer's work of redemption.

Second, we are redeemed from the law and its curse. Paul's letter to the Galatians can be most helpful to us here. There he explains that when the fullness of time had come, God sent forth His Son, born of woman and born under law, in order that He might redeem those under law (4:4-5a). All we who sinned were all brought under God's law automatically, and not only brought under His law but also under the curse of His law. Why? Because we had sinned against the law of God.

Had any of us ever kept all the law of God—and kept all of it not only in letter but in spirit? Who has ever been able to do that? No one! We had all therefore come under the curse of the law; for as Paul further explained, quoting from the Old Testament, cursed is anyone who fails to keep all of the law (3:10). And so, the Lord Jesus, having been born of woman, came under God's law in order that He might redeem us from the law. Furthermore, Paul makes clear that the Lord Jesus not only redeemed us from the law itself but also redeemed us from its curse, in that He became a curse for us; for the word of the law had declared that anyone who is hanged on a tree is cursed (3:13). And we know that Jesus our Redeemer was hung up on a tree, as it were, by having been crucified. Consequently, according to God's law, He became a curse for us so that he might redeem us—set us free—from the curse of the law.

I would pause for a moment to inquire of anyone present with us today who has not yet experienced the redemption of the Redeemer of the world: Is it your intention to try keeping

God's law? Is it your belief that you can take pride in your having thus far lived a good life? I would remind you of what was referenced from God's word a few moments ago, that if you transgress even just one small item of the law, you are deemed by God as having transgressed the whole law; and hence, you can no longer be blessed by the law but you shall fall under the curse of the law and shall be condemned by the law. The only remedy is for you to embrace the Lord Jesus as your Redeemer, who out of love has become a curse on behalf of all of us so that we who trust Him may be delivered from the curse of the law. And that is a second aspect—though again a negative one—in the limitless scope of Christ's redemption.

I am here today to tell you, however, that Jesus' redemption includes more than even that. For His redemption further embraces a third negative aspect of deliverance—the aspect of His having redeemed us from the vain conduct of traditional living and from a life of lawlessness and rebellion. Now as to the first of these two lifestyles, it may sound quite strange, yet that is the very way the Bible has put it. Let us turn again to the apostle Peter's first epistle where we read once more these words in its opening chapter: It was not by perishable things such as silver or gold by which you have been redeemed from your vain way of life handed down from your forefathers (v.18). In other words, the apostle wrote that his readers have been redeemed from their empty style of life that conducts itself according to the tradition of this world. Is it not true that at one time we all had lived our lives according to the traditional way by which our fathers had themselves lived, and that we have since then found it to be so empty? Such a way of living we today regard as vain, for by Christ's redemption we have been delivered out of such an empty, traditional, dead life. Oh, that we may be a living people towards God. Now that, in part, is what redemption has done for us in having delivered us from a vain and dead lifestyle.

And as for the second of these two lifestyles, both of which have existed side-by-side in all of us, we learn from Paul's letter to Titus that Christ "gave himself for us, that he might redeem us from all lawlessness" (2:14). We may at times wonder why there is so much lawlessness in the world today. Indeed, the spirit of rebellion against any authority is greatly on the rise in our world today. Yet let us not be surprised at this because that is the normal condition of this wicked world, and we Christians were at one time a part of such expressions of lawlessness and rebellion; but Christ has redeemed us from such a lifestyle.

We need to ask ourselves, Might there still be traces of the spirit of lawlessness within us? Let us be reminded of what the Scriptures have said concerning our flesh, that there is nothing good which dwells there, and that includes lawlessness (Romans 7:18). Were we, in our past conduct, law-abiding persons? We were not. There was a spirit of rebellion in our hearts. We had rebelled against God and against anything that had anything to do with God. And the world continues to live today under the rule of the lawless one (II Thessalonians 2:3), and hence, it is no wonder that the world is lawless. But thank God that Christ has redeemed us from all lawlessness and the spirit of rebellion: He has redeemed us from such a life and placed a new spirit and a new heart in us (Ezekiel 36:26a, Romans 6:22).

There is a fourth aspect—though once again a negative one—which Christ's redemption includes within its all-embracing scope: He is one day to redeem us, that is to say, deliver us, from these corrupted and corruptible bodies of ours as well as from this corrupted world. We are told in Paul's Romans epistle that we are eagerly waiting for our adoption as sons, which event will be brought about with the redemption of our bodies (8:23). We who are currently in these decaying physical bodies of ours sense an ongoing perishability in them; for because of man's fall, these bodies of ours have taken on that which is perishable. And they shall continue to deteriorate in that state until, thank God, there comes the day when they shall take on and be clothed with the imperishable—even the redemption of our bodies. That is what we are eagerly awaiting: the change that shall occur in the twinkling of an eye (cf. I Corinthians 15:51-53)—even the transforming of our bodies. They shall be transformed from shameful and vainglorious bodies into glorious spiritual ones (cf. I Corinthians 15:35-44a).

Then, too, if our bodies are decayed and decaying, so also is the created world for it likewise has been affected by the Fall. The created world is subject to decay everywhere, and Paul informs us further that the entire creation has been groaning and groaning, as though in the pains of childbirth, up to this very moment. Even we ourselves, adds Paul, groan inwardly. Yes, writes Paul in his Letter to the Romans, both creation and those who are the Lord's are groaning today—for what?—for the glorious freedom of the sons of God to arrive. On that day all of creation shall be set free from its bondage to decay, and God's people shall receive glorious spiritual bodies free at last from corruption (cf. Romans 8:18-23). The day is indeed coming when we shall be delivered from this ongoing corruption.

Now those are the points which redemption covers negatively. Oh, if that is how redemption is negatively spoken about in Scripture, what are the ways it is positively spoken about? Yes, redemption has its negative side, but redemption also has its positive side in Scripture. Christ has redeemed us out from this and that in order that we may be redeemed into and unto.

So the fifth point or aspect of Christ's redemption is that He has redeemed us to God. Take note of Revelation chapter 5 verse 9: "Thou, slain Lamb, hast, by Thy blood, redeemed us to God." His redemptive work accomplished on the cross is not merely a matter of our being purchased out of, and thus set free from, the slave market but is also a matter of our being bought to God. Let us therefore not assume that because our sins have been forgiven, we can now live our own life and can do whatever we like. Yes, we are free men and women, but free for what? Free for ourselves? Not so; we are free solely for God and for the fulfillment of His will and purpose. Let us forever recognize that we are not our own but we have been bought at a costly price; therefore, let us glorify God in our bodies (I Corinthians 6:19b-20).

Have we forgotten this? How we rejoice that he has redeemed us from our sins and has forgiven our offenses. How we rejoice in that, and yet we are prone to forget that we are redeemed to God, and thus we belong to Him, having no right over ourselves nor over our bodies. To the contrary, our time, money, future, and family—indeed, anything and everything pertaining to ourselves—are not ours but God's because we have been bought by Him and to Him. And for what purpose?

Well, that verse 14 of Titus chapter 2 cited earlier continues by declaring that Christ gave himself for us in order not only to redeem us from a life of lawlessness but also to make of us a peculiar people zealous to do what is good. In other words, He has redeemed us from all lawlessness and purified for himself a peculiar people eager to do good works. We are to be a peculiar people, yet not in the sense of our trying to be strange but in the sense that we are to be an altogether different kind of people from what we had been. Now if we claim that we have been redeemed by the Lord Jesus but we are no different from the world, will that not be a contradiction to our supposed testimony? We are to be a different people from the people of the world, and for what purpose? That we may be zealous in doing good works. Yet let us be clear that the good works referenced here is not meant to be what people commonly consider as being good works. Rather, the phrase, good works, in the Bible has reference to the work of God. We have been bought to God to do His will. And in this respect, this is what redemption really means.

A sixth aspect in the limitless scope of the Redeemer's work of redemption—it being a second positive one—is that we are redeemed to receive the promise of an eternal inheritance. This is explained in Hebrews 9:15. It is said there that the called ones of God may receive the promised eternal inheritance. This is further explained in Ephesians 1:13b-14: we are redeemed so that we may receive the promised eternal inheritance; for the Holy Spirit has put his seal in our hearts as a deposit guaranteeing that one day we shall acquire our possession in Christ Jesus—all to the praise of His glory.

Oh, what a possession we have in Christ Jesus. At one time we were so poor that we had to sell ourselves and everything else of ours; but now we have become so rich as to have acquired an eternal inheritance in Christ Jesus. Oh the glory of that!

The all-embracing scope of Christ's redemptive work at Calvary covers a seventh aspect, and that aspect constitutes a third positive one: we are redeemed into sonship. The Scripture passage for this is Galatians 4:5. We are informed there that God sent His Son to this world to be born under law for the purpose of redeeming those under the law so that they might receive sonship. How wonderful that we are redeemed to be sons and daughters of God! We have been redeemed in order that one day we may be praised not only for being children of God (John 1:12) but also for being God's fully grown-up sons and daughters (Romans 8:19) who will have been transformed (Romans 12:2b) and fully conformed to the image of His Son (Romans 8:29a), our Redeemer Lord Jesus.

And lastly, the slain Lamb of God's all-inclusive redemptive work on the cross includes an astounding eighth aspect, it being the fourth and final one among the positive aspects I wish to address today. This aspect we learn about from the very Song of Redemption we have been focusing attention upon in our fellowship together today: we have been redeemed to God in order that we may be for Him both kings and priests who shall reign over the earth. How astounding it is, indeed, that criminals and beggars—such as we all once were—have now become kings and priests who shall one day co-reign with Christ our Redeemer over all the earth!

Now this is the far-reaching effect of the all-embracing redemption of Jesus Christ. No wonder the twenty-four elders and the four living creatures fell down before the Lamb of God and felt moved to sing the Song of Redemption. They *had* to sing it!

Finally, there is one other matter which needs to be addressed before concluding our time together today. And here I would like to speak specifically to those present with us today who may not yet be believers in Christ Jesus, the Redeemer of all mankind. And here I have in mind the matter of the acceptance of redemption. It is true that when Jesus paid the price of redemption in shedding His blood on the cross He redeemed all of creation, including especially all of mankind, to God. Which means that there is no one in this world who has not been redeemed—that is to say, there is no one in the world who need remain any longer in a state of spiritual lostness and eternal death. And why? Because Christ has paid the full price that was required in redeeming the whole of creation to God's satisfaction.

Nevertheless, Christ's redemption of the entire created world does not mean that you automatically enjoy the benefit of redemption. Not true. Universalism—the doctrine that holds to the belief that all of mankind shall be saved from eternal death—has no place in the economy of God. Yes indeed, the redemption accomplished by Jesus is universal in scope, but every person's enjoyment of it must be made individual and personal.

Is there a Biblical basis for holding to this latter belief? There *is* such a basis. This we find in Romans 3:24-25; for there the reader is told that saved people have been justified freely by God's grace through the redemption which is in Christ Jesus, whom God has set forth as a mercy seat *through faith in His blood.* In this passage Jesus' redemption is being discussed: God is said to have set forth Christ as a mercy seat. That is what He still is today: a mercy seat. Now what was the mercy seat back in the olden days of Israel? The mercy seat was situated above the ark of God's covenant and both of which together were placed within the holiest area of all inside the tabernacle, and later inside the temple of God; and when Israel's high priest entered the holiest of all, he never did so without taking blood of a sacrificial animal with him on behalf of all the people of Israel. He had been instructed by God through His servant Moses to bring sacrificial blood with him and to sprinkle it before the mercy seat and also to turn around towards the veil (Leviticus 16:14).

What does all that signify or symbolize for people of the world today? It signifies that God has set forth His Son Jesus as the One who represents God's mercy towards everybody. But who is able to receive God's mercy? Only those who have faith in Jesus' blood which He shed on Calvary's hill. For those who, as it were, bring the blood with them and sprinkle it, that would be the exercise of living faith.

Let no one present here today assume that because Christ's redemption covers the whole created world, Jesus has brought all of mankind—including you yourself—to God, and that therefore you do not need to believe and trust in His blood by applying His blood upon your heart—that you have automatically been reconciled to God. No, no, no. You must apply the blood personally to yourself, for it is only through faith in Jesus' shed blood that your sins can be forgiven.

Thank God that the day is coming when the number of all those who are to be saved shall finally be fulfilled, that the day is coming when the body of Christ shall be completed; for then the sons of God shall be revealed and manifested and the whole creation shall be redeemed—liberated—from vanity and corruption (cf. Romans 8:19-21).

In the light of all the foregoing words of explanation based upon the word of God, I would make this public appeal: Do not any of you present here today be complacent. Those who refuse God's mercy and resist to the end will be cast into the lake of fire, and thus they shall be outside the kingdom of God forever. That should be a warning which should be taken most seriously to one's heart. I say again that the work of redemption has long since been accomplished by this fallen world's Redeemer. Anyone who is desirous of enjoying the benefit and blessing of His redemption can come to Christ and simply receive it. Trust the Redeemer by putting your faith in Him, and you shall be redeemed in actuality and shall experience the blessing of His redemption. But if you personally fail to accept Christ's redemption, and even though it has covered the entirety of creation, including all of mankind, you will nonetheless be lost, and lost forever.

So may you accept and receive by faith the Redeemer's merciful redemption.

Chapter Four

The Seven Seals (1)

And I saw when the Lamb opened one of the seven seals, and I heard one of the four living creatures saying, as a voice of thunder, Come and see. And I saw: and behold, a white horse, and he that sat upon it having a bow; and a crown was given to him, and he went forth conquering and that he might conquer.

And when it opened the second seal, I heard the second living creature saying, Come and see. And another, a red horse, went forth; and to him that sat upon it, to him it was given to take peace from the earth, and that they should slay one another; and there was given to him a great sword.

And when it opened the third seal, I heard the third living creature saying, Come and see. And I saw: and behold, a black horse, and he that sat upon it having a balance in his hand. And I heard as a voice in the midst of the four living creatures saying, A choenix of wheat for a denarius, and three choenixes of barley for a denarius: and do not injure the oil and the wine.

And when it opened the fourth seal, I heard the voice of the fourth living creature saying, Come and see. And I saw: and behold, a pale horse, and he that sat upon it, his name was Death, and hades followed with him; and authority was given to him over the fourth of the earth to slay with sword, and

> with hunger, and with death, and by the beasts of the earth.
>
> And when it opened the fifth seal, I saw underneath the altar the souls of them that had been slain for the word of God, and for the testimony which they held; and they cried with a loud voice, saying, How long, O sovereign Ruler, holy and true, dost thou not judge and avenge our blood on them that dwell upon the earth? And there was given to them, to each one a white robe; and it was said to them that they should rest yet a little while, until both their fellow-bondmen and their brethren, who were about to be killed as they, should be fulfilled.
>
> Revelation 6:1-11

I do hope, as we read together this next Scripture portion—it being from the Gospel of Matthew—that we will carefully compare it with what we just read from Revelation 6:

> And Jesus answering said to them, See that no one mislead you. For many shall come in my name, saying, I am the Christ, and they shall mislead many. But ye will hear of wars and rumours of wars. See that ye be not disturbed; for all these things must take place, but it is not yet the end. For nation shall rise up against nation, and kingdom against kingdom; and there shall be famines and pestilences, and earthquakes in divers places. But all these are the beginning of throes. Then shall they deliver you up to tribulation, and shall kill you; and ye will be hated of all the nations for my name's sake. And then will many be offended, and will deliver one another up, and hate one another; and many false prophets shall arise and shall mislead

many; and because lawlessness shall prevail, the love of the most shall grow cold; but he that has endured to the end, he shall be saved. And these glad tidings of the kingdom shall be preached in the whole habitable earth, for a witness to all the nations, and then shall come the end.

Matthew 24:4-14

Our key verse for this series of messages on the book of Revelation continues to be that fragment from that book's chapter 19 verse 10: "... the spirit of prophecy is the testimony of Jesus." As has been noted before, God is concerned with but one matter, and that is, the testimony of Jesus. The reason God may seem to be interested in many things, many events, and many people is not because those things, events and people are so interesting but because they are closely related to the testimony of Jesus. It is my hope from the outset of our various considerations together on this prophetic book of the Bible that we have a clear understanding that if God is interested in you and me it is not because you and I are so interesting but is because you and I are related to the testimony of Jesus. Or may I put this understanding in a somewhat bizarre way: If the enemy of mankind—Satan—is disturbed by you and he becomes interested in you, it is not because of you, it is because the testimony of Jesus is in you. The one issue which really matters in this universe is the testimony of Jesus, and this testimony of Jesus is today entrusted to the church.

That is why we find in the book of Revelation that the first vision which John saw while in exile on the Aegean island of Patmos was that of the Son of man standing in the midst of the seven golden lampstands. It is the testimony of Jesus as centered upon the Son of man, and this testimony of Jesus is portrayed as being played out in the midst of the seven golden lampstands—the latter of which collectively represent the church. Due to time constraints I am not able to go back and review what we have already covered in our discussion together concerning that first vision. Nor can we review in detail what was said about the second vision which John beheld while on Patmos Isle. Briefly stated, that vision—recorded in Revelation chapters 4 and 5—consisted of two parts: the glory of the Creator as covered in chapter 4 and the glory of the Redeemer as presented in chapter 5. To sum up, this vision concerns the testimony of Jesus towards the world. In other words, the world that God created is redeemed by His Son.

Permit me to say that it would have been the easiest and most natural action for God to have taken if, after the world had fallen away from Him by man's rebellion against His will, He had simply wiped His creation out completely. I think that would have been the simplest and quite logical thing for God to have done. Strangely enough, however, God did not do that. Instead of wiping out the world and everything in it, He commenced the work of redeeming it all back to himself. Now that is love—redeeming love—in action.

Let us next recall that no one was able to take the book from the right hand of Him who sits upon the heavenly throne—God the Father. No one was found worthy to open its seals. But then John was shown a lamb—newly slain—even the lion of the tribe of Judah. The Lamb of God is worthy, steps forward, takes the book from the Father's hand, and then is heard the song of redemption: Thou art worthy to take the book and to open its seals because Thou hast been slain and hast redeemed to God by Thy blood out of every tribe and tongue and people and nation, and hast made them to our God both kings and priests, and they shall reign over all the earth. And when the twenty-four elders and the four living creatures commenced singing the song of redemption, John learned that the whole angelic host likewise responded; yet, not only all the angelic beings but also all the created things in heaven, on earth, and underneath the earth responded with praise and worship.

Now in reading the fifth chapter of Revelation does it not give you a feeling that all things are now reconciled to God? that all things which heretofore had been torn apart and which had been disintegrating into pieces and had reached the point of seemingly being impossible to be put back together have now appeared to have been reconciled to God through the redemption of the Lord Jesus? But as you look away from John's vision and look around the world, do you see that all things have found their focus and reconciling center in Christ Jesus? Do you believe all things have indeed been harmonized and reconciled and united towards God in His Son?

Granted, from God's viewpoint the moment the redemption price was paid, at that very moment the world was redeemed, because with God it is ever and always the present, there being no past and no future. But viewing the world from our human perspective, it is not so. Rather, the world is to be gradually reconciled on the basis of the redemption of Jesus Christ. This is because we find that the world puts up a very stiff resistance. The world resists to be reconciled; and hence, the Lord, on the basis of His redemption, has to reconcile the world unto himself gradually step by step until all things shall have been reconciled.

Let us recall again that verse in Hebrews chapter 2 where the writer is found quoting from Psalm 8: What is man that You, O God, remember him or the son of man that You visit him? You have made him a little inferior to the angels and have crowned him with glory and honor; in fact, You have subjected all things under his feet.

We see here that the psalmist declares concerning man that the Lord God has made him a little inferior to the angels and yet He has crowned him with glory and honor and has subjected all things under his feet. But after quoting these declarations from Psalm 8 the writer of Hebrews went on to say this: But now we see not yet all things subject to him; but we see Jesus, who was made a little inferior to angels on account of the suffering of death crowned with glory and honor so that by the grace of God He should taste death for everyone.

The author of Hebrews is correct, for we have not yet seen all things subjected to man, but we do see Jesus, and because of the suffering of His death He is now crowned with glory and honor. This we see, and because we have seen Him crowned with glory and honor, we know that He will bring all things under His feet.

I believe that the process and the procedure whereby Jesus' redemption is made a reality to this world is provided to us in the book of Revelation: the unfolding of the seven seals followed by the seven trumpets and ending with the seven vials. Yes, the world has been redeemed; for the Lord Jesus has paid the price—even with His blood—to redeem the world back to God; but currently the world is in the *process* of being reconciled to God. And it is a two-fold process: on the one hand the Lord is preparing a people, and on the other hand He is purifying the world as if by fire. Let us bear in mind that nothing which is of God is mechanical. Whatever has anything to do with God must be morally right and spiritually suitable. Legally speaking, the world has been redeemed; so that one could correctly say that the world is doubly the Lord's because He is the Creator/Maker as well as the Redeemer. At any moment since Calvary He could take the world to himself by legal right, but the Lord does not wish to do that. Yes, indeed, He has the legal and the moral right to the world, but He will not take possession of it until it is morally and spiritually suitable for Him. This is the mystery of our God and His Son.

God the Son needs some suitable people to rule with Him over the world. If He does not obtain that people He is not going to immediately take the world to himself. God the Son needs to purify the world. To those who receive Him as the Lamb of God, the testimony of Jesus to the world is, in the first place, that He is the sacrificial lamb who takes away the sin of the world. To those who receive God the Son as the Lamb, they become His people and He will further make them ready to rule with Him over the world. But for those who persistently refuse to accept Him as the Lamb of God, they shall encounter Him as the Lion. The Lord will purify the world until He brings all things under His feet.

I am not interested in giving a detailed exposition on the book of Revelation. Again I say, I am very tempted to do so. There are so many different interpretations afloat that a person does not know which one is the right interpretation. Many claim that they have the correct interpretation and say that other interpretations do not satisfy them, and I suspect that you too may say this if I were to give you an interpretation. But my interest currently is solely in the testimony of Jesus and how it is to be worked out in seeing that testimony established on earth as it is in heaven. And because such is what I am interested in, therefore, my approach to the book of Revelation will be entirely from that point of view.

I would repeat here that the process and the procedure whereby the testimony of Jesus is established in the world is presented to us in Revelation in terms of the seven seals, the seven trumpets, and the seven vials. Some Bible commentators say that the seals have reference to government, that the trumpets betoken a religious interpretation, and the vials have to do with tradition. That approach might just be so. Allow me to say that the way to understand the book of Revelation is not to make it difficult to understand. I think the best way to understand Revelation as well as all the other Bible books is to follow the easiest and simplest approach, because surely it is the Lord's will that we should understand the Bible. So when we approach the book of Revelation, let us not do so with a very complicated mindset by trying to change and change until we end up not knowing what we are talking about. Let me repeat that the best approach is to be as simple as possible. For as Scripture tells us, to the simple God will give wisdom to the wise and prudent in heart (cf. Matthew 11:25, Luke 10:21).

I will not try to tell you that the seven seals and the seven trumpets and the seven vials are all contemporaneous to each other—that they are the same thing. No, I will simply conclude from the Bible what it says: that out of the seven seals come the seven trumpets and out of the seven trumpets come the seven vials. I think that is the simplest way to approach the matter. If we take the fifth chapter of Revelation as being the historical record of the concluding phase of the ascension of the risen Lord—I say if here, because if you do not agree, it is perfectly all right. Here in this fifth chapter we see the Lamb as newly slain standing in the midst of the throne of God almighty, and who then takes from the hand of the One who sits on the throne the book that as was discussed before is the title deed to the world.

As cited in a previous message in this series, I would bring to our attention once again that passage from Psalm 2 wherein God is quoted as declaring to His Son: "Ask of Me, and I will give You the nations for an inheritance, and for Your possession the ends of the earth" (see v.8). In light of that passage, therefore, it makes good sense to me that after the risen, glorified Son of man had ascended up on high—and on the basis of His accomplished work of redemption—He as the Lamb of God newly slain comes before the Father's throne and asks of the Father and immediately obtains the world as His possession by taking from the Father's right hand the held-forth book which is the title deed to the entire world and all things within it. And hence, it is my view that if one wishes to place historically the moment of the Lord Jesus' inheritance of the earth, that event occurred during the concluding phase of the risen Lord's ascension back to the Father as was revealed to the apostle John which he recorded in Revelation chapter 5. Which brings the reader of Revelation to what is described in chapter 6 following upon the Lamb having taken the book into His hands and John having heard the response of praise and worship offered up to the One on the throne and to the Lamb by all creatures in heaven, on earth, under the earth, and upon and in the sea. For, in fact, chapter 6 commences with John beholding the Lamb beginning to open the first of that book's seven seals.

Here, though, I need to pause and express an opinion as to why I cannot agree with those who say that none of those seven seals has as yet been opened. For it is difficult for me to think that the Lord Jesus would take the book from the Father's hand and not commence opening its seals until—I do not know how long—all these nearly twenty centuries. It is simply too difficult for me to think in those terms. And why? Because the very reason—as clearly stated several times throughout chapter 5—for the Lamb to take that book is to open it, look inside it, and to read it (vv. 2, 3, 4, 5c). Therefore, I do not believe it to be presumption on my part to state that upon obtaining the title deed to the entire created universe, the Lamb immediately begins to open the book's seals. And if that be the case, then the opening of the seven seals has its beginning at the time when the risen, glorified Son of man concluded His ascension back to heaven's throne.

Before going further into this matter, I would bring to your attention this: If seals have reference to government, then all which follows in chapter 6 concerning the first four seals is but the reflection of the governmental dealings of the Lord with the world. After the Lord has taken the world as His possession He begins to deal with His world according to His governmental hand. In short, we may say that the Lord's governmental hand is now upon the earth.

In Matthew chapter 24 we read that when Jesus' disciples asked Him about the things which are to happen in future, the Lord said the following: "Be careful after I have left. There will be many who will come and say, 'I am the Christ.' There will be false prophets and false teachers and they will deceive many. And there will also be wars and rumors of wars, famines, earthquakes, and persecution." However, the Lord made it clear that such would not be the end. Yes, He declared, nation shall rise up against nation, kingdom against kingdom, and so forth, but these things are just the beginning of the "throes"—or as some Bible versions read: these are but the first birth pangs or pains. And then, the Lord added, it follows that those who are His disciples will be hated—indicating persecution of the brethren—and the love of many will grow cold. But, concluded the Lord, whoever endures to the end shall be save and the glad tidings of the kingdom shall be preached to all the nations as a testimony, and then the end shall come.

Now if we lay Matthew chapter 24 verses 4 to 14 side by side with Revelation chapter 6, can we detect a similarity between these two Bible passages? Many people, of course, have been trying to figure out who or what the four horsemen of chapter 6 represent. I must acknowledge here that after I was saved I became deeply interested in these four horsemen. Oh how I read book after book, tract after tract in an attempt to find out who or what these four horses or horsemen are: the white horse followed by the red horse and then the black horse followed by the pale or green horse. How greatly I wished to know what these horses or their riders really symbolized. In my investigation I had read so many books, and so many people had given me so many different interpretations that I did not know which book or whose interpretation I should advocate.

But, dear brethren in Christ, let us be simple. Let us not try to figure out these things by imagining that somehow Nazis or Nazism, Communists or Communism, and so forth and so on, are the answers; rather, just be simple. Take into account what the Lord Jesus himself has said, that after His departure there would be primarily four things arising: false christs, wars, famines, and persecution ending in death—that also the gospel of the kingdom must be preached to all the nations as a testimony, and that only then will the end come. With this simple interpretation in mind, could it therefore be that the white horse represents false christs? I know that many say that this horseman is Christ. But in carefully comparing Revelation

6 with Matthew 24 one comes up with the following discrepancy concerning the white horse and its rider: Yes, the man has a bow, but where is the arrow? The picture presented of a bow without an arrow constitutes a false gesture. The conquering victory is therefore a false one; and hence, could it be that the rider on the white horse represents not Christ but a false christ? And then there is the red horse who makes not peace but war—an echo, is it not, of Jesus' remarks about wars and rumors of wars. This second seal's horse is followed by the third seal's black horse—conceivably representing famine, for when one is dying of famine due to lack of food (see Revelation 6:6) one's face and skin will turn black. And finally there appears the pale or green horse, on which Death itself rides, taking away the fourth part of the earth.

Let us discern from this that the governmental hand of the Lord upon the earth is seen in false christs, wars, famines, and death. After the Lord has redeemed the world, after he has reconciled all things to himself, surely there should be no false christs, no wars, no famines, and no death; however, we see all such things. And so, the question arises, Why should the Lord allow these things to occur, for of course, He is not the author but simply allows them to happen and to be manifested in order that the normal immoral and/or abnormal condition of the world and its people should be exposed.

So many are playing God, they saying that if there is a God why does He allow wars? why does He allow famines? why does He allow death? why does He allow this, that and the other? In fact, many blame God for all such circumstances. Instead of blaming God they should recognize and acknowledge that the governmental hand of the Lord is heavily active upon the earth and that His governmental dealing is merely His way of exposing the negative moral condition of the world. It is a world that rejects Christ and refuses to believe in truth.

The Bible declares that because people of the world have refused to believe in truth, therefore, God will give them a teaching of error in the last days (II Thessalonians 2:10b-11), and the last days have come upon the earth. Indeed, because people of the world refuse to listen to the truth, they will heap upon themselves many erroneous teachers. Their ears are itching for what they would like to hear and not what God wants them to hear (II Timothy 4:3-4).

It is because this world has rejected Christ and does not love the truth but loves unrighteousness that therefore the Lord in His governmental action allows lies to come forth. Because the world does not want peace but rejects the Prince of Peace, therefore, God says, All right, you will have wars come upon you. Because the world rejects life in Christ who is the Bread of Life—therefore, says God, you will have death. Such is the governmental hand of God being manifested. It is as though all this is what the world has asked for, and as a consequence, the unrighteous moral condition of the world is exposed and manifested as well for all to see. Such are the moral consequences of a world that rejects Christ and does not wish to be reconciled to Him. And I believe that that explains in great part what we are witnessing all around us today.

I believe these four horses and their riders represent the governmental dealings of God upon the people of the world. What can anyone expect if people reject the truth? What can anyone expect if people refuse the Prince of Life? In fact, what can anyone expect but these four horsemen? These symbolize the consequences of the ongoing iniquity and rebellion of this world, and so we witness the hand of the Lord upon this earth. So let no one say that God does not care. Oh, how people are tempted to say that very thing. Not so, for God *does* care, and because He cares, He deals with the world. It may be hard, nevertheless, it is towards a world without our Lord Jesus.

There will be false christs and false prophets, wars and rumors of wars, famines, earthquakes, persecution, and death; and these things will gather momentum and be intensified and increased as these last days draw to an end. Throughout these twenty centuries since the ascension of the Lord Jesus these things have been occurring repeatedly and gathering increased momentum and strength; and in coming to the end of the twentieth century, what do we find? We find that all these things have increased in great measure and intensity to an indescribable degree.

We are under the force and power of the enemy but the Lord explained to His disciples that these developments are but the first birth pains. Let us consider for a moment a mother who is pregnant and is going to bring forth her child, and so the day arrives when there will be the first pains of labor. Those first labor pains are not a false alarm. In meaning, they are very real; nevertheless, the child is not born following those first labor pains but they do indicate that the child is soon to come forth. Oh, as she is in labor she is travailing in pain. Indeed, it can be quite sorrowful and painful for her to experience. But after the child is born the mother forgets all those pains and sorrows, for she is happy because the child is born.

We know that the world is in great pain and in much suffering. It continues to suffer under wars, under famines, and under death. If a person has a heart, that one can hardly live with the thought of how much the world suffers. The world as it were is in great labor and pain, but let us understand that it does not labor in vain.

Now many people may ask what is the meaning of all these evil things happening all around them. Is it simply a great amount of pain and suffering without any meaning? To the worldly people it makes no sense, but to us who are the Lord's we know the world is in travail and experiencing as it were its first birth pains. What will come forth out of the sufferings and travail of this world?

In the apostle Paul's Letter to the Romans chapter 8 the Spirit of God tells us very clearly what is happening to the world and its meaning. For there we learn that the whole creation groans and travails together in pain until this very hour. And why? In hope, writes Paul, that the creature itself also shall be set free from the world's bondage to corruption and decay into the liberty of the glory of the children of God. It is for this that the whole world is in travail. Do we hear the groanings of the world? Do we hear the agony, the cry, the sufferings of this world? Now, then, what is all this for? What will come forth as a result? The Spirit of God is working through all these sufferings for the purpose of bringing forth in fullness the manifestation of the Son of God.

The testimony of Jesus is to be worked in and worked out through a believing, faithful and prepared people. Christ is going to claim the world as His own, but this is to be a new mankind that is to rule with Him over the earth. It is to be the one new man (Ephesians 2:15, 4:24). Hence, the world is groaning for that one new man: Christ as the head and His church as the body. God has secured His Man—even Christ; and now this man Christ must be worked in and must be worked out through a body that will be the child that is born through the travail of the world, and this child is to rule over the world.

Oh, the travail in the world is with a purpose. Is it not true that suffering often drives us to the throne of God? If He allowed us to always live peacefully and prosperously, there would never come forth a people prepared for the kingdom. It is through frustration and suffering and trial that man's heart turns to God. Do we now see the love that lies behind His governmental hand? It may be hard, but out of that divine governmental dealing a people will be raised up who have the testimony of Jesus. Oh, yes indeed, the travail of the world is for the furtherance of the testimony of Jesus. Oh that that testimony may be secured in the lives of many; and when that testimony is fully secured, the world shall bring forth that one new man in Christ who is to rule the earth. Can the Lord Jesus publicly claim the world without first having His people ready? If so, He would have no one to live and reign with Him. To put it quite frankly, the Lord needs them.

Oh, we must acknowledge that there is much suffering in the world, but we come to understand that that much suffering purifies. For those of us who live in prosperity and peace, how easy for us to forget God—how easy it is for us to sit back, relax, and enjoy ourselves; but those who are in great suffering press on towards the goal (cf. Philippians 3:14).

Which brings us to the fifth seal, for when this seal is opened by the Lamb John is given to see underneath the altar the souls of them that had been slain for the word of God and for the testimony of Jesus. Oh, throughout the generations and ages God has been working out the testimony of Jesus, and many of those who have the testimony of Jesus have voluntarily sealed that testimony with their blood. And all these martyred souls John saw underneath the altar, who cried out with loud voice: How long will it be, oh holy, true and sovereign Ruler, that You do not judge and avenge our blood on those who dwell on the earth? And there was given to each one of them a white robe; and it was said to them to wait until the number of their fellow bondmen and their brethren who were about to be killed as they had been, should be fulfilled.

We need to compare this passage of Scripture with what I believe are the corresponding words of the Lord Jesus recorded in Matthew 24. There we earlier learned that in the last days the world would suffer greatly under falsehood, wars, famine, and death. But now we learn from Revelation 6 that those in the past who have had the testimony of Jesus had suffered much at the hands of the world. And we learn from Matthew 24 that the same thing will occur to God's faithful followers in these last days. For the Lord Jesus himself prophesied that people of the world would rise up against, persecute, and deliver up to be killed many of Jesus' followers. Moreover, declared the Lord, the love of many will grow cold, but whoever of His own endures to the end shall be saved. And only after the gospel of the kingdom has been preached to all the nations as a witness and testimony to them shall the end come.

Here we find that throughout the generations and ages there has been a people, apprehended by God, who have had wrought into them the testimony of Jesus. They have spread and continue to spread the testimony of Jesus to all the nations as a testimony to all the world that Jesus is Lord, and because they bear this testimony they are killed. In fact, they seal their testimony with their blood. They are seen by John underneath the altar, and towards the end, when they shall have cried out—"How long?"—the answer is given for them to wait a little longer till many more of their brethren shall be slain. Does that not indicate that towards the end of this world there will be a great persecution of Christians everywhere? Many have yet to seal the testimony of Jesus with their blood. The testimony of Jesus must be spread throughout the nations as God's testimony to this world, but in the process many more must give up their lives.

We are told by the Lord that in these last days the love of many shall grow cold but the one who endures to the end shall be saved. We cannot expect to die a martyr's death if we do not live daily a martyr's life—which is to say, a life that is wholly given over to God and a life that is committed to the testimony of Jesus. I believe that this is the lesson for us today. God is allowing the birth pains to occur throughout the entire universe. Things are coming to an end. But how about the testimony of Jesus? What is our relationship with the testimony of Jesus? Do we hold to that testimony or do we let it slip away? And are we willing to seal that testimony in blood? Then the end will come.

Chapter Five

The Seven Seals (2)

And when it opened the fifth seal, I saw underneath the altar the souls of them that had been slain for the word of God, and for the testimony which they held; and they cried with a loud voice, saying, How long, O sovereign Ruler, holy and true, dost thou not judge and avenge our blood on them that dwell upon the earth? And there was given to them, to each one a white robe; and it was said to them that they should rest yet a little while, until both their fellow-bondmen and their brethren, who were about to be killed as they, should be fulfilled.

And I saw when it opened the sixth seal, and there was a great earthquake; and the sun became black as hair sackcloth, and the whole moon became as blood, and the stars of heaven fell upon the earth, as a fig tree, shaken by a great wind, casts its unseasonable figs. And the heaven was removed as a book rolled up, and every mountain and island were removed out of their places. And the kings of the earth, and the great, and the chiliarchs, and the rich, and the strong, and every bondman and freeman, hid themselves in the caves and in the rocks of the mountains; and they say to the mountains and to the rocks, Fall on us, and have us hidden from the face of him that sits upon the throne, and from the wrath of the Lamb;

because the great day of his wrath is come, and who is able to stand?

Revelation 6:9-17

But of that day and hour no one knows, not even the angels of the heavens, but my Father alone. But as the days of Noe, so also shall be the coming of the Son of man. For as they were in the days which were before the flood, eating and drinking, marrying and giving in marriage, until the day on which Noe entered into the ark, and they knew not till the flood came and took all away; thus also shall be the coming of the Son of man. Then two shall be in the field, one is taken and one is left; two women grinding at the mill, one is taken and one is left. Watch therefore, for ye know not in what hour your Lord comes. But know this, that if the master of the house had known in what watch the thief was coming, he would have watched and not have suffered his house to be dug through into. Wherefore ye also, be ye ready, for in that hour that ye think not the Son of man comes.

Matthew 24:36-44

It was mentioned last time that the world we live in today is under the governmental dealing of the Lord. In the vision which John was shown by God while exiled on the Isle of Patmos he saw the risen, glorified and ascended Son of man as the Lamb of God, who is also called the Lion of the tribe of Judah; and John observed that at a certain point the Lamb stepped forward and took the book—the title deed to the created world—from the hand of Him who was seated upon heaven's throne and began to open that book's seven seals.

And with the opening by the Lamb of the fifth seal John saw underneath the altar the souls of them who had been slain for the word of God and for the testimony which they had held. In other words, throughout these past twenty centuries there have been many in every land who have given their lives for the sake of the gospel of the kingdom and for the testimony of Jesus. The slain souls of all these martyrs from throughout the generations and ages John beheld underneath the altar.

A little background may be helpful in providing a better understanding of what John saw. It so happened that within the Jewish temple at Jerusalem was located the altar which had been built on a huge highly elevated rock. Though today the temple is no longer there (except for its wailing wall), the altar rock still exists. For instead of the temple there is today a Moslem mosque; and in the middle of that mosque can be found a huge rock. The Moslems look upon this rock as being a most sacred object because they believe that their prophet Muhammad had ascended to heaven from atop that rock. However, Jews and Christians know that this rock was the original site of the Jewish altar over which had been built the temple of Jerusalem.

Now if you were to look at this rock today you would notice that there is a cleft in the rock whose opening extends all the way down through the rock's interior. In fact, visitors inside this Dome of the Rock Mosque are able to go downstairs and observe this opening in a room which has been constructed there. In ancient Jewish times, therefore, whenever the priests would offer up an animal sacrifice on this altar rock, the blood would flow down through that hole or opening underneath. Hence, that is the historical background to the scene which was pictured for John: the souls of all those martyrs were underneath the altar, symbolizing the fact that they had offered up their life for the testimony of Jesus—that down through all these generations and centuries the souls of those who have been martyred for the word of God and for the testimony of Jesus are there.

But as was pointed out in an earlier message, we must take note of a great change having occurred in the attitude and spirit of these martyred souls as reflected in the words of their recorded loud cry here: "How long, O Sovereign Ruler, holy and true, do You delay judging and avenging our blood on those who dwell upon the earth?" Let us remind ourselves that while on the cross the Lord Jesus said to the Father, "Forgive them, for they know not what they are doing" (see Luke 23:34a). Let us also remind ourselves what the very first martyr for the testimony of Jesus, Stephen, while on his knees and being stoned to death, had cried out: "Lord do not lay this sin against them; forgive them" (see Acts 7:59-60). The cry of the martyrs throughout these twenty centuries past has been this: Forgive. Indeed, the very spirit and attitude of Jesus have been theirs; just as the Lord Jesus had voiced the word forgive, so also on the lips of the dying martyrs one could hear that same word uttered: forgive, forgive. And this has been the characteristic of this Age of Grace continually. Whenever the gospel has been preached throughout the world that sentiment of forgiveness has invariably come forth. The cry of those martyrs has been: "Lord, forgive; lay not this charge upon them."

But now at this moment of the fifth seal being opened, we are given to hear a far different cry from these martyrs: "Lord, how much longer must we wait? When will You judge and avenge our blood upon those who dwell upon the earth?" That is clearly not the same spirit or attitude as before which these martyrs now have. They instead are voicing an opposite cry: a cry for revenge—yet not so much for themselves but more so for the vindication of the name of the Lord. Now why is it that they say such a thing? It is thought that because these martyrs have been in such full sympathy with their Lord that they themselves could sense that a radical change is about to come upon the world. And because they have sensed this soon-coming change in time, these martyrs give expression to this sensing by together offering up a prayer of supplication.

It has been pointed out by our brother Watchman Nee that whenever heaven is about to undertake a desired action, God puts a desire for that action in the hearts of those who are near to Him as a way of prompting them to pray and thus open the path for heaven to work.* And hence, these martyrs, sensing the approaching end to this present age, and being in such close affinity and sympathy with God and His interests and desires, begin to cry aloud that the time is soon coming when He shall vindicate himself upon the earth. The answer from heaven to their cry, however, was for them to wait a little while longer for that time of vindication to come until the number of their fellow bondmen and fellow brethren who were yet to be killed should be completed. Surely, this answer means that great persecution shall break forth on the earth towards the end of this Age of Grace.

Following the opening of the fifth seal the sixth seal is opened and ushers in a vast catastrophe: a great earthquake occurs, the sun becomes dark, the moon becomes like blood, the stars fall to the earth, and the mountains shall be moved out of their places. And at this point all the world over shall begin to realize that the end has come. So severe will be this catastrophe that both rich and poor, kings and great men, and slaves and free men shall attempt to hide in the caves and among the rocks of mountains, and shall even say to the rocks and mountains to fall upon them and hide them from the presence of Him who sits on the throne and from the wrath of the Lamb; for, they shall say, the great day of the wrath of the Lamb has come—and who is able to stand? Surely, they shall believe, the end has come.

---

* A presentation of this Biblical understanding can be found in Watchman Nee, *The Prayer Ministry of the Church* (New York: Christian Fellowship Publishers, 1973), the opening chapter, pp. 8-35. —*Publishers*

Allow me to pause here to ask a question, which is this: that in spite of the fact that there are wars and rumors of wars, famine, earthquakes, death, and wickedness prevailing on every hand in this world, does the world really know that the end is approaching? Yes, there are some people who do warn that doomsday is coming upon the world or that should the hydrogen bomb or atomic bomb or whatever other destructive bomb is available to usher in that kind of warfare, the whole world will be destroyed in the course of such war. Yet, in spite of the fact that people are warned that if the world continues in such condition, sooner or later the earth's doomsday will surely come, nevertheless, do they truly know it? Are they really prepared for that day of the world's doom? Indeed, do they actually live as though they have that knowledge?

No, I would have to say that many people in this world are still dreaming of a coming golden age of peace, prosperity and perfection. They are still intent on bettering the world and do not believe that it will come to an end but insist on making the world their permanent home. In other words, in spite of all these warnings concerning the heavy governmental hand of the Lord on the world, they refuse to believe them and instead are intent on changing it into what they consider to be an improvement. We will recall from Genesis that after Cain killed his brother Abel God placed a curse upon him and told him that henceforth he was to be a vagabond, a wanderer. But what did Cain do? He went away and commenced building cities. God had said that Cain was to be a wanderer, but Cain's response was that, "No, I will live in cities." God had placed upon Cain a wanderer's curse, but in response he said, "Not so, I will try to improve my living condition"; and so there came forth from his descendants musicians, craftsmen and artisans and all such people (4:8-22). In other words, Cain did not submit himself to God's governmental hand and instead rebelled against it.

Is that not the spirit of the world? People's attitude should be that when they see all these devastating things happening in the world, they should submit themselves to the Lord and acknowledge, saying, "Lord, this is because of our sins and iniquities." They should repent. They should come to God and humble themselves under His governmental hand. Such would be the right attitude, yet the world does not assume that attitude but adopts the opposite kind: If, God, You want to deal with us governmentally, we will resist and try to make the world a much better place; we will improve conditions to such an extent that we will be able to live comfortably and live according to the pleasures of the world. Is that not the answer of the world to God's dealing? Instead, we see the spirit of rebellion on every hand. The world does not believe the warnings nor does it accept God's governmental hand. The world continues on its ill-conceived and rebellious way.

In this very connection the Lord Jesus observed to His disciples that as in the days of Noah so shall be the days of the return coming of the Son of man. What were the days of Noah like? They were characterized by the people eating and drinking, marrying and giving in marriage. Now there is nothing wrong with eating and drinking and with marrying and giving in marriage. These are legitimate activities; but though they are legitimate they can be turned into excessive sins. In other words, these pleasures can become the purpose of people's lives. Instead of these activities serving as supports in their life so that they may live wholly for God and His interests, these very things become their world; in fact, they become their god. By making these things their purpose in life, the people of the world immerse themselves in eating, drinking, marrying and giving in marriage, and by so doing they neglect their very souls—by so doing they are diverted from an awareness of the governmental hand of the Lord upon them.

Jesus also remarked to His disciples that just as had happened in the days of Lot so shall it be in the return coming to the earth of the Son of man. Now what exactly had characterized the days of Lot? The people of the world were buying and selling, planting and building (Luke 17:28, 30). Again, let me say that there is nothing wrong with engaging in these activities, for people must certainly buy and sell every day; likewise, people must plant and build. However, if these things become the characteristic of the age, then they become illegitimate, and the danger is that they become the very aim and purpose of people's lives. And by occupying themselves with these activities and pleasures of the world, the people end up having no sympathetic feeling for the Lord. By immersing themselves in these various interests the world's people are totally unaware that the Lord is soon coming, that their world will soon be coming to an end, that the world will not last forever.

I do not say, of course, that there are no individuals warning the world about this. As a matter of fact, even the scientists are warning it. Even so, however, generally speaking, it can be said that the world is not awakened; far from it, people are sleeping. We may here recall God's word through the apostle Paul in I Thessalonians chapter 5 which declares:

> ... the day of the Lord so comes as a thief by night. When they may say, Peace and safety, then sudden destruction comes upon them, as travail upon her that is with child; and they shall in no wise escape. But ye, brethren, are not in darkness, that the day should overtake you as a thief: for all ye are sons of light and sons of day; we are not of night nor of darkness. So then do not let us sleep as the rest do, but let us watch and be sober (vv. 2-6).

Here God's word tells us that the Lord is coming as a thief in the night. Now, of course, we are not to take that statement in the bad sense of that word thief. No, that word is being used as an underlying thought to illustrate something else here. We may therefore ask, What is a thief? and what does a thief do?

Basically, a thief comes to steal. The Gospel of John chapter 10 tells us that a thief has only one motive: he comes to steal. And, of course, a thief comes at the most unexpected hour—usually at night in the darkness. Let us further inquire, What does a thief come forth to steal? Does he come to a person's house and steal that person's garbage? Never! On the contrary, when a thief comes to somebody's house, he will steal the best of what is there. Indeed, more than likely he will go into the master bedroom to see if there are any diamonds or other precious objects which he would want. So, when Jesus comes back to the earth, He will come as a thief. But sad to say, the world today is completely unaware.

Oh! I do not know how to say it, but in my heart I have a burden. I feel that the Lord has given the world enough warnings. He has given it warning after warning after warning. Surely, certain circumstances and situations all around people are serving as warnings, and yet the world is seemingly incapable of discerning them as warnings. The people of the world are still asleep and having a good time. The world is grossly unaware that the Lord is coming and that sudden destruction shall come upon its people.

However, with the opening of the sixth seal people shall begin to realize that the day of the wrath of the Lamb has come. Yes, indeed, the Lord shall come as a thief, but must He come to you and me as a thief? We read earlier from Matthew 24 the words of Jesus that no one knows the day or the hour of His return coming. Yet people today try their best to figure out when the Lord will come. In this connection, I can still recall that when I was a young Christian I was quite interested in prophecy. In fact, I spent years studying prophecy and bought book after book on the subject and read them all; and I still remember coming across a picture of someone who had seen a vision and the vision had to do with the year which had the digits 193 displayed, and in that vision a hand covered the remaining fourth digit. The first three digits of the year prophesied for the Lord's return was displayed as 193, but I did not know what was underneath the hand; but could it be that very year 1935, I mused? Lots of speculations like that were occurring back then, and many other foolish things like that have been occurring ever since.

The Lord himself had clearly told us that no one knows the day or the hour except the Father. But does that mean that because we do not know the day or the hour that therefore we do not know that He is coming?—that therefore His coming must be looked upon by us His followers as that of a thief? that the Lord will somehow pass us by because we, too, like the people of the world, are unaware that the precious object which He wants has disappeared? Of course not! The world's people are sleeping because they are sons of night and sons of darkness; but Paul said that you and I are sons of the day and are sons of light. We should thus not be sleeping but should be those who watch and are sober. Then, at whatever time the Lord may in fact come, we are ready; yet not in the sense that we can predict when the Lord is coming, for He can come at anytime; but in the parallel passage found in Luke's account of the Lord's words we find that He mentioned "in the second watch" and "in the third watch" (12:38a). Yes, we do not know exactly when the Lord shall come, but if we are ready—if we are prepared—then in whatever watch He may come we are prepared. We are watching and waiting for Him.

Thus, the question before us all who are His disciples is: Are we ready? Are we prepared? Are we watchful? Do we live day by day in the light of the Lord's coming? Do we desire to please Him in all things by His Spirit? If so, when the Lord comes, He shall find us ready. Whereas the world is sleeping and does not recognize Him, we ought to be those who watch and can hence recognize Him at His coming.

I think it may be quite helpful for us to go through the New Testament and see how many times the coming of the Lord is described as that of the coming of a thief. I believe it will be most enlightening. For instance, we have already read I Thessalonians chapter 5. There Paul said that the day of the Lord shall come as a thief by night.

Then there is the apostle Peter who declared the same thing. In his second letter Peter wrote in chapter 3 verse 10: "… the day of the Lord will come as a thief, in which the heavens will pass away with a rushing noise, and the elements, burning with heat, shall be dissolved, and the earth and the works in it shall be burnt up."

Jesus himself is recorded by John as having uttered a similar statement; for in Revelation chapter 3 verse 3 He is quoted as having said: "Remember therefore how thou hast received and heard, and keep it and repent. If therefore thou shalt not watch, I will come upon thee as a thief, and thou shalt not know at what hour I shall come upon thee."

Then also, in this same book of Revelation, in its chapter 16, the angel of God is seen by John pouring out the sixth bowl of judgment; and in the course of recording what in the vision he witnessed happening, the apostle inserted the now familiar exhortation of the Lord's and adds an additional word-picture of his own: "Behold, I come as a thief. Blessed is he that watches and keeps his garments, that he may not walk naked, and that they may not see his shame" (v.15). There is a most sobering historical background to this passage. The Jerusalem temple of old was guarded during the night at various strategic points within its premises. Guards would be placed on watch in different parts of the temple lest an intruder might come in the darkness. This was considered such an important duty that the captain of the temple guard (Acts 4:1) would inspect these guards at their posts at irregular hours. Perhaps at midnight, perhaps at 2 o'clock, etc., etc. Thus, at any time of the night that captain would go around the temple to see how these guards were watching. If he should find them sleeping, the punishment would be that they would be stripped of their uniforms and be required to walk naked before their companions.* That was the punishment.

So the apostle John had this as background when recording what the angel had uttered. Today, the church as the house of God is representative of the temple of old. And today we are in the nighttime of the world's history, we are perhaps nearing its midnight hour and God has set us as guards in His house and we should be watching and thus maintaining the testimony of Jesus through the earth's dark hours. But if the Lord should find us sleeping instead of watching, what will be the result? We shall be stripped of our garments as punishment. Can the Lord come to His church as a thief? Can the Lord come to you as a thief? Yes, He shall most certainly come as a thief, but can it be that He comes to *you and me* as a thief? If you and I are not watching, then His coming to us will indeed be as a thief. And we shall suffer loss.

Now in that passage read earlier from the third chapter of Revelation, the words written there are addressed by the risen, ascended Son of man to the church in Sardis: "I know thy works, that thou hast a name that thou livest, and art [actually] dead." The Lord went on to say that if they did not repent, then He would come upon them as a thief, and that they would not know at what hour He would come upon them. The Son of man said, "I will come upon you." In other words, He would pass them by because He would not consider them as precious treasure for Him to take away in rapture.

Let us now turn again to Matthew chapter 24. In that chapter we find Jesus speaking to His disciples of His return coming, and states that His coming shall be as in the long-ago days of Noah. Back then, as in our own day, people were eating, drinking, marrying and giving in marriage as though nothing unusual or adverse would happen—indeed, as though the world

* For further details on the rounds of the captain of the temple guard see Alfred Edersheim, *The Temple* (London: James Clarke & Co. Ltd., 1959), chapter 7, "At Night In the Temple," pp. 147-9. —*Publishers*

would continue onward in this manner forever. All like this continued to occur till the day on which Noah entered the ark, and the people knew not of what was about to happen until the flood came and took all away. Thus also, added Jesus, shall be the coming of the Son of man. So here we find the Lord saying that His coming would be like what occurred in the days of Noah.

Let us look, though, at what Jesus *next* said: "Then two shall be in the field, one is taken and one is left; two women [shall be] grinding at the mill, one is taken and one is left. Watch therefore, for ye know not in what hour your Lord comes." Do we get what the Lord is saying here? The world today will go on unconsciously doing as was done in Noah's day as though nothing will happen out of the ordinary until, like Noah who entered the ark, the Lord does something unusual—He returns to the earth. And when that occurs, what will happen? Jesus explains to the twelve what will happen: Two will be in the field, one is taken and one is left. Two women will be grinding at the mill, one is taken and the other is left. And in Luke 17 we read that Jesus also said that in the night two will be on one bed, one shall be taken and the other shall be left (v.34 ASV).

Actually, these passages in Matthew and Luke are an indirect confirmation that the earth is round; for the three activities described—all taking place simultaneously when the Son of man returns—shall be occurring at three different places on the earth as it rotates on its axis around the sun. For notice that two women shall be grinding at the mill: that is an indication of early morning. Also, two persons shall be working out in the field: a reference in time to daylight around noon. And two persons shall be in one bed sleeping: an activity which obviously happens during nighttime. We can therefore infer from all this that the earth is truly round.

Let us additionally take notice of the repetition here of the word two: two, two, two. Two in Scripture is the number having to do with being a witness: by the word of two or three witnesses a matter shall be established or confirmed (Deuteronomy 19:15, Matthew 18:16b, 20). And at the time of the Son of man's return to the earth one person in each of these two-person activities, declares the Lord, shall be taken and the other person shall be left behind.

Outwardly both persons within each couple are engaged in the same activity, but inwardly they are quite different in heart and attitude. Accordingly, declared Jesus to the Twelve, when He shall come back to the earth, one of the two is taken and one is left. And hence, the precious treasure for which the Lord will be coming back shall be separated from the non-precious. This is because, like a thief in the night, the Lord will naturally take to himself the best, thus meaning that the person taken is considered most precious by the Lord but the person left behind is not deemed to be good enough to be taken at that time.

Oh, how sobering are the concluding words of Jesus to His disciples: "Watch, therefore, for you do not know in what hour your Lord comes." The Lord Jesus cannot expect the people of the world to watch because they do not believe in Him; but He does expect us who are His followers to be watchful and ready for His return coming. Let us therefore be those who are continually watching and making themselves ready, for in the hour when, said Jesus, we think the Son of man will not come, He will.

Related to those words of Jesus' warning are similar warning words of His to His disciples which are recorded in Luke's Gospel chapter 21:

> ... then shall they see the Son of man coming ... Take heed to yourselves lest possibly your hearts be laden with surfeiting and drinking and cares of life, and that day come upon you suddenly unawares; for as a snare shall it come upon all them that dwell upon the face of the whole earth. Watch therefore, praying at every season, that you may be accounted worthy to escape

all these things which are about to come to pass, and to stand before the Son of man (vv. 27a, 34-36).

And, then, in like manner, the risen, glorified and ascended Son of man is quoted in Revelation chapter 3 as writing the following to the church in Philadelphia: "Because thou hast kept the word of my patience, I also will keep thee out of the hour of trial, which is about to come upon the whole habitable world" (v.10).

Here is the lesson for us to learn, that so far as the people of the world are concerned the Lord shall come upon them as a thief—that they are completely unaware, but may it not be so with us who are the Lord's. He does not desire that this should happen to us, but that we should be watching and praying. We should be delivered from the things, desires and cares of this world and be ready so that when the Son of man shall come back, He shall look upon us as a precious treasure and will thus take us first.

Perhaps, because of the constraints of time, I must conclude our discussion together today with the following few remarks regarding the coming again of the Lord Jesus as ought to be mentioned when considering the New Testament Greek term *parousia*. That term conveys the thought that His "coming" or "presence" includes within its meaning besides those words the idea of there not being just one event but a series of events covering more than a moment of time. And here I would attempt to lay the matter before us in very simple fashion as I have come to understand it. Yet, you need not accept my understanding, should you not like it.

The *parousia* or coming of the Lord, then, covers a period of events which commences with the rapture of the man-child as presented in Revelation chapter 12 and concludes with the Lord's appearing upon the earth that is visible to all—just as is lightning which shines from east to west

(Matthew 24:27, 30a, c). The one event marks the beginning of *parousia* and the other denotes the end.*

Let us also take note of how the Son of man was received up into heaven after His resurrection, as is laid out for us by Luke in his book of Acts chapter 1. There we are told that Jesus was received up into heaven as the disciples looked and looked upward until they could no longer see the ascending Lord because of the cloud which ultimately had enveloped Him. At which point two men in white apparel appeared on the scene and explained to these Galilean disciples of Christ that He who had just then been taken up from them into heaven would come back in exactly the same manner as they had seen Him ascend up into heaven (vv. 10-11). Thus, in the same way as the Lord Jesus had gone up, so shall He return.

Now, then, how did the risen Son of man depart into heaven? Verse 9 of this same passage in Acts 1 tells us that as He was taken up while His disciples watched, they beheld Him ascending until a cloud received the Lord out of their sight. At first they saw Him, and then they saw Him not any longer. Such was the initial stage in Jesus' ascending and it was visible to His disciples, whereas the second stage—which occurred unseen behind the cloud—was invisible to them. And hence, in accordance with the testimony of those two men in white, the Son of man's return coming to the earth will likewise be in two

* For a helpful explanation of this Greek New Testament term, see W.E. Vine, *An Expository Dictionary of New Testament Words* (Old Tappan NJ: Fleming H. Revell Co., 1966, 1st published 1940), Vol. I, pp. 208-9. In part it reads: "*Parousia* ..., lit., a presence, *para*, with, and *ousia*, being ..., denotes both an arrival and a consequent presence with. ... When used of the return of Christ ... it signifies, not merely His momentary coming ..., but His presence with [His saints] from that moment until His revelation and manifestation to the world. In some passages the word gives prominence to the beginning of that period, the course of the period being implied, ... 1 Thess. 4:15; 5:23; 2 Thess. 2:1 ... In some, the course is prominent, Matt. 24:3, 37; 1 Thess. 3:13; 1 John 2:28; in others the conclusion of the period, Matt. 24:27; 2 Thess. 2:8." —*Publishers*

stages, but in *reverse* order: His return's first stage being *un*seen and the second stage being seen. He will come as a thief during that first stage (Matthew 24:42-44, Revelation 3:3), whereas in the visible second stage of His return coming He shall appear as the King of kings and Lord of lords, as He is called in Revelation 17:14 and 19:16.

Let us be clear that the Lord does not desire that we should be sleeping and thus be caught unaware but He desires that we should be watching and waiting for His coming. His great desire is that He would be able to take us to himself because we are most precious. But what if we live as do the people of the world? In that case the Lord will be compelled to come upon us as would a thief and we shall find ourselves left behind instead of taken. You may ask, Who will be taken and who will remain? It is clear to me that those who have been true to the testimony of Jesus will be taken but those who have been false to the testimony of Jesus cannot be taken because they are not ready.

This is a most serious matter. I realize, of course, that there are Christians who naively comfort themselves by saying that it does not really matter how we live on this earth—whether that be watching or sleeping; for when the Lord comes, they believe, we shall all go together and experience a happy reunion. Yes, it is true that there will come a day when we who are the Lord's will all be united; but when will that happen and under what circumstances?

I must state again that anything and everything which concerns the Lord is moral and spiritual in nature and is never something mechanical. Hence, even in this matter of the Lord's return coming, it too is moral and spiritual in character. May the Lord use these simple words to awaken us so that we may watch and pray and be saved from all which is contrary to Him.

Finally, let me say that I realize that there are many different interpretations regarding the end-times. I do not ask you to accept what I believe to be true. Yes, you may hold to other interpretations, but you believe the Bible just as I do. It is not my intention to impose upon you any interpretation; but no matter what your interpretation may be, there is one very important consideration: What is your and my present relationship with the testimony of Jesus? Let none of us push that aside, regardless the interpretation we may hold. What is most central and vital is the testimony of Jesus. How true, then, is it in your life and mine? We shall discover that the answer to that question will make all the difference.

So may the Lord be merciful to us all.

Chapter Six

The First through Fourth Trumpets

And when it opened the seventh seal, there was silence in the heaven about half an hour. And I saw the seven angels who stand before God, and seven trumpets were given to them. And another angel came and stood at the altar, having a golden censer; and much incense was given to him, that he might give efficacy to the prayers of all saints at the golden altar which was before the throne. And the smoke of the incense went up with the prayers of the saints, out of the hand of the angel before God. And the angel took the censer, and filled it from the fire of the altar, and cast it on the earth: and there were voices, and thunders and lightnings, and an earthquake.

And the seven angels who had the seven trumpets prepared themselves that they might sound with their trumpets.

And I saw, and I heard an eagle flying in mid-heaven, saying with a loud voice, Woe, woe, woe, to them that dwell upon the earth, for the remaining voices of the trumpet of the three angels who are about to sound.

Revelation 8:1-6, 13

When therefore ye shall see the abomination of desolation, which is spoken of through Daniel the prophet, standing in what is a holy place, (he that reads let him understand,) then let those who are in

> Judaea flee to the mountains; let not him that is on the house come down to take the things out of his house; and let not him that is in the field turn back to take his garment. But woe to those that are with child, and those that give suck in those days. But pray that your flight may not be in winter time nor on sabbath: for then shall there be great tribulation, such as has not been from the beginning of the world until now, nor ever shall be; and if those days had not been cut short, no flesh had been saved; but on account of the elect those days shall be cut short.
>
> Matthew 24:15-22

It was mentioned last time that the coming of the Lord is as a thief who will come suddenly, unexpectedly, and who will take away what is most precious to Him. The risen, glorified, ascended Son of man shall come to this world as a thief and come upon it unawares. But must it be that way with us who are His? It should never be so because we are sons of day and sons of light; nevertheless, it *can* happen to us. Let us recall once more the warning which the Son of man gave to the church at Sardis: If you do not repent, then I will come upon you as a thief—I will come and pass you by—I will leave you there when I take up with Me what is most precious to My heart. Let us realize afresh that the coming of the Lord is imminent, and because of that, we must be ever watchful and prepared.

I would like to bring to your attention one other point, which is that there is nothing standing in the way of the Lord's coming. Which is to say that He can come at any moment; for whatever needed to be fulfilled prior to the beginning of His *parousia*-presence has already been realized or is currently in the process of being realized. As I shall shortly make clear, I believe there is but one circumstance which must occur first and then the Son of man will come. Hence, if we know God's word rightly, we can safely say that there is nothing which blocks His coming and He can therefore come at anytime. There is, of course, a reason why the Lord has not returned to the earth yet and that is because the man-child is still in the making. However, as soon as the man-child is completed and born, the *parousia*-presence of the Lord shall occur.

But someone may raise an objection and begin to quote II Thessalonians chapter 2 where Paul the apostle mentions the coming of the Lord, as follows:

> Now we beg you, brethren, by the coming of our Lord Jesus Christ and our gathering together to him, that ye be not soon shaken in mind, nor troubled, neither by spirit, nor by word, nor by letter, as if it were by us, as that the day of the Lord is present. Let not anyone deceive you in any manner, because it will not be unless the apostasy have first come, and the man of sin have been revealed, the son of perdition ... (vv. 1-3).

Here Paul is saying that no believer should be deceived, for the day of the Lord (that is, the day of the Lord's judgment upon the world) will not come until there first comes apostasy—a falling away from faith—and then the man of sin—the son of perdition, the lawless one—shall appear. That one, Paul goes on to explain, is he

> who opposes and exalts himself on high against all called God, or object of veneration; so that he himself sits down in the temple of God, shewing himself that he is God. ... And now ye know that which restrains, that he should be revealed in his own time. For the mystery of lawlessness already works; only there is he who restrains now until he be gone, and then the

> lawless one shall be revealed, whom the Lord Jesus shall consume with the breath of his mouth, and shall annul by the appearing of his coming ... (vv. 4-8).

The apostle is saying here that the man of sin, the son of perdition, who is the embodiment of lawlessness, will come and do away with everything pertaining to God as the object of man's veneration and thus present himself as God and henceforth require everyone on earth to worship him and no one and nothing else. Paul makes clear that until all of this shall appear on earth, believers can be sure that the day of the Lord—the day of His judgment upon the earth—has not yet come. Only after the lawless one shall have been revealed shall the Lord return, who will then consume the lawless one with the breath of His mouth and thus annul and bring to an end the lawless one by the appearance of the Lord's *parousia*-presence.

Yes, these are what the Scriptures tell us; and yes, from these particular scripture passages someone could make the case that the Lord cannot come until apostasy makes its appearance and until the man of sin, the Antichrist, has been revealed. For does this Scripture not say here that unless the man of sin shall appear, the day of the Lord shall not come? Moreover, we know today, as did the Thessalonian believers in their day (2:6a), who it is who is restraining the appearing of the lawless one; and only when he that restrains is taken away will the lawless one be revealed and then the Lord shall come and bring him to an end by the appearing of His *parousia*-presence. Yes, all that is in fact true, according to these Scriptures.

However, if we read all the relevant passages of Scripture carefully, we will see what I have pointed out before: that the *parousia*-coming of the Lord back to the earth has about it two distinct stages. The first stage is characterized by His coming as a thief, and as we well know, a thief will not issue a warning first before he comes; for if he should warn of his coming tonight to someone's home, that one would wait up for the thief. So because a thief will come forth without warning it means that the thief's coming will be a hidden action. And thus we see that in that same manner the first stage of the Lord's *parousia*-coming is likewise a hidden action.

On the other hand, the second stage of the Lord's *parousia* or return coming to the earth will be marked by many advance warnings, and thus this stage will be open and apocalyptic or revelatory in nature. We therefore find in verse 8 the mention of "the appearing of his [the Lord's] coming," which is an open appearing, and thus we also learn from this quoted passage in II Thessalonians 2 that this second stage must be preceded by both apostasy and the revealing of the son of perdition.

Let us therefore be reminded that there is nothing which must be fulfilled before the *beginning* stage of the Son of man's coming. At the *end* of His coming—at the end of His *parousia*—yes, that will be true: the apostasy must first come, also the man of sin or son of perdition must be revealed, whom the Lord shall then slay by the very appearance of His coming—all of that is quite correct. However, as for the initial stage of *parousia*, its occurrence can happen at any moment without any advance warning or indication of its soon-taking place.

Let us next notice again these words from this same II Thessalonians passage:

> And now ye know that which restrains, that he should be revealed in his own time. For the mystery of lawlessness already works; only there is he who restrains now until he be gone, and then the lawless one shall be revealed ...

We know that lawlessness has already been at work on this earth for quite some time. Everywhere one looks there is lawlessness: in the world situation, in every nation, in nearly every city, in any association and society. There is even lawlessness in political and religious systems. Everywhere one may look, one can find lawlessness present. The mystery of lawlessness is very much at work on earth. But let us thank God that the lawless one himself has not as yet been revealed. And why? There is that which restrains and holds back the full measure of lawlessness. Yes, the world is marked already by much lawlessness, and it is sickening to our hearts to have to behold it on every hand. But we do thank God that there is still something or someone that restrains the mystery of lawlessness in its current manifestation in the world, which is bad enough as it is. However, when that restraining one is gone, then the deepest mystery of lawlessness shall break forth in full force and fury, the likes of which the world has heretofore never seen.

Who is that one? Who is the one that when he is gone the lawless one shall be revealed in the worst light? Now when writing his second Thessalonian letter Paul had taken for granted that the Thessalonian believers knew the answer (2:5-6); and we today ought to know as well who he that restrains is. Personally, I believe that the "he" here is an allusion to the company of the overcomers. It is their presence on this earth in bearing a pure testimony of Jesus which holds back the fiercest lawlessness in the world. Jesus has called those who are His "the light of the world" (Matthew 5:14). Paul has written elsewhere that the world looks upon believers as the offscouring of the world (cf. I Corinthians 4:13, Lamentations 3:45). Nevertheless, it is because of those who are faithful to the Lord and to His testimony that the world is not worse off, for the lawlessness throughout the world at its current worst could still be far more severe. If we read the Scriptures most carefully we must acknowledge that the day is coming when the world shall be thrown into a situation that no one can imagine. No wonder the Bible calls it the *Great* Tribulation.

Oh, a great and most severe tribulation is about to come upon the world. A tribulation that the world has never witnessed before and shall never witness again: the Great Tribulation. Oh, when he who restrains is taken away, that shall be the time that the lawless one is revealed and makes his appearance on the world's stage. At that time all hell shall break forth, for then there is nothing in the world to provide restraint of any kind. Yet we must thank the merciful God that in the world today there is still he that restrains.

Now the pronoun he in this passage is a collective term, and it includes all in the world at that time who have the testimony of Jesus and who are faithful to God. However, when the time comes that the "he" be gone, which, I believe, is when the male child of Revelation 12 is "caught up to God and to his throne," then it shall happen that there will be "war in the heaven": Michael and his angels shall fight against Satan and his host and shall prevail. And because of this, there shall be found no more place for Satan in heaven and he shall be cast down upon the earth (vv.5b, 7-9). And if Satan and his angels shall be cast down to the earth, what can the world expect but the greatest degree of tribulation?

Now what we need to take to heart from all this is the following. The coming of the Son of man is near. He may come at any moment. Will you and I be found ready? Will He consider us as most precious to His heart and take us to himself, or will He be compelled to leave us behind? One day the world shall suddenly become aware that many of the saints of God have disappeared from the earth, and my prayer is that by the grace of God we may be those who are ready to be taken up.

Now we learned last time that with the Lamb opening the sixth seal, there shall be a great change which shall occur in the heavens and on the earth, and because of that great change the world shall be awakened to the fact that the wrath of the Lamb of God will have finally come; and, says Revelation, "who is able to stand?" (6:17) Let me inquire, Have you ever actually seen a lamb in wrath? We are very much aware, of course, that a lamb is the very symbol of meekness, lowliness, gentleness and kindness. I myself have never seen a lamb in anger or in wrath. But I would imagine that a lamb in wrath must be a very terrible thing to witness. When the Lord Jesus was on the earth, he was the Lamb of God who takes away the sin of this world, and how lowly and meek He was. The prophet Isaiah tells us that He was led to the slaughter as a lamb and He was dumb as a sheep before its shearers: He as the Lamb of God did not open His mouth (53:7). Such was the Lord while He was on earth the first time. Oh, how gentle, how meek, how lowly and long-suffering He as the Lamb was on earth—so much so that one could do most anything to Him and He simply accepted it all. That was the Lord while on earth as the meek and lowly sacrificial Lamb of God.

But did we ever have pictured for us in Scripture the Lord Jesus in anger while He was on earth? Yes, we will recall that on one occasion He had gone up to Jerusalem and, observing the gross temple environment that day—people buying and selling and money changers conducting business—the zeal and fury of God so devoured Jesus that He made a scourge of cords for himself and drove the much oxen and sheep away, overturned the tables of the money changers, and ordered those who sold doves to cease doing so. Declared Jesus in righteous anger: "You are making My Father's house a place of merchandise!" Oh, how angry He was! Could anyone resist Him that day? In their reaction to this scene, the priests and Pharisees were all angry, but none of them dared to confront the Lord (John 2:13-17). The Lamb of God was in anger, and who among men is able to stand? (cf. Revelation 6:17)

We may perhaps recall another interesting occasion of this kind. Jesus, upon entering the synagogue in Capernaum one sabbath day, saw a man with a withered hand. Standing about inside the synagogue were some scribes and Pharisees who were very carefully observing Jesus to see whether He would heal on the Sabbath or not, they seeking something of which to accuse Him. Though He was aware of their thoughts, at this point He was not angry; but He did take a very strong stand against unrighteousness on their part. So the Lord commanded the man with the withered hand to stand up and stretch forth his hand, and it was soundly restored. Then turning to all the onlookers present, Jesus inquired of them as follows: "Is it right, is it lawful, to do good or harm on the Sabbath—to save life or to destroy?" And no one responded.

Now because of their unwillingness to respond, and to respond rightly, the Lord Jesus at this moment became very angry, becoming so because of the hardness of these people's hearts. They were supposed to be worshipers of God, and yet they were so hardhearted (cf. Luke 6:6-11, Mark 3:1-6, Matthew 12:9-14). Nevertheless, in this moment of His anger, Jesus as the Lamb of God on earth was nonetheless meek. Those who were opposed to Him could do anything they pleased to Him—even crucify Him if they so wished—but there was no resistance on His part. The only response to their crucifixion of the Lamb of God was this: "Forgive them, Father, for they know not what they are doing" (see Luke 23:34). Such, then, was the conduct of the precious Lamb of God during His first visit to this earth.

The day is coming, however, when the Lamb shall be in wrath, and when the Lamb is in wrath, the whole world shall cry out, Who is able to stand? The kings and princes, the great men and commanders, the rich and poor, the freemen and bondmen—everybody shall cry out, Who can stand it? The Lamb shall manifest His wrath (Revelation 6:12-17). Oh, may I warn those of you here who may not be His followers, Do not provoke the Lord too much. Yes, He suffers long. Yes, you can provoke Him again and again and He suffers and suffers as if there is no end. But I would advise you to be careful. The day shall come when the Lamb shall be in wrath and then, what shall happen next?

That was the opening of the sixth seal; but with the opening of the seventh, something quite different shall appear to happen at that time, for when the apostle John saw the Lamb open this final seal there was silence in heaven for half an hour (8:1). As the well-known adage declares, this shall be the calm before the gathering storm, and portends that something unusually great is about to occur. But first there shall be the silence. Why this silence? The seven angels who having received seven trumpets stand before God; they are ready to sound their trumpets, yet they are seen waiting. Waiting for what? They are waiting for the prayers of the saints to ascend upward to heaven. We considered together this principle before, that whenever heaven is desirous of making a move, it waits for the prayers of the saints to ascend to God. In other words, the signal for the movement of heaven to occur is given by the church down on earth. The heaven is ready, the seven angels are there with their seven trumpets—ready to be sounded, and yet they and heaven are waiting—waiting for a signal, and the signal comes by means of the prayers of the saints. When their prayers shall rise up to the throne, then the angel with the golden censer shall take the fire from the golden altar, fill the censer with the fire, and shall cast it upon the earth; and with that there shall come forth voices, thunders, lightnings and an earthquake; and only then shall there begin the sounding—one by one—of the seven trumpets by the seven waiting angels (8:2-5).

We see here that heaven is ready to act, but are we who are the church ready? Let us not say that we are waiting for *the Lord* to act; no, He is waiting for us to act. How often we pray, "O Lord, how long must we wait? Why do You delay?" The Lord may answer, "I am waiting for the church to be ready. Are you ready?"

It was mentioned last time that the seals speak of the governmental dealings of God. Trumpets, though, speak of military action. Upon reading the opening of the first four seals we discover that all these can be considered as that which shall cause human woe of many kinds. These are various man-made disasters: wars, famines, earthquakes, and death—all these are man-made human woes, and they are the natural consequences of the sins and iniquities perpetrated by the people of this world. And we all are suffering today as a result.

But when considering the various upcoming outcomes of the sounding of the trumpets, their character appears to be so unnatural. We may say, in fact, that these shall be *heavenly* disasters when heaven strikes; which is to say that heaven shall have declared war upon this world's corruption; and especially when considering the fifth and sixth trumpets, we learn that heaven shall let loose all the evil forces in the universe and that such phenomena shall begin to appear which has never before appeared even up to this day.

We do not have time left today to go into this matter in detail, but probably I can say this much. At the beginning of our time today we read together what the Lord Jesus very clearly told His disciples, that when there shall be seen the abomination of desolation standing in the holy place, as prophesied by Daniel, then it will be known that the end has come. For there shall be great tribulation upon this earth such as has never happened before nor ever shall be thereafter. Indeed, this great tribulation will be a most terrible period in world history. And whether you hold to the notion of the great tribulation being seven years or three and a half years in length, we can all agree that there will at least be three and a half years of great tribulation.

But why, you may ask, is it called a great tribulation? In response, let me say that I believe it is described as such in Scripture because during this end-time the trinity of evil shall be on this earth. First of all, we learn from Revelation 12 that the great dragon, that ancient serpent, who is called Devil and Satan, he who accuses the brethren and deceives the entire habitable world, will end up being cast down upon the earth and, knowing that his time is short, he shall pour out his wrath upon the remnant of the seed of the woman who will have given birth to the man-child: that remnant being those who keep the commandments of God and have the testimony of Jesus (see

12:9, 10b, 12b-c, 17). This is what will happen when the first of the trinity of evil, Satan himself, shall be cast down to the earth. For immediately following the rapture of the man-child to God and His throne, war shall break out in the heaven between on the one hand the archangel Michael with his angels and on the other the dragon Satan and his angels (12:5, 7).

This which has been foretold and described in Revelation 12 regarding Satan being cast out of the heaven will actually be a fulfillment of Jesus' words recorded in Luke 10. Those words were uttered on the occasion of the seventy disciples who having been sent forth two by two by the Lord in advance of His coming later to each place to be visited, returned to Jesus with great joy and reported the fact that even the demons had been subject to them through His name. To which the Lord declared: "I beheld Satan as lightning falling out of heaven. Behold, I give you the power of treading upon serpents and scorpions and over all the power of the enemy …" (vv.1, 17-19). In other words, Jesus has given power to His church and that shall cause the downfall of Satan. Indeed, it will be the rapture of the man-child which shall cause the devil's downfall.

But second with regard to the trinity of evil on earth, we are told in Revelation 13 that there will rise out of the sea a horrible-looking beast who will turn out to be the Antichrist (vv.1-9) and the little horn that Daniel had prophesied about (8:9-12, 23-25). And as to the third of this evil trio, there shall come forth another beast, this one arising out of the earth and looking like a lamb but speaking like a dragon (Revelation 13:11ff.). This will be the false prophet who shall work great deceptive signs among the world's populace. And thus shall there be this trinity of evil upon the earth in the last days; and therefore, what can anyone expect to be the condition of the world other than the Great Tribulation?!?

Hence, I think it is probably appropriate to simply close with the words of the Lord Jesus recorded in Luke chapter 21:

> The heaven and the earth shall pass away, but my words shall in no wise pass away. But take heed to yourselves lest possibly your hearts be laden with surfeiting and drinking and cares of life, and that day come upon you suddenly unawares; for as a snare shall it come upon all them that dwell upon the face of the whole earth. Watch therefore, praying at every season, that ye may be accounted worthy to escape all these things which are about to come to pass, and to stand before the Son of man (v.33-36).

Here the Lord said for us to watch and pray that we may be accounted worthy. Worthy of what? Worthy to escape all these terrible things which are about to occur, and to stand before the Son of man. So who shall be those who escape? Will it not be the collective man-child of overcomers who shall escape in that day, as intimated in Revelation 12:5? And again, let us note what the Son of man tells the overcoming church at Philadelphia: "Because thou hast kept the word of my patience, I also will keep thee out of the hour of trial, which is about to come upon the whole habitable world" (Revelation 3:10). These overcoming saints in Philadelphia will not be there but they will have escaped as part of the raptured man-child.

So let us not be dwellers of the world. Let us not make this world our home and be rooted in it. Let us not fill our lives with the cares of this life. Let us instead be watchful and praying always that we may be deemed to be worthy to escape all this and to stand before the Son of man.

Chapter Seven

The Fifth and Sixth Trumpets

And I saw, and I heard an eagle flying in mid-heaven, saying with a loud voice, Woe, woe, woe, to them that dwell upon the earth, for the remaining voices of the trumpet of the three angels who are about to sound.

Revelation 8:13

And the fifth angel sounded his trumpet: and I saw a star out of the heaven fallen to the earth; and there was given to it the key of the pit of the abyss.

Revelation 9:1

And there was war in the heaven: Michael and his angels went to war with the dragon. And the dragon fought, and his angels; and he prevailed not, nor was their place found any more in the heaven. And the great dragon was cast out, the ancient serpent, he who is called Devil and Satan, he who deceives the whole habitable world, he was cast out into the earth, and his angels were cast out with him.

And I heard a great voice in the heaven saying, Now is come the salvation and the power and the kingdom of our God, and the authority of his Christ; for the accuser of our brethren has been cast out, who accused them before our God day and night: and they have overcome him by reason of the blood of the Lamb, and by reason of the word of their testimony, and have not loved their life even unto death. Therefore be full of delight, ye heavens, and ye that dwell in them. Woe to the earth and to the sea, because the devil has come down to you, having great rage, knowing he has a short time.

And when the dragon saw that he had been cast out into the earth, he persecuted the woman which bore the male child. And there were given to the woman the two wings of the great eagle, that she might fly into the desert into her place, where she is nourished there a time, and times, and half a time, from the face of the serpent. And the serpent cast out of his mouth behind the woman water as a river, that he might make her be as one carried away by a river. And the earth helped the woman, and the earth opened its mouth and swallowed the river which the dragon cast out of his mouth. And the dragon was angry with the woman, and went to make war with the remnant of her seed, who keep the commandments of God, and have the testimony of Jesus.

Revelation 12:7-17

Up to this point our discussion together on the book of Revelation has brought us to the sounding of the first four of seven trumpets following the opening by the Lamb of all seven seals that enclosed the book containing the title deed to the entire created universe which the Lamb had taken from the right hand of Him who sits on heaven's throne. And as was pointed out last time, these trumpet soundings shall carry within them the projection of military action; which is to say that there is coming a day, sooner rather later, when heaven shall declare war upon this sinful wayward earth. For the nature of the various disasters which shall immediately follow the sounding of these first four trumpets can in no way be considered to be man-made but heavenly-propelled in character. As the relevant passages in Revelation inform us, the third part of the earth, of the sea, of the rivers, and even the third part of all the heavenly bodies—sun, moon and stars—shall all be affected disastrously (vv.7-12). And thus it becomes clear that calamitous events shall be closing in upon the entire habitable world as the end-days themselves approach closer and closer.

Now following the sounding of the fourth trumpet but before the sounding of the fifth, the apostle John beheld a most spectacular sight. Reported the apostle:

> I saw, and I heard an eagle flying in mid-heaven, saying with a loud voice, Woe, woe, woe, to them that dwell upon the earth, for the remaining voices of the trumpet of the three angels who are about to sound.

In other words, one can infer from this that there will be even greater disasters coming upon this earth—that which the world has never witnessed before. We may think that we are living in an extremely troublesome time already and that the troubles of this world appear to be quite enough for us; however, the Bible predicts that the world has yet to see and to experience a series of disasters which it has never known before. Woe—woe—woe: are these not the words indicating that the long prophesied Great Tribulation will have now come upon them that dwell upon the earth?

That word dwell conveys a very definite thought in the Bible. It conveys the thought of earth-dwellers: those who make the earth their home: those who are rooted and grounded in this earth: those who make the earth their primary aim and goal of life: those whose lives are primarily if not fully occupied with the things of the earth: those whose hearts are being enticed and filled to excess with eating and drinking and cares of life (Luke 21:34a). Such are the earth-dwellers.

The Lord Jesus has delivered us out of this world. Yes, we are still *in* the world but we are no longer *of* the world. Let us recall the apostle Peter's word that we believers are strangers and sojourners on this earth (I Peter 2:11a). Let us also recall what the writer of Hebrews declared: that we, like Abraham of old, are looking for a city with foundations whose builder is God himself (11:10), and that city is our permanent home. We are not to be earth-dwellers anymore. Yes, we still live on this earth but we are merely passing through as heaven-bound sojourners and travelers. We know that "we are but strangers here" and no longer earth-dwellers.

But we can also infer from this description—"Woe to them that dwell upon the earth"—a further thought being conveyed, namely, that there are some who have lived upon the earth but who are no longer there. And sure enough, as one continues to read in Revelation, we learn that there are those who shall be tabernacled in heaven, for they shall be translated or raptured to heaven (the collective man-child told of in chapter 12). But, cried out the flying eagle, "Woe to those who, still living on this earth, have become earth-dwellers"; for then shall the Great Tribulation come upon them and none shall escape.

We who have been redeemed by the precious blood of the Lord Jesus, are we here on the earth as strangers and sojourners or do we occupy ourselves with the things of the world to such an extent that we too have become earth-dwellers? If so, we shall not dwell in heaven.

Let us remind ourselves what the Son of man promised to the church at Philadelphia: "Because thou hast kept the word of my patience, I also will keep thee out of the hour of trial, which is about to come upon the whole habitable world, to try them that dwell upon the earth" (Revelation 3:10). A time is coming, and it is coming soon, that there will be a great trial—even the Great Tribulation—which shall come upon the entire world to try those who are earth-dwellers. If, however, a person keeps the word of the Lord's patience, He has promised to keep that one out of the time or hour of that trial.

There is a difference between being kept *through* the trial and being kept *out of* or *from* the trial and being kept out of or from the *hour* of trial. Being kept through the trial means that a person is living in the trial but is being preserved. Being kept out of the trial means that when the trial comes upon a person, he or she is off somewhere else. However, being kept out of the hour of trial means that when the hour of trial for tribulation appears, that hour never comes to you personally. Thus, the Lord's promise here is that if anyone maintains the word of His patience, He will keep that one not only out of the trial but even out of the hour of the trial itself. In other words, when that hour strikes, the faithful believer will not be there. So what is the condition for the believer to be spared from even the hour? Answer: the believer has been faithful in having kept the word of the Lord's patience.

The question which therefore needs to be asked is this: Are you and I losing patience with regard to the Lord's coming? How many of God's children have lost their patience in this regard? How many have grown impatient? Impatient with the Lord, we say to Him: Lord, You have not yet come, so we have commenced loving and enjoying the world and immersing ourselves in the cares of the world and occupying ourselves once more with the pleasures of this world. We have the tendency of growing impatient with the Lord Jesus over the matter of His return coming. Oh, how many Christians are impatient to see the coming kingdom. And because of the Lord's delay, they turn to enjoying themselves in the world instead of waiting patiently for Him to come. Instead of living for that which is invisible they live for that which is visible. They forget that what is visible is transient but what is invisible is eternal. Many of God's people have lost patience.

When Jesus walked on this earth, how patient He was. When offered by the devil all the kingdoms of the earth, the Lord refused because He was most patient—He was patient enough to wait until God the Father should give Him the kingdom legally and rightfully and after His going through the cross. Are we growing very impatient? Or are we willing to take up our cross and follow Him? Are we still denying ourselves in following the Lord, knowing that our reward is with Him and not with this world? Or are we becoming impatient? If we keep the word of His patience, we shall be kept out of the very hour of trial which is about to come upon the entire habitable world to try those who dwell upon the earth.

We need to take most seriously to heart what Jesus himself declared to His disciples towards the end of His teaching ministry on earth:

> Take heed to yourselves lest possibly your hearts be laden with surfeiting and drinking and cares of life, and that day come upon you suddenly unawares; for as a snare shall it come upon all them that dwell upon the face of the whole earth. Watch therefore, praying at every season, that ye may be accounted worthy to escape all these things which are about to come to pass, and to stand before the Son of man (Luke 21:34-36).

Praise the Lord that God's people are able to escape all these things if they meet the Lord's conditions which He set forth in these words of His. Yes, the Great Tribulation is coming upon the earth, but it is not meant for those who are not earth-dwellers and are watchful unto prayer. If faithful, you and I may escape all these things which are about to come to pass and to stand before the Son of man.

There are other Scriptures I could quote but I think these I have already quoted are enough. The long prophesied Great

Tribulation is coming upon this whole world, but it is not the will of God that His own shall pass through it because He expects us to be not earth-dwellers but strangers and sojourners on this earth. The Lord does not expect us to be so occupied with eating and drinking and the cares and worries of life that that day should come upon us as a snare. He expects better things from us and for us, in that we are watching unto prayer and that we are keeping the word of his patience and that He may take us out of the hour of the Great Tribulation.

So, you may ask, what is the Great Tribulation? We may recall that one sign of its coming was given by the Lord Jesus to His disciples as is recorded in verse 15 of Matthew chapter 24: "When therefore ye shall see the abomination of desolation, which is spoken of through Daniel the prophet, standing in what is a holy place, (he that reads let him understand,)" and so on and so forth. And verses 21-22 of this same warning passage reads: "for then shall there be great tribulation, such as has not been from the beginning of the world until now, nor ever shall be; and if those days had not been cut short, no flesh had been saved; but on account of the elect those shall be cut short."

Jesus declares very clearly that the day shall come when those still living on the earth shall see the abomination of desolation standing in the holy place, and that when they see this they will know that the Great Tribulation has come. And in telling of this, Jesus cites as His Old Testament source the prophet Daniel. And in Daniel chapter 9 we find that this faithful prophet is being shown by the Lord through His angel Gabriel what things will happen in the long-range future. Daniel was exercised before the Lord concerning the future of his own people Israel, and as he was praying and confessing and waiting upon the Lord, the Lord through Gabriel revealed to him what should happen in the distant future.

Let us now read forward from verse 24 of chapter 9:

> Seventy weeks are apportioned out upon thy people and upon thy holy city, to close the transgression, and to make an end of sins, and to make expiation for iniquity, and to bring in the righteousness of the ages, and to seal the vision and prophet [prophecy], and to anoint the holy of holies. Know therefore and understand: From the going forth of the word to restore and to build Jerusalem unto Messiah, the Prince, are seven weeks, and sixty-two weeks. The street and the moat shall be built again, even in troublous times. And after the sixty-two weeks shall Messiah be cut off, and shall have nothing; and the people of the prince that shall come shall destroy the city and the sanctuary; and the end thereof shall be with an overflow [a flood], and unto the end, [there shall be] war,—the desolations determined. And he shall confirm a covenant with the many for one week; and in the midst of the week he shall cause the sacrifice and the oblation to cease, and because of the protection [on the wing] of abominations there shall be a desolator, even until that the consumption and what is determined shall be poured out upon the desolate (vv.24-27).

Be advised that I am not going to explain Daniel's seventy sevens, for that would require quite some time today; but let me simply say this much, that Jesus is quoting the prophecy of Daniel, and accordingly, we come to understand that God's dealing with His people Israel is apportioned out in seventy sevens and that during the last seven, in the midst of that week we find that the prince—a Jew—shall come who will bring in the abomination of desolation. And that what is determined shall be poured out upon the desolate.

Let us first understand from this passage in Daniel that the foretold Prince of verse 25 is a reference to the Lord Jesus: From the going forth of the word to restore Jerusalem unto the Messiah, the Prince. Jesus is the Prince of Life and is the Messiah Prince who is sent by God to His people; and yet, He was not accepted by His people; for just as John's Gospel has indicated: Messiah Jesus "came to his own, and his own received him not" (1:11). The Messiah Prince was "cut off"—that is to say, He was crucified. But we remember that before His crucifixion Jesus had lamented over Jerusalem, saying: "Oh Jerusalem, Jerusalem, how often have I wanted to gather your children together to myself as a hen gathers her chicks under her wings, but you would not. Therefore, your house shall be left to you desolate. You shall not see me again until you shall say, Blessed is the one who comes in the name of the Lord" (see Matthew 23:37-39).

We may also recall what Jesus had said in the early days of His ministry on earth. Said Jesus to the unbelieving Jews: "I come in the name of My Father and you do not receive Me; but if someone else comes in his own name, you will receive him" (see John 5:43). The Lord Jesus came in the name of the Father, and yet they did not receive Him. He who is the Prince of Peace, the Prince of Life, even the Messiah himself had to come into this world of sinners, but He was rejected. And according to the prophet Daniel, after the cutting off of the Messiah Prince, there will come another prince, who is the prince mentioned in Daniel 9:26. And the people of that prince shall come and shall destroy Jerusalem and the sanctuary. This is the prince who will come in his own name, and he will be received. Through deceit he shall conquer the world and bring it under his wing. Indeed, he shall be the superman whom the world is looking for—the world ruler. He will come in his own name and it will be during his reign that the abomination of desolation shall stand in the place that is called holy.

Probably I have gone too far forward regarding the end-time situation. Let me therefore go back a little because there is a need for a little more background. As we by now well know, the Great Tribulation has been prophesied in the Bible. The prophet Jeremiah has quoted Jehovah God as calling it "the time of Jacob's trouble" (30:7). Daniel himself had referred to it as "troublous times"—times of distress (9:25c). And we also see referenced in the Bible on more than one occasion in nearly all cases the following numerical terms having to do with the prophetic end-times: "a time [year] and times [two years] and half a time [half a year]"—thus signifying three years and a half (see, e.g., Daniel 7:25, 12:7, Revelation 12:14); "in the midst of the week" or, as strictly understood, "in the dividing of the week" or "half of the week" (see, e.g., Daniel 9:27); "forty-two months" (see, e.g., Revelation 11:2c, 13:5b); and "a thousand two hundred and sixty days"—i.e., 1260 days (see, e.g., Revelation 11:3b, 12:6b). Yet all these numerical terms have reference to one and the same thing. And no matter one's interpretation, it can accurately be stated that it is prophesied in the Bible that a great trial or tribulation shall come upon the whole earth and shall last in length for at least three and a half years. And furthermore, none, we are told, shall escape who are under the enemy's rule (Revelation 13:7-8).

Why is this horrific trial called the Great Tribulation? Why is it that such woe shall come upon this earth? As was explained last time it is because by this time that is under discussion the trinity of evil shall all be together upon the earth. At the beginning today we read together from Revelation 9 that when the fifth trumpet shall be sounded, a star out of the heaven shall fall to the earth and the key to the pit of the abyss shall be given to that fallen star, and thus it shall become the king over a most evil place—the abyss. Indeed, he is called "the angel of the abyss" and his twin name—in Hebrew and in Greek, respectively—is Destruction and Destroyer (vv.1, 11).

Similarly, we will recall from Revelation 12 that when the man-child shall have been born and is immediately caught up and raptured to God's heavenly throne, war shall break out in heaven between Michael and his angels and Satan and his followers until there shall be no more place in heaven for Satan and his angels, resulting in their being cast out of heaven to the earth.

Similarly, further, an incident in the earthly ministry of Jesus was touched upon last time in which the seventy disciples, having been sent out by the Lord two by two, returned to the Master and reported with great joy how even the demons had been subject to them through His name. To which Jesus had declared, "I beheld Satan as lightning falling out of heaven" (Luke 10:1, 17-18).

Two of the great Old Testament prophets have prophesied as follows concerning the archangel Lucifer, who according to Revelation 12 turned himself into the great red dragon and the ancient serpent, he who is called Devil and Satan (vv.3, 9): Once upon a time Lucifer, called in Isaiah the bright morning star, whose very name means Brilliant Star, shall one day soon become that falling star of Revelation 9:1 and the lightning-like falling one of Luke 10:18. This greatest archangel of God's creation had been created with unique perfection and beauty and had been endowed with extraordinary talents and power and who had even been "the anointed covering cherub" covering and protecting the ark of God in heaven (Revelation 11:19a). He it was who was the masterpiece of God's creative hand: beautiful, talented, and most powerful among all angels and archangels of heaven, and perfect in all his ways from the day of his creation—until, that is, unrighteousness was found in him: gross pride had taken over Lucifer's heart, for he who had been placed on the holy mountain of God had subsequently wanted to take the place of God his Maker, to exalt his throne above the stars of God, and to be like the Most High. So because of that, Lucifer was cast out as profane from the mountain of

God (Isaiah 14:12-14, Ezekiel 28:2, 6, 12-16). But then, after he had been cast out, Lucifer now Satan made the air surrounding the earth—what we humans refer to as heaven—his dwelling place and commenced directing affairs upon the earth from his base and headquarters in the airy heaven (Ephesians 2:2b, 6:12, cf. John 12:31b).

As was made clear in our earlier discussions together, however, the risen, glorified and ascended Son of man has gone through the airy heaven of Satan's headquarters and upward into the very highest heaven where His Father's throne is situated. Which is to say that the Lord Jesus has overcome Satan who was unable to block the Son of man's way through to His Father, nor will Satan be able to do so when the Lord again comes to the earth. The way of the Lord's path of return shall have been prepared, for it shall be by means of the Lord's overcomers. They, too, will have gone through the enemy's territory, and the enemy cannot hinder or impede the way through. As we have come to realize from our earlier discussion of the man-child in Revelation 12, the overcomers, when their full number will have been realized, shall have been raptured up to God's throne; and because of this double victory over Satan—that of both the Son of man and of the man-child—the devil shall not be able to remain in his aerial heavenly headquarters but for a second time he will be cast out from there down upon the earth itself. And we further realize that Satan shall later on be cast from the earth into the bottomless pit and shall even still later be taken up out of the pit and cast into the lake of fire—which is what the Scripture calls the second death (Revelation 20:14b) and the final end of God's archenemy.

We thus see sentenced here the dragon, the ancient serpent, the devil, Satan the Accuser of the brethren. God's enemy shall be cast upon the earth, and when that happens, he shall become very angry, for he realizes that his time on earth is short, that his days are numbered. So he pours out his anger upon the remnant of the seed of the woman (who had given birth to the man-child). The remnant of this woman's seed shall be those who have kept the commandments and word of God and the testimony of Jesus. We see, therefore, that when Satan himself—the preeminent member of the trinity of evil—shall be cast upon the earth, the Great Tribulation shall begin.

Then, too, we read about the second member of this evil trio—the Antichrist. This is the beast that emerges up out of the sea, as is described in Revelation 13:1-9. The sea represents the people and nations of the world. Out of the turmoil, chaos and troubles of the world there shall arise the Antichrist superman who will control the whole earth and exercise world dominion. This is none other than "the little horn" prophesied about by the prophet Daniel (7:8, 20-21, 24; 8:9ff.). And Daniel tells us that this one shall make war upon the saints to wear them out (7:21, 25b). Let us remember this statement and not forget what this second member of the trinity of evil shall do on the earth.

But, then, we saw during our last time together that the third member of the trio of evil is to be another but smaller beast, this one rising from out of the earth. This shall be the false prophet. This third member of the evil trinity shall perform lying wonders and shall cause an image to be made of the first beast—the Antichrist—and this image—the abomination of desolation spoken of by the Lord Jesus—shall be set up in the holy place (Matthew 24:15a), and all people on the earth shall be seduced into worshiping this image by the false prophet's treacherous and deceitful magic. And should anyone not worship it, that one shall be killed. Moreover, the mark of this beast shall be required to be upon the forehead or upon the right hand of everyone. For without that mark no one shall be able to buy or sell (Revelation 13:11-18; see also II Thessalonians 2:3-4; Daniel 8:9-13, 9:27, 11:31; Matthew 24:15; Mark 13:14).

Thus shall there be this triple evil upon the earth: the dragon, the first beast, and the second smaller beast—that is to say, Satan, Antichrist, and the false prophet. And these three will combine to make this earth a most unbearable place.

Indeed, Jesus himself declared what would happen when, He said to His disciples, "ye shall see the abomination of desolation ... standing in [the] holy place, ... then shall there be great tribulation, such as has not been from the beginning of the world until now, nor ever shall be" (Matthew 24:15, 21). But please understand that my purpose here is not to explain the details of prophecy. Though they are most fascinating to inquire after, that is not my purpose. Rather, the purpose is for us to see and to grasp hold of the testimony of Jesus.

Let us realize that even during the most difficult of times—even during the Great Tribulation—there shall be a remnant who shall be those who will have kept the commandments of God (Revelation 12:17). Could it be that those who have the commandments of God are the 144,000 of the twelve tribes of Israel who have the first seal? This you find in Revelation chapter 7:1-8: 144,000 out of the twelve tribes of Israel shall have the first seal that they may not be hurt as they go through the Great Tribulation. Are these the faithful remnant of Israel who will bear witness for God and His commandments during this most difficult time in world history?

Now we know from Scripture that the Antichrist will entice even the nation of Israel to enter into a covenant with him for a week, that is, for seven years. But in the middle of that week of years he shall break that covenant (Daniel 9:27b). Why? Because he wants to wipe out all religions of God so that he can make himself the supreme God; nevertheless, the faithful remnant of Israel shall maintain the commandments of God. Those who shall comprise this remnant of the faithful towards God will not worship the idol, for to them there is no God but Jehovah, and they shall faithfully bear solitary witness for God during the upcoming "troublous times" (Daniel 9:25c). And they shall be helped by two witnesses sent especially by God: who are believed shall be Moses and Elijah (Revelation 11:3-4; cf. Zechariah 4:3, 11, 14).

But there are also those who have kept or maintained the testimony of Jesus. They are those who in Scripture are termed "the saints." Recall from earlier today that passage in Daniel 7:21 where we are told that the beast shall war against the saints. What place are these saints in at this end-time period, and who are they? If, as we are told, they keep the testimony of Jesus (Revelation 12:17c, 14:12) they must be believers. Now whether you consider them as part of the church or as not part of the church is perfectly all right. Even so, there is one fact which cannot be denied, which is, that even during the Great Tribulation there will be saints who bear the testimony of Jesus. There will be those who refuse to worship the idol image of Antichrist and who refuse to bear the mark of the beast on their forehead or their right hand; and we know what shall be the consequence of such faithfulness to the Lord: they can neither buy nor sell; they shall be deprived of the merest means of physical life, and more than that, the beast will make war against them and kill them. In short, they shall be martyred. But thank God, this is the endurance and faith of these saints (Revelation 13:10c). They will rather starve to death or be killed rather than join themselves with evil. They shall maintain the testimony of Jesus during the most troublous of times.

Do we realize what all this means? Towards the very end of his career the devil will go all out to gain total worship of himself among all of humanity. Throughout the generations and centuries and ages he has been engaged in achieving the sole supremacy over all. He has been desirous of gaining all glory for himself. In brief, Lucifer turned Satan has wanted to be God. All through his career he has wanted to get rid of the living God and be God instead. And in endlessly wanting to become the supreme one, towards the very end, Satan will pull out all stops to achieve that purpose. And why? Because if he can create such an environment upon the earth wherein nobody can live without joining himself/herself to him, he will have gained for himself the fullest pleasure. Yet here shall be a remnant of those who, because they have the testimony of Jesus, shall rather prefer to starve and even die than give homage to the image of Antichrist and bear his mark. In other words, they shall frustrate Satan's purpose. They shall be those who frustrate his age-long desire to be the supreme one by maintaining the testimony of Jesus. By their speech and by their life and even, if necessary, by their martyr's death they shall proclaim that Jesus and not the devil, that Jesus and not the beast, that Jesus and not the false prophet is supreme and worthy of all worship. Such, then, is the hallmark of those who keep the testimony of Jesus, and there shall be those who will maintain that testimony even during the Great Tribulation. Yes, indeed, here is the endurance of the saints (Revelation 14:12a).

But we are told in Revelation chapter 13 that those who kill shall themselves be killed and those who lead others into captivity shall themselves be brought into captivity (v.10a, b). Moreover, we read in Revelation chapter 20 these fitting words of reward:

> And I saw thrones; and they sat upon them and judgment was given to them; and the souls of those beheaded on account of the testimony of Jesus, and on account of the word of God; and those who had not done homage to the beast nor his image, and had not received the mark on their forehead and hand; and they lived and reigned with Christ a thousand years (v.4).

That is the reward for those who shall be faithful even during the most troublous times at the very end.

Oh how we too must maintain the testimony of Jesus. It must be maintained throughout the generations and ages, and, dear brothers and sisters, this testimony is today entrusted to the church. May we be those who keep it.

Chapter Eight

The Seventh Trumpet

And the angel whom I saw stand on the sea and on the earth lifted up his right hand to the heaven, and swore by him that lives to the ages of ages, who created the heaven and the things that are in it, and the earth and the things that are in it, and the sea and the things that are in it, that there should be no longer delay; but in the days of the voice of the seventh angel, when he is about to sound the trumpet, the mystery of God also shall be completed, as he has made known the glad tidings to his own bondmen the prophets.

Revelation 10:5-7

And the seventh angel sounded his trumpet: and there were great voices in the heaven, saying, The kingdom of the world of our Lord and of his Christ is come, and he shall reign to the ages of ages. And the twenty-four elders, who sit on their thrones before God, fell upon their faces, and worshipped God, saying, We give thee thanks, Lord God Almighty, He who is, and who was, that thou hast taken thy great power and hast reigned. And the nations have been full of wrath, and thy wrath is come, and the time of the dead to be judged, and to give the recompense to thy servants the prophets, and to the saints, and to those who fear thy name, small and great; and to destroy those that destroy the earth.

And the temple of God in the heaven was opened, and the ark of his covenant was seen in his temple: and there were lightnings, and voices, and thunders, and an earthquake, and great hail.

Revelation 11:15-19

And I saw another sign in the heaven, great and wonderful: seven angels having seven plagues, the last; for in them the fury of God is completed. ... And after these things I saw, and the temple of the tabernacle of witness in the heaven was opened; and the seven angels who had the seven plagues came out of the temple, clothed in pure bright linen, and girded about the breasts with golden girdles. And one of the four living creatures gave to the seven angels seven golden bowls, full of the fury of God, who lives to the ages of ages. And the temple was filled with smoke from the glory of God and from his power: and no one could enter into the temple until the seven plagues of the seven angels were completed.

Revelation 15:1, 5-8

We have been considering together for some time the testimony of Jesus in relation to the world, we having previously considered together the testimony of Jesus in relation to the church. And having also considered the seven seals—representing the Lord's future governmental dealing towards the world in the end-time—we saw during our past two times together that the opening of these seven seals shall be followed by the sounding of seven trumpets, the nature of which, not surprisingly, shall be military in character, with our having come to see that the highest heaven shall ultimately declare war against the earth.

For whereas with the opening of the seven seals the fourth part of the world shall be affected disastrously (Revelation 6:8b), the sounding of the first four trumpets shall bring about a disastrous impact upon the third part of the land of which its trees and green grass shall be burnt up, the third part of the seas shall become blood, the third part of the rivers and fountains of waters shall become wormwood in taste, and the third part of the earth's immediate heavenly bodies—sun, moon and stars—shall be darkened (8:7-12). But as calamitous as that shall be, with the sounding of the fifth and sixth trumpets the entire habitable earth shall be disastrously affected because that shall be the time of the Great Tribulation whose trumpet soundings shall be introduced by the threefold pronouncement of "Woe, woe, woe" upon "them that dwell upon the earth" (8:13b)—a tribulation, prophetically declared the Lord Jesus, which the world shall not ever have witnessed previously nor shall ever witness afterwards (Matthew 24:21). It will be a tribulation which shall prevail over the entire earth.

Now we inquired last time as to why there shall come upon the earth such an unparalleled troublous period. And we came to see that it shall be due to the fact that the trinity of evil—Satan, Antichrist, and false prophet—shall all three be present together on the earth. God shall finally allow evil to run its full course and allow iniquity to reach its full measure. And why? In order that He may judge this sinful, wicked world.

Now such was what has been shared previously. Today, however, I would like for us to focus our attention upon the seventh trumpet. The character of this final trumpet sounding is to be quite different from all the previous trumpet soundings, in that with the sounding of this seventh and final one "the mystery of God also shall be completed, as he has made known the glad tidings to his own bondmen the prophets." I personally believe that the impact of the fifth and sixth trumpet soundings shall cover the three and a half years of the Great Tribulation, although should you not agree with me it is perfectly all right since that is a matter of interpretation.

Here we read that with the sounding of the seventh trumpet the mystery of God shall have been completed. What is the mystery of God? We realize, of course, that the word mystery here does not refer to something mysterious, strange, or hideous. Rather, the word mystery refers to that which is known to God but unknown to man and waits to be revealed or unveiled. That is what the use of the term mystery in the Bible is meant to convey. It is that which has been in the mind of God all the time. We may even say it is what has been in the heart of God well before the foundation of this world and throughout the generations and ages of time. This mystery had been hidden from man throughout the Old Testament period but it has now been revealed to us through both the prophets and the apostles.

So what *is* the mystery? Well, it must be something great and tremendous, if it has been in the mind of God even before Time was, and if it has been that which has been so near and dear to the heart of God and has itself been present with Him all these years and generations and centuries in Time, and to which He has been ceaselessly working for its fulfillment. Yes, this mystery of God is indeed great, and if that be the case, then this mystery ought to be that which should attract our attention. And if this mystery has been the focus of God all along, then it must be our focus, too. And we are told that at the sounding of the seventh trumpet God's mystery shall be finished—shall be completed.

What, then, is the mystery? It is today an open secret, for the mystery of God cannot be anything less than His Son, Jesus Christ. The mystery of God is none other than Christ himself (Colossians 2:2b-3 ASV). Christ himself is the mystery of God. That which has always been in the heart of God is Christ His Son. All the counsels of God throughout the generations and ages have always been planned with Christ in mind. All the operations of God's power have been working towards the realization of Christ, who is truly the mystery of God.

We think too small of Christ. Thank God, we know Him as our Savior. God has sent Him into this world to save us, but is that all? Not according to Paul's Letter to the Colossians. There we read that the full knowledge of God's purpose is that "in all things [Christ] might have the preeminence" (1:18c ASV). Now this is the will of God. This is the full knowledge of God's will. God wants His Son Christ Jesus to have "the first place in all things" (1:18c Darby). God wants Him to have the first place in your life. God wants Him to have the first place in the church. God wants Him to have the first place in the world. God wants Him to have the first place in all of creation.

And this saying of "the first place" does not mean that Jesus is the first and you or I are the second. First place means in the Scriptures that "Christ is all and in all" (Colossians 3:11b). He is to be everything to the believer. This, then, is the mystery of God concerning Christ: He has the preeminence over all things, He is to fill all things, all things shall express Him and shall magnify Him; indeed, He is to be the "head over all things" (Ephesians 1:22b). In other words, not only all things shall take their instructions, orders and commands from Christ but all things shall be filled by Him (Ephesians 1:23b, 4:10b) and express Him. He has been appointed by the Father to be the heir of all things (Hebrews 1:2b). God the Father has thus given His Son all things as His possession. He is to be the heir, owner, and possessor of all people and things throughout the universe.

Yet, I would ask this of you, Have we seen this mystery fulfilled yet? Yes, we have seen Jesus made a little lower than the angels. We have seen Him manifested on the cross. Yes, we have even seen Him as having been raised from the dead and as having been crowned with glory and honor (Hebrews 2:9a-b ASV). Yes, all this we have seen realized, but let us understand that only at the sounding of the seventh trumpet shall the mystery of God be fulfilled and completed. That is to say, only then shall all things be subjected to God's Son (cf. Hebrews 2:8c): every knee shall bow to the Lord Jesus, every tongue shall confess that He is Lord (Philippians 2:10-11). Christ shall then have the first place in all things, He shall be the Head over all things, and He shall inherit all things. Hence, only at the sounding of the seventh trumpet shall the mystery of God be completed (Revelation 10:7a). And then the apostle John, as he is led by the Spirit of God, further explains, as follows: "And the seventh angel sounded his trumpet: and there were great voices in the heaven, saying" (11:15a). Let us listen closely to what those great heavenly voices shall at that moment say: "The kingdom of the world of our Lord and of his Christ is come, and he shall reign to the ages of ages." The mystery of God is Christ and His kingdom—that He shall be the King of kings and the Lord of lords and shall reign over the earth to the ages of ages.

We must pause here and inquire of ourselves as to what exactly is the gospel—what are the glad tidings which we know and preach to the people of the world? Yes, it is quite true that when we preach the gospel, it is the good news of Christ's humiliation: oh how God came to this world in the person of His Son Jesus, lived a humble life, and finally was humiliated to the extreme beyond humiliation, He having been crucified on Calvary's cross; and that because He died on that cross He shed His blood and His body was broken so that we might be saved. Yes, indeed, that is the gospel. But the gospel we preach is too often restricted exclusively to Christ's humiliation. The cross is indeed the basis of the gospel, that is true. We have to preach Christ crucified because none can be saved if He had not been crucified. In the days of His humiliation (Acts 8:33a) Jesus accomplished salvation. That is all true and we must preach it.

Even so, the glad tidings of God are much, much more than that. The gospel is not only that of Christ's humiliation but is also the gospel of His glorification. The glad tidings are not only those concerning Jesus' cross; they are also those concerning

His crown. Here we find expressed by those great voices in the highest heaven the mystery of God in its totality and as has been made known what are the glad tidings to God's bondservants (see again Revelation 10:7 with 11:15). The mystery of God is the glad tidings in their totality. So what are the glad tidings? What is the good news? The good news of the gospel is not only that Jesus has emptied himself and was obedient to the Father even unto death, and that the death of the cross, but that He has also been lifted up on high and has been given a name which is above all names, so that at the name of Jesus every knee shall bow and every tongue shall confess that He is Lord (Philippians 2:7-11). And that is the whole gospel.

Let us not present only half a gospel to this world. Let us present to the people of the world the full gospel of Jesus Christ: that He had come to die and now He is in glory and shall come back to receive the world to himself. At the sounding of the seventh trumpet the kingdom of the world of our Lord and of His Christ shall come. And all of that is the complete gospel.

As we all know, of course, we have four Gospels in the New Testament. Yet we also know that we have only one gospel. The apostle Paul declared that if anyone preaches another gospel, then cursed is that person (Galatians 1:8-9). There cannot be another gospel. Thus, we have the Gospel according to Matthew, the Gospel according to Mark, the Gospel according to Luke, and the Gospel according to John. Nevertheless, they together actually constitute but one gospel concerning the Lord Jesus Christ as presented in four accounts of that one gospel. Now which of these four Gospel records stands first in the New Testament canon? That is the Gospel according to Matthew.

Now we have been correctly shown that the Gospel according to Matthew emphasizes Christ as the King—His kingship. And that the second Gospel in the canon is the Gospel according to Mark which emphasizes the servanthood of Christ as God's servant, and so on with respect to the other two Gospels. But do we know the total gospel of Jesus Christ? Have we received the full gospel of God's Son? Or have we only received Jesus Christ as our Savior—that is, as the Crucified One? Have we fully received Him not only as the Crucified One but also as the Glorified One? If we have received the Lord Jesus only as our Savior, that is not enough. We must go further and receive Him as our Lord and King. Unless we also receive Jesus as Lord and King we have not received the whole gospel, and thus we have not received Christ in His fullness. Oh, how important it is that we see and receive Him as the King of kings and the Lord of lords—that we willingly and gladly yield ourselves to Christ completely so that He may have absolute sway over our lives.

Then next we are told by John that the twenty-four elders shall fall on their faces and worship God, and that after they worship Him they shall give thanks to God; and in offering thanks they shall further describe the mystery of God or the kingdom of His Christ by revealing four distinct and important details. Now let us be reminded that the content of these details are all included in the seventh trumpet-sounding. That is why I say that the seventh trumpet is unique, in that at its sounding the content of all these details concerning the mystery of God shall come to pass; and when all of them shall come to pass, then the mystery of God shall be completed because the kingdom of the world of our Lord and of His Christ shall have come. Now what are these four details as shall be expressed by the twenty-four elders at the sounding of the seventh trumpet?

First, these elders shall say, "We give thee thanks, Lord God Almighty, He who is, and who was, that thou hast taken thy great power and hast reigned." This first detail we have in essence already mentioned, namely, that at the sounding of the seventh trumpet the kingdom of Christ shall come and he shall reign upon the earth. We are taught by the Lord Jesus himself to pray the following: "Our Father who art in heaven, Hallowed be thy name. Thy kingdom come" (Matthew 6:9 ASV). The kingdom of this world today is not God's kingdom. Therefore, we are praying for His kingdom to come. Look at the world's kingdom of man today: what utter confusion, wickedness, and chaos the world of man is in today! Yet the Lord has taught us to pray for His kingdom to come, and the church, too, has been praying that prayer all these centuries.

If you have been praying that prayer, are you expecting it to be answered? Well, at the sounding of the seventh trumpet the answer shall come: the kingdom of God and of His Christ shall finally come upon the earth and Christ shall reign to the ages of ages. And if, further, you are praying for God's kingdom to come, then according to the Lord Jesus himself you should be seeking first the kingdom of God and His righteousness (Matthew 6:33); for these two actions must go together: on the one hand, you cannot pray, "Thy kingdom come" and on the other hand be seeking after the things of this world. That would be a contradiction. What if the Lord's kingdom should come today, where will you be in relation to it—in what state will it find you to be? Yes, the Lord's kingdom will one day come but, meanwhile, we who are His followers must live in, and according to, the spirit and attitude of that kingdom, which is for us to be seeking first the kingdom of God and His righteousness; and when His kingdom shall come, we shall not be caught unawares and ashamed at His coming (I John 2:28c).

Here is the second detail: "… and the nations have been full of wrath, and thy wrath is come." The word of these elders is that the nations of the world have been full of wrath! Now I wonder, is there any good reason for the nations to be angry? They have good reason to be angry with themselves; but they themselves are not the object of their wrath; rather, they are angry with God! They suffer because of their iniquity and wickedness, and yet, they have become irrational: instead of being angry with themselves they are angry with God. Oh! When Satan gains control over the thoughts of man, how irrational man's mind can become.

Is there anyone present here today who is angry but is angry with God and not with himself or herself? If there is, then I would remind you that that is irrational behavior. You ought to be angry with yourself, and if you do become angry with yourself then there is the possibility of salvation for you. Yet, how irrational the nations' people have become. They have become angry with God, and by the time of that seventh trumpet's sounding the nations will have become fully enraged with Him.

However, the twenty-four elders shall go on to say this: "... and Thy wrath is come." Oh, today the earth is angry with God, but God is currently silent. He is loving and patient and suffers long (cf. I Corinthians 13:4a Darby/ASV). You may point your finger of blame at heaven and even perhaps curse God, and in response there is no thunder because of the long-suffering kindness and love of God. But, dear friends, the day shall come at the sounding of the seventh trumpet that though *your* wrath is full, God's own full wrath will have come. The wrath of God shall come upon this earth and this wrath shall be poured out upon the earth from those seven golden bowls or vials mentioned in Revelation 15 and whose passage we read together at the beginning of our time together today. As one of the consequences of the seventh trumpet-sounding there shall appear seven angels to whom shall be given those seven bowls or vials. And those seven golden vessels, we are told, are "*full* of the fury of God." Thus, the content of these seven vessels represents His wrath and fury. God's anger shall be poured out fully upon the kingdom of the beast, for the kingdom of this world is under the beast's control (cf. Revelation 16:10). However, we cannot stay to explain here the many and various details regarding the contents of those seven bowls, but I would simply mention this overall second detail of what the twenty-four elders shall say in their offering of thanksgiving to God concerning the completion of God's mystery.

Here is the third detail: "... and the time of the dead to be judged [is come], and to give the recompense to thy servants the prophets, and to the saints, and to those who fear thy name, small and great." I do not know how you feel about this passage, but personally I think the dead here who are to be judged does not have reference to the dead of the world of unbelievers but the dead of those who will have died in Christ. Of course, I have a reason for believing that. The passage declares that the time has come for judging the dead—the servant prophets, the saints and those who fear God's name—and who by their obedience to Him are to be recompensed or rewarded for what they have done or suffered. And thus the dead mentioned here are all related to the giving out of a recompense or reward.

All this, says the passage, shall be fulfilled at the sounding of the seventh trumpet. I would refer you to several verses in I Thessalonians chapter 4 which together are a passage often quoted by God's people. There Paul the apostle is comforting those saints in Thessalonica by telling them that they should not be ignorant concerning those who have fallen asleep in Jesus (vv. 13-14), and then he continues in verse 16—

> For the Lord himself, with an assembling shout, with archangel's voice and with trump of God, shall descend from heaven; and the dead in Christ shall rise first; then we, the living who remain, shall be caught up together with them in the clouds, to meet the Lord in the air; and thus we shall be always with the Lord.

Do please notice here the mentioning of the trump or trumpet of God. At the sounding of the trumpet the Lord shall descend from heaven, and then the dead in Christ shall rise up first, and then we who live and shall have remained on the earth up to that time shall all be caught up together in the clouds to meet the Lord in the air and there to be with him forever. This is therefore the time when all shall be raptured and meet the Lord in the air—both the dead in Christ as well as those in Christ who at that moment are still living. Such is what shall occur at the trump of God.

Let us next turn to another related Bible passage, I Corinthians 15:51b-52: "We shall not all fall asleep [or, die], but we shall all be changed, in an instant, in the twinkling of an eye, at the last trumpet; for the trumpet shall sound, and the dead shall be raised incorruptible, and we shall be changed." Now these two passages from the Thessalonian and Corinthian letters of Paul speak of the dead in Christ being raised up from the grave incorruptible and of those who are alive in Christ and remain being changed. When shall all this come to pass? Both say it is at the sounding of the trumpet, and one describes it as the last trumpet. Now if one speaks of a *last* trumpet, then it can be correctly inferred that there must be a *series* of trumpets involved. Otherwise, a person cannot describe a trumpet as being the last one. Hence, the event being described in these passages is going to occur at the seventh and final trumpet-sounding.

But what exactly is it that shall occur? It shall be the final harvest together of both those who have died in Christ and those in Christ who, at the coming of the Lord, are yet alive and remained on the earth. The dead in Christ shall all be raised from the grave and shall be clothed with incorruptibility, and those who at the last trump are still living and have remained on earth shall also be changed, they too shall be transformed. (Oh, I must pause here for a moment to say how I like that little descriptive phrase—"the living who remain." This signifies that there shall be some believers who were still alive but at the last trump shall no longer be among those who remain on the earth. And why? Because they will have already been raptured and thus have gone to their home with their Lord—a subtle allusion by Paul to the overcomers: to the man-child described in Revelation 12.) Then both those who had died in Christ and are now being raised incorruptible, and all those who will still be alive and have remained on the earth shall be caught up together to meet the Lord in the air (I Thessalonians 4:17a). Where, though, is the Lord today? He is in the third heaven at the right hand of the Father. But at the seventh trumpet-sounding He shall descend from heaven to the earth's immediate airy heaven. How so? Because, as was discussed earlier, Satan will have already been cast out from his airy headquarters down to the earth. Therefore, the dead in Christ and the believers in Christ still living and remaining on the earth shall all be caught up together to meet the Lord in the air because He shall be there. And such shall be the final rapture. But what, you may ask, shall happen there? Recall what this third detail expressed by the elders has described: the dead shall be judged and the recompense shall be given out to all his bondservants and saints. In other words, here shall be the assembling together of the whole church in the air and here also shall be when the event surrounding the judgment seat of Christ shall begin.

At this juncture in our discussion it will be helpful to turn to Revelation chapter 14:14. For there we find the unfolding of yet another vision which John beheld:

> And I saw, and behold, a white cloud, and on the cloud one sitting like the Son of man, having upon his head a golden crown, and in his hand a sharp sickle. And another angel came out of the temple, crying with a loud voice to him that sat on the cloud. Send thy sickle and reap; for the hour of reaping is come, for the harvest of the earth is dried [and ripe]. And he that sat on the cloud put his sickle on the earth, and the earth was reaped (vv. 14-16).

Now this is a description of the grain harvest, and whenever the idea of grain harvest is being mentioned in Scripture, it is related to those who belong, or shall belong, to the Lord (cf., e.g., John 4:34-35). Symbolically speaking, we are the wheat and we are His spiritual harvest. The time of the final general harvesting will have finally come.

As has been pointed out and discussed earlier, the firstfruits have already gone up to the Lord. As was described in a previous message dealing with the man-child of Revelation 12, before the general harvest in ancient Israel there would be the gathering of the firstfruits which have been cut and which would then be presented at the tabernacle or temple as a most pleasing offering to God. But then there would be the waiting for the time of the general harvest. The grain harvest can only occur when the crop is fully dried. The stem of every stalk of grain must be so dry that it can easily be pulled up out of the soil, and is an indication that the crop has ripened.

Spiritually speaking, therefore, those believers who had not been ready before have—like the scorching of the sun on the grain crop—finally been made ready through the dealings, discipline, and arranged circumstances of the Spirit of God. They are now ready and, according to I Thessalonians 4, are taken up together to the cloud in the air. And following that harvest there will be yet another harvest, but a most ominous and terrible one: the gathering of the grapes of the wrath and fury of God (Revelation 14:17-20). And this harvesting points to the war at Armageddon and its horrific consequences (Revelation 16:14b, 16).

So it shall come to pass that we who are the Lord's shall all be gathered together and shall all be present at the judgment seat of Christ, which shall have its setting in the cloud (see again Revelation 14:14). We believers shall not be present and be judged at the great white throne (Revelation 20:11-15) because that is the place of judgment determining eternal death and life. Our Lord Jesus on Calvary's cross has already been judged for us. Therefore, we shall not come to the judgment of the great white throne, which shall be the judgment of the world.

But please be advised and warned that that does not mean we believers shall never be judged. Let us accordingly be very careful here, because there are some Christians, perhaps many, who subscribe to the notion that because Christ has been judged for us on the cross, therefore, we shall never be judged. In one sense that is correct, but in another sense not completely correct. We shall not be judged at the great white throne because the matter of our eternal destiny has already been judged and settled for us by Christ on the cross. But as children of God let us not deceive ourselves into thinking that we, having accepted Christ as our Savior, may do anything we like thereafter and that, hence, there will be no unpleasant consequence for us at the coming of the Lord. Not so, for there will be the judgment seat of Christ before which we all shall appear.

Three Scripture passages which are most relevant to this matter are I Corinthians 3:8b-15, II Corinthians 5:10, and Romans 14:10c-12. In the first of these passages a judgment as though by fire is mentioned. The day shall come when fire shall appear and it shall cause all our works to be judged whether they be of gold, silver and precious stones or wood, grass and straw. And we learn from the other two passages that we must all appear before the judgment seat of Christ and be judged according to what we shall have done on this earth. Nevertheless, we must thank God that this is not the great white throne but is the judgment seat of Christ.

Now in the New Testament's original text there is a difference between a throne (Greek: *thronos*) and a seat (Greek: *bema*). *Thronos* means a governmental throne or chair, and the judgment involved shall be governmental in character and is therefore a judgment regarding the issue of life and death; whereas *bema* conveys the idea of an uplifted seat.

In the olden days in the East and sometimes still true today, there were large families comprising a clan. And the clan was so closely knit together that everything important was decided, done or determined not at the small family level but as it were at the clan level. And hence, in a given Eastern country there was the habit of having a room set aside for a special purpose, and alongside that room there was a spot where a special seat was placed in an uplifted fashion—a *bema*—and having but one seat in that uplifted place. And from time to time the whole clan or large extended family would be gathered together in that room for the purpose of determining something special or significant confronting the entire household. And the person presiding would be the father of the clan, who would be seated on that uplifted place while the members of the extended family or clan would be standing before him. And then, if there was a member of that household who had done something so good as to have brought fame and prosperity to the whole clan, he or she would be recommended and rewarded, and the reward would be given out at that very time. But if any member had done something which shall have brought disgrace or shame to the clan, this was the occasion on which that one would be reprimanded and punished in the presence of all the rest of the clan.

Such, then, is the meaning of the notion conveyed by the Greek word *bema*, an uplifted seat of judgment. It is not governmental in nature, but has to do with a household or clan matter. If you did not belong to that household, you were not qualified even to come into that gathering. But if you *were* of that household you would be required to come and you *would* come—yet, if not joyfully then reluctantly. This time of gathering should normally be one of great rejoicing but it could instead be a time of great sadness and sorrow. We who are the children of God can readily thank Him that the issue of eternal life and death has already been resolved for us: we have eternal life and shall therefore not perish: none can pluck us out of the hand of our heavenly Father nor out of the hand of our Lord Jesus Christ (John 10:28-29); and thus we shall not be required to appear before the great white throne and be judged *there*; that is a fact most certain. But since we have the life of Christ in us, we are now children of God, and on the basis of that life we shall nonetheless be judged as to whether that life has been properly developed in us or has been abused or misused.

This is a serious matter. Yes, as the apostle Paul has asserted in his I Corinthians letter, the foundation, which is Jesus Christ, has been laid, and there can be no other foundation. But Paul also said for us to be careful how we build upon it. If we build upon that foundation with gold, silver and precious stones, we shall be joyfully rewarded. If, however, we build upon it with wood, grass and straw, then fire shall appear, it shall try that kind of work, and it shall burn up all which we have built on that foundation. Of course, the judgment fire cannot consume away the foundation—the foundation shall still remain; but we ourselves shall barely be saved.

Under such a circumstance as *that*, a believer cannot enter the kingdom of God richly or abundantly. As the apostle Peter once wrote, it is the will of the Father that we should enter His kingdom abundantly and richly (cf. II Peter 1:11). Oh, it is the good pleasure of the Father to reward His children, but He cannot reward indiscriminately; He can only reward those who are deserving of such; otherwise, it cannot be considered to be a reward. Do we deserve a reward? Then, too, is it by *our* working out? Or is it the working out of His grace which we have received? It is still a matter of God's grace, but it is to be the working out of His grace in the development of the Christ-life in us, and the recompense shall be, and can only be, according to that principle.

Hence, according to my understanding of Scripture, we learn—from the worshipful prayer of thanksgiving which the twenty-four elders shall offer up to God at the sounding of the seventh trumpet—what is the third detail concerning the completion of the mystery of God. It is the final rapture of the entire church, the family of God, to the judgment seat of Christ.

And then the fourth and final detail to be expressed and thus revealed by those elders in heaven as they shall fall upon their faces and worship God, shall be this: "… and the time has come to destroy those that destroy the earth." At the sounding of the seventh trumpet those that destroy the earth shall themselves be destroyed; for at the last battle, the battle of Armageddon (Revelation 16:14b, 16), the beast—who is the Antichrist—and the false prophet shall both be taken alive and shall be cast into the lake of fire (19:19-20). And Satan himself shall be bound and cast into the bottomless pit (20:1-3a). And all those who shall have followed this trinity of evil shall themselves be killed (19:21). Thus those who destroy the earth shall themselves be destroyed, but the kingdom of our Lord and of his Christ shall come upon this earth at the sounding of the seventh trumpet (11:15).

Chapter Nine

The Seven Bowls: Babylon vs. Jerusalem

And the seventh poured out his bowl on the air; and there came out a great voice from the temple of the heaven, from the throne, saying, It is done. And there were lightnings, and voices, and thunders; and there was a great earthquake, such as was not since men were upon the earth, such an earthquake, so great. And the great city was divided into three parts; and the cities of the nations fell: and great Babylon was remembered before God to give her the cup of the wine of the fury of his wrath.

Revelation 16:17-19

And one of the seven angels, which had the seven bowls, came and spoke with me, saying, Come here, I will shew thee the sentence of the great harlot who sits upon the many waters; with whom the kings of the earth have committed fornication; and they that dwell on the earth have been made drunk with the wine of her fornication. And he carried me away in spirit to a desert; and I saw a woman sitting upon a scarlet beast, full of names of blasphemy, having seven heads and ten horns. And the woman was clothed in purple and scarlet, and had ornaments of gold and precious stones and pearls, having a golden cup in her hand full of abominations and the unclean things of her fornication; and upon her forehead a name written, Mystery, great Babylon, the mother of the harlots, and of the abominations of the earth. And I saw the woman drunk with the blood of the saints, and with the blood of the witnesses of Jesus. And I wondered, seeing her, with great wonder.

Revelation 17:1-6

After these things I saw another angel descending out of the heaven, having great authority: and the earth was lightened with his glory. And he cried with a strong voice, saying, Great Babylon has fallen, has fallen, and has become the habitation of demons, and a hold of every unclean spirit, and a hold of every unclean and hated bird; because all the nations have drunk of the wine of the fury of her fornication; and the kings of the earth have committed fornication with her, and the merchants of the earth have been enriched through the might of her luxury.

And I heard another voice out of the heaven saying, Come out of her, my people, that ye have not fellowship in her sins, and that ye do not receive of her plagues: for her sins have been heaped on one another up to the heaven, and God has remembered her unrighteousnesses.

Revelation 18:1-5

And there came one of the seven angels which had had the seven bowls full of the seven last plagues, and spoke with me, saying, Come here, I will shew thee the bride, the Lamb's wife. And he carried me away in the Spirit, and set me on a great and high mountain, and shewed me the holy city, Jerusalem, coming

> down out of the heaven from God, having the glory of God.
>
> Revelation 21:9-10

During these past several weeks we have been considering together the subject: the testimony of Jesus in relation to the world. And in our last discussion on that overall topic we focused our attention on the seventh and final trumpet. And we learned that at about the time of its sounding by the angel, the mystery of God shall be fully realized and completed, in accordance with the glad tidings which God had announced and made known to His bondservants the prophets.

Today, however, we will focus our attention on the seven bowls; for subsequent to the sounding of the seventh trumpet there shall come forth seven angels to whom shall be given by one of the four living creatures seven bowls or vials, and the contents of these seven vessels constitute the wrath of God—His full fury—which shall be poured out upon this sin-cursed earth. From each one of these bowls the fury of God shall be poured out upon the earth because the earth has been under the complete control of the trinity of evil. When this shall occur, it shall no longer be a matter of disastrously affecting one-fourth of the earth and shall no longer be that which shall disastrously affect one-third of the earth; instead, the effect of the contents of these seven bowls shall concern the whole earth because the entire earth has been under the control of the trinity of evil. And with the pouring out of the last of these seven bowls, a great voice shall come forth out of the heavenly temple from the throne declaring that it is done—it is all done. Now, everything shall be finished and brought to an end, or shall be brought to a new beginning. And at that moment something unusual shall happen: God will be reminded of Great Babylon to deliver to her the cup of the wine of the fury of His wrath which she shall be compelled to drink.

Now we find that the last few chapters of the book of Revelation are devoted to a delineation and description of two cities: chapters 17 and 18 are concerned with Babylon and chapters 21 and 22 describe Jerusalem. In fact, it becomes clear that as all things draw to a close, all shall be focused upon those two cities—either upon Babylon or upon Jerusalem. From Revelation and world history we discern that these two cities shall come into conflict with each other, with Babylon on the one side and Jerusalem on the other. Jerusalem is reflective of the Son of God and His character, whereas Babylon reflects the thought and character of Satan.

At the very beginning God had Jerusalem in His thought when He created the earth and then created man. Perhaps, however, you may ask, Where was Jerusalem in all of that? We will recall that there was a beautiful garden in Eden in which God had planted all kinds of trees and in the midst of the garden there was the tree of life and by its side the tree of the knowledge of good and evil. And then God put His created man Adam in this garden which was without a wall. But was there a wall there, after all? Let us remind ourselves that God had said to Adam that he was to till the ground and guard the garden. So God created the Edenic garden, then created a man, and told that man to guard the garden. Spiritually speaking, therefore, God did have a garden wall—which must be built with man and must be constructed with man's cooperation. And once that human wall would be successfully erected, Jerusalem would come into being.

Hence, from the very beginning God had Jerusalem in view. Yet, though Jerusalem was to be built by God, it must be built with man as the material and with man's cooperation. That was God's wish. He wanted a city—Jerusalem—but as we now know the enemy of God slipped into the situation. Before the wall was built he tore down the building of it and ruined the garden; and instead of there being God's city of Jerusalem, His enemy—after getting hold of man—began using man to build for himself a city of his own.

Now one of the men whom the enemy used was Nimrod, the mighty hunter and great rebel. He was the leader of all the people of the world at that time and told them, Let us build a city and a tower; let us do that and make a name for ourselves, lest we be scattered and be left unknown. And thus, they commenced building a tower up to heaven; but God soon came down to see the city and the tower and confused their tongues so that the work was stopped (Genesis 10:8-10, 11:1-9). Nevertheless, though the beginning of the kingdom of Nimrod was fatal, there emerged from his effort the nascent outlines of the city and kingdom of Babylon.

So we come to see from the very opening of God's word that there is the city of Jerusalem in God's mind and there is the city of Babylon in the enemy's mind. And the existence of these two cities one can trace throughout the whole Bible. In fact, we will notice from the historical record of these two cities how they have frequently intertwined and crossed each other's path; moreover, we will observe that whenever Jerusalem was strong Babylon was weak and whenever Jerusalem was weak Babylon was strong. Furthermore, we come to learn that it was Babylon which captured Jerusalem and took its people into captivity. And it was back to Jerusalem that its people returned to rebuild the temple of God.

All of this is what we find spread out upon the pages of the Bible and in extra-Biblical historical records. We do not have the time here to look into the detailed history of these two cities. Even so, it will be enough if we simply bear in mind that in Jerusalem we have displayed the fullness of God's thought concerning the world and in Babylon we have revealed Satan's forethought concerning this same world.

At its core, what is Jerusalem? The very name Jerusalem in Hebrew means peace—Salem, city of peace. Its name has also been translated as meaning possession or foundation of peace.

Briefly stated, therefore, Jerusalem can be said to be built on the principle of peace. It is meant to be a peaceful city. Now what is peace? The apostle James tells us that the wisdom which is from God is first pure then peaceful (3:17a). You cannot have peace if you do not have purity. If there is a mixture of things together whose natures are totally different, then naturally these things will be in conflict with each other and thus there cannot be peace. But if all things are in pureness, the result will be oneness, with no foreign particles but all shall be in perfect unity, oneness and harmony. And consequently, there is peace. Let us thus recognize that Jerusalem is built on the principle of peace; which is to say that Jerusalem is built with such pureness and such oneness that there can be no disharmony, disunity nor discord. Everything is at peace with God and with one another. And the reason for that is that everything is of God.

In this connection, let us inquire with regard to the new creation. What is the difference between the new and the old creation? Well, in the old creation we observe that all things are at odds with each other, whereas in the new creation all things are in harmony with each other: If anyone be in Christ, declares God's word, that person is a new creation; old things are passed away and, behold, all things are made new (II Corinthians 5:17), and, it was added, this is because all things are of God (v.18a). God is building a city, even Jerusalem, and He is building it on the basis of peace. That is to say, every stone and every other piece of material that is used is of God, and even the very fitting together of all material is of Him (Ephesians 2:21-2, 4:15-16; cf. I Kings 6:7). As a matter of fact, everything speaks of God, and whatever is not of Him shall not be there. And that is the reason there is such unity present in God's city, Jerusalem: there is such peace therein. His heavenly city is built on the principle of peace.

On the other hand, what is Babylon? The very name Babylon means confusion. In contrast to Jerusalem, Babylon is built on the principle of confusion. The more confused its builders and inhabitants are, the higher its builders build. Is it not true that the enemy of mankind has continually been causing confusion of all kinds? Why are the world's people so confused today? It is because mankind's enemy has been furiously building his city. If everything should be peaceful then the enemy would be defeated in his intentions. That explains why all is instead confusion. But those who are God's people will not be confused if what the enemy does is all evil; however, they *will* be confused whenever they discover that in the enemy's evil there seems to be some good, if in the falsehood there seems to be some truth. That *will* confuse God's people because they do not know where they stand in relation to a mixture of falsehood and truth. That, indeed, is the very tactic the enemy has been employing all these years, generations and ages up till this very day: great confusion through mixture. And he has been building his city on that very principle.

There is another aspect to be noted about Jerusalem—this city is a woman. In Revelation 21 we are told that Jerusalem is the Lamb's wife. Thus Jerusalem is presented as a woman, and when Scripture speaks of woman, it betokens an inward life experience. Whereas man in the Bible stands for truth, woman in the Bible represents inner experience. And we see that Jerusalem is presented as a woman in God's word.

Then, too, we know from God's word how this woman is built. Think back to the Genesis account. God created Adam and then said that it was not good for man to be alone. So God put Adam to sleep, and then He opened up his side and took out something that was most likely a rib, and God built a woman around that something of Adam's. That Hebrew word translated as built in the relevant Genesis passage is a term employed in matters of architecture, and is therefore not a commonly used word. And thus we can conclude from this architectural term that the woman is built or made differently from the way of Adam: woman is built with the rib of man, which is to say that Adam in Scripture represents Christ, whereas the woman represents Jerusalem that is thus built with Christ; and such, we may say, is an architectural effort—it is a building process. God builds Jerusalem with Christ. The city is all of Christ but Christ as expressed in a corporate entity or body. And that is how Jerusalem is built.

Then, further, still another feature of this city of God is the fact that Jerusalem is naked—at least in three ways: in purity, in transparency, and in radiancy. By reading chapters 21 and 22 of Revelation we discover that so much of this city is constituted of one hundred percent pure gold. There is no mixture whatsoever. And with respect to transparency—everything about this city is transparent. One can see through its features without any shadow or cloudiness—no opaque appearance at all. And with regard to the city’s radiancy, it is brilliant, shiny and bright everywhere within her precincts.

Now because Jerusalem is symbolically a woman, because further, we have the age-old understanding that a woman is to be united to her man, therefore, God’s thought is that Jerusalem is built for the purpose of being united to Christ. God has had this thought even from before the beginning of mankind’s history—that He has desired to have a woman as bride for His Son Jesus Christ. But in order for her to be suitable for His Son she must be built with His Son so that they can be united together into one. Such, then, is the Jerusalem woman whom God has desired from eternity past to have for His Son.

On the other hand, though Babylon is also woman, she is a harlot and therefore not a good woman. She will be marked by riches of every kind. She will be clothed in scarlet and pearl and precious stones and will be like a beautiful tree sitting there, but we know she is built on the foundation of falsehood, lies, deceit, and hatred. She, too, is to be united, but she is to be united with Satan, which is what he has long wanted. Satan has desired to have a woman to be united with him so that he could claim her as his own and that that would represent him and magnify him.

There is another similarity between these two cities—both are habitations for their respective builders. With regard to Jerusalem, it is a habitation for God. Because it is a city it is a corporate entity, and in that corporate establishment God desires to dwell with man; and we know how true that desire is (see, e.g., Leviticus 26:11-12, Ezekiel 37:27, Revelation 21:3). God wants a corporate city that is built together and fit together in order that He may dwell among His own people and display His fullness through that corporate expression. This is what God has wanted from before the existence of Time itself.

Babylon is also a place of habitation—yet not for God but for His archenemy. Satan is building that city in order that he may dwell in it and express himself through it. We can thus readily see that these two—Jerusalem and Babylon—in their outward appearance have several features in common, but in actuality they are as different from each other as heaven is from hell, because one represents God's thought and the other represents Satan's.

Before we go into more detail I would like to mention one more aspect concerning these two cities. From reading the history of these two cities one can discern the fact that Babylon seems always to come forth first in terms of action and movement. It appears that Babylon has always been one step ahead of Jerusalem. It persecutes Jerusalem and puts her under Babylon's aggressive thumb. But we know from God's word that it is going to be Jerusalem that finally defeats Babylon. That is true prophecy. So we learn from their history that these two cities have been in spiritual conflict with each other throughout the generations and ages of mankind and that Babylon has probably been the one in the ascendancy more often than not. On the other hand, Jerusalem seems for the most part to have been hidden, but we know from Old Testament prophecy and the book of Revelation that there shall come a day when Babylon shall be destroyed; and she will be destroyed by Jerusalem. So from these few chapters which we read together at the beginning of our discussion today we learn that at the pouring out of the seventh bowl, Great Babylon shall be destroyed, and subsequent to that, Jerusalem shall be established.

Let us now consider this subject of Babylon as we find it described in much detail in the book of Revelation. At the time of the pouring out of the seventh bowl God was reminded about Great Babylon. It would seem as though God had forgotten about her—that He had allowed Great Babylon to develop and develop and develop until she had spread herself out and filled the entire earth. And we may sometimes have wondered whether God had indeed forgotten about Babylon because He had allowed her to develop at such speed and in such fullness.

And thus, this result has become a test of our faith. Oh, if only God would do something and not let evil develop to such an extent. It seems to us as though there has been no end to Babylon's spread on earth. So we wonder why it is that God has not interfered, that He has not intervened, that He has not taken some action that would put a stop to Babylon's advancement. Now sometimes we do have such thoughts, questions and feelings. But let us ourselves be reminded that there shall come a day when at about the time of the pouring out of the seventh bowl God shall be reminded of Great Babylon. Yet, it is not really that God has ever forgotten anything, but with respect to Babylon and her advancement it is simply this: that God has allowed her to develop to her fullness so that when God's remembrance is brought forth, He can effect the full end of her evil advancement and spread.

Now the two aspects or sides to Great Babylon which have already been mentioned and briefly discussed are actually presented in the vision which John informs us about in Revelation chapters 17 and 18. In chapter 17 Babylon is presented to us as a woman and is presented to us in chapter 18 as a city. Let us take up each one separately. First of all, the aspect as woman which is presented to us is the religious side of Babylon. Let us not think that Great Babylon is atheistic. She is not. This is because "Mystery, great Babylon" is "the mother of the harlots and of the abominations of the earth."

I do not know if you have read a book entitled, *The Two Babylons*. It is a very learned volume, the author having accomplished much research. And in his book he tells us the result of that research—that all the man-made religions in the world can be traced to their one source of Babylon. If one becomes familiar with Babylonish mystery cults he will see very clearly that the humanly-devised religions in this world have many things in common with the Babylonish mystery cults and that thus one can conclude that the source for them all is there in Babylon. Whether those religions bear the name of Buddhism, Hinduism, Islamism, or even Christianity—if it is not revealed by God or is not purely revealed, then most every feature in those religions can be traced back to Babylon. She is truly the mother of the religious abominations of the earth.

Satan knows that man needs religion. He is too clever to try to remove that inborn instinct in man—an instinct for things spiritual and religious. Such an instinct is born in us. It cannot be wiped away or eradicated. For example, even though Russia has been trying all these years since the Soviet Communist revolution's attempt to eliminate all vestiges of religion, she has had to acknowledge that she has failed. This especially became clear during the Second World War (1939-1945). Many of her soldiers, who were born and brought up after the revolution broke out in 1917, and who had thus received an atheistic education all those years, when those young soldiers entered Western Europe in the final years of the war, they, of their own volition, entered church buildings and meditated and prayed. Whenever man is faced with the stark issues of life and death, he can only think of that which is beyond, of that which is unseen, of that which is real. It is an inborn instinct which can never be totally eradicated.

Now Satan has well known that, so he has attempted to divert the object of that instinct of worship from God to himself. We will recall that he even challenged the Lord Jesus with that. So, he said to Jesus, you want to worship? All right, you worship *me* and I will give you all the powers and authorities of the kingdoms of this world. Yes, Satan is too clever to eradicate religion altogether. He knows that the pretense of being religious is necessary.

Hence, the woman side is the religious aspect of Great Babylon. Babylon represents the concentration of the world which Satan is building up, and in that world there is a place for religion—indeed, a very large place. In fact, during the end-time (which is fast approaching) there will come forth a world religion. By which is meant that all religions will be combined in this one woman, and accordingly, there will be but one religion in this world.

Please note in this regard that Revelation describes this woman as sitting upon many waters—the term waters there representing all peoples, all nations, all tongues, and all tribes. Oh, how many religions there are today in the world. Everybody has his or her own idea; nevertheless, there is a growing tendency today—which is very prevailing—in attempting to bring all religions together into one. And the notion underlying this attempt is as follows: Since we are all seeking for heaven, why not combine all our separate pursuits into one? The present-day ecumenical movement in Christianity is an example of such thinking, and it is so strong that it has come to dominate Protestant Christianity. If anyone should differ, these ecumenical exponents respond by saying, Well, now, you want to maintain divisions! But let us be aware that this ecumenism is only a union; it is not a unity. It is nothing more than a man-made union and not a God-given unity. It is merely an imitation and not a true expression of what God is after.

Yet, not only are there different sects in *Protestantism* which are trying to be united; there is a similar desire within the

Roman Catholic Church whose expressed desire is couched in the following language: "Now you separated brethren, it is time for you to come back into the fold. Let's be united." Yet this uniting task is not only aimed at uniting Roman Catholics and Protestants together, but even the Orthodox Church ought to be included, say these ecumenical advocates. Moreover, it is not only the Orthodox who are being reached out to but also Buddhists: they, too, should be included, because, after all, we are all religious.

Are we aware of such a movement in the world today? Such a development is actually according to prophecy that is to be found in the word of God. This development is definitely coming; in fact, it is bound to come; and the day shall arrive when all religions in this world will be united into one world religion, and it shall be quite rich and powerful.

We must next notice that this religious side of Babylon shall have had a tight relationship with the world of politics; for let us observe that in John's vision this woman rides astride a scarlet beast. Babylon's religious aspect has been marked by its collusion with the political world as a means of gaining for itself an ascendancy in secular affairs. A review back into history reveals how religion has made use of the political arena as a way to gain influence and power. And the day is coming when this relationship shall have been developed to the nth degree.

But the apostle John—to whom all of this was prophetically revealed in a vision—beheld what was for him a most amazing sight. He beheld this woman drunk with the blood of the saints and the blood of Jesus' witnesses. And upon seeing this, the apostle was amazed and wondered with great wonder. How could this be? he wondered to himself. For had the person in this vision been instead the founder of Islam, Mohammed, John would have had no reason to be amazed, since that would have been the natural act for the Moslem leader to have done, in that should Mohammed have been seen killing Christians, then such an act would have gained merit and heaven for himself, since that is prescribed in that religion's holy book, the Koran. However, what John beheld was this woman—representing as she does the religious feature of Great Babylon—drinking to the full the blood of Christ's faithful followers; and that caused great amazement to rise up in John.

Now why was that John's reaction? It is because it shall be in the form and name of *Christianity* that world religion shall experience its final downfall. And because of that, John was greatly amazed to witness such a contradiction. In name and form this woman is supposedly a kind, gentle and loving Christianity, but in reality she shall have been ruthless, unloving and cruel in having fully consumed the blood of Christian saints and the blood of Jesus' many witnesses.

The days are rapidly approaching when those Christian believers who desire to be faithful to the Lord Jesus shall be persecuted, killed and martyred—yet, not by the world directly but by the world religion of Christianity. This is most serious, with that day coming quickly when the world religious system shall be revealed in its final form.

Now as mentioned earlier, Revelation chapter 18 presents Great Babylon in its other aspect—that of a city. Symbolically speaking, it is the capital of the world. We need only recall one very prominent period in its history: King-Emperor Nebuchadnezzar and the construction of his great and opulent capital Babylon. The unity of the Bible's contents is readily exemplified by the fact that in world history's final period we find mentioned once again, and prophetically described in much detail in the Bible's final book, the great city of Babylon. And here in chapter 18 this city is portrayed as an intertwining mixture of politics and economics—an eco-political world system that shall have become the final form of world government.

In fact, this city shall control all mankind through both its commerce and its politics. One political economy and one government, and its motto or slogan shall be—"Prosperity,

prosperity." Interestingly, someone has observed that this being the last form of world government, it is more likely to be socialistic than communistic in character. That is because in this chapter 18 communism is not there but socialism. And people in Great Babylon buy and sell all sorts of commodities: they buy and sell not only gold and silver, not only incense and perfumes, but they also buy and sell even the bodies and souls of men—just think of that for a moment: not only people's bodies can be bought and sold but their souls can also be bought and sold as commodities. And because of this city's expansive commercial activities, everyone shall seem to be able to be enriched and shall be able to live in unparalleled luxury. Oh, what great prosperity shall be evident!

Will this not be the golden age of utopia? What would anyone want and desire more than that? In the entire world only one religion, one economy, one government. I would ask, however, How shall this world system have been built? It shall have been built totally on confusion: the ingredients of which will have been treachery, sin, wickedness, falsehood, hatred, and lies. Outwardly, all aspects of this supposedly utopian system shall appear to be the best—one undivided religion, one benign government, one unfailing economy. Has that not been the aspiration of the world throughout mankind's history? And has that not been the philosophic quest of many wise men?

Nevertheless, we find that all of it shall have been marked through and through by confusion. And how shall the enemy accomplished this? By having continually brought in mixture—a mixture of truth and lies so as to confuse. That is why the Spirit of God presents such things to us in God's word so that we may not be deceived and carried away (Ephesians 4:14); and God's word to His people is:

> Come out of her, my people, that ye have not fellowship in her sins, and that ye do not receive of her plagues: for her sins have been heaped on one

> another up to the heaven, and God has remembered her unrighteousnesses (Revelation 18:4b-5).

That is God's word to His people today concerning the world as symbolized by Great Babylon, because she represents the world. The people of the world are in Babylon and God's call is to come out of her. And He is calling His people to come out of not only her political and economical system so that they may not be buried under it, but also to come out of her advancing world religious system.

God summons His people to come out of confusion, mixture, and external greatness. God says for us not to have fellowship with those sinners. For if we do have fellowship with them, we will share in their punishment. This call of God has continually been sounded throughout the generations and ages of mankind's long history.

As was indicated earlier, this call can be found, for instance, in the book of Isaiah chapter 48 where the prophet informs the people that God says for them to "go forth from Babylon, flee from the Chaldeans [i.e., the Babylonians] with a voice of singing" (v.20a). Let us ask ourselves, Have we taken heed to that call?

It is true that Babylon has been building and building and building. As we saw earlier today it began with that rebel leader Nimrod which we learn from reading Genesis chapter 10 and verse 10 and from reading chapter 11:1-9. And the building has been continuing throughout the generations and ages and will only reach its final form as described in Revelation chapters 17 and 18. Even so, are we aware that this is what Satan has been building right up till today? He has been about the building of a great and monstrous Babylon for himself. He has been constructing everything according to his idea in order that all shall express him, and that that shall be his habitation and his dominion over which he shall be supreme. Yes, he is clever enough to let man have some semblance of a god as an appearance of religiosity in order that he may infuse into it all kinds of evil. He has been using, and shall continue to use, confusion by which to nefariously complete his work. And as we look about, we must acknowledge that the world today has already become a great Babylon. Oh! How seemingly complete it already is. What a mystery is Great Babylon, indeed! Even the religion of Christianity today is a confusing mixture—there being some truth in it, but where lies that truth? And because the lies are so many, it becomes difficult for people—even Christians—to discern the difference between lies and truth. And the result: utter confusion.

Oh, how many of God's people are lost in the world today! They are lost not only in the eco-political world system, they are likewise lost in the religious world system. They are greatly confused. You who are not in religious Babylon and have talked with those who are, the impression you have received is that they are very confused, greatly confused. And the only way for them to extirpate themselves from the confusion is to come out of Great Babylon. God has said to come out of her; yet not to come out with reluctant sighing but with joyful singing (again, Isaiah 48:20a). Let any who are presently trapped within religious Babylon take heed to what God has said: Come out of her.

However, if God tells us to come out of Babylon and we afterwards enter a vacuum, then we will very soon be back in Babylon; but thank God, what He tells us to do after coming out of Babylon is for us to enter Jerusalem. God has His city and He is building that city on the principle of peace. He wants to draw His people out of that corrupt secular and religious system and have them enter into His heavenly entity in order that in that heavenly body He may express himself and we may enjoy Him together. Blessed are those who can enter the gates of the city of Jerusalem and eat of the fruit of the tree of life (Revelation 22:2), for that has always been God's thought. Let us ever be reminded that God is still building today. From the very beginning of Time God has been building. The book of Hebrews tells us that there is a city with foundations of which God is the designer and the builder (11:10). He has designed that city and continues to build that city today. Abraham looked for that city (11:10a). Jacob too looked for that city (cf. 11:21). Joseph also looked for that city (cf. 11:22). They and many others were and are strangers and sojourners on the earth (11:13b). They do not belong to Babylon but to Jerusalem, and God is preparing for them that heavenly city (11:16) and is building them into Jerusalem.

Oh, what a blessed hope that is! What a work God has been doing! Even so, God does not expect you and me to sit by passively. He wants our cooperation. God can create a garden without us but He cannot build a city without us. He needs you and me. He wants to deal with and discipline us and build us into Jerusalem. Hence, it really comes down to but this one thing: Come out of Babylon and enter Jerusalem.

Now we have previously discussed together about New Jerusalem and its description, so I will not enlarge further upon it here except to say the following. God's answer to this world is Jerusalem. It will be Jerusalem which shall bring forth the downfall of Babylon. As long ago as in the days of God's prophet Isaiah it had been prophesied that Jerusalem shall destroy Babylon. Indeed, Isaiah, speaking of Jehovah God's declaration, reported Jehovah as asserting the following:

> "Hearken unto me, Jacob, and thou Israel, my called. I am he; I the first, and I, the last. ... All ye, gather yourselves together, and hear: ... He whom Jehovah hath loved [i.e., Jerusalem and Israel] shall execute his pleasure on Babylon, and his arm shall be on [or, against] the Chaldeans [i.e., the Babylonians]" (48:12, 14).

It is Jerusalem that will displace Babylon, and Jerusalem shall be established forever.

So may the Lord use these words to help us in gaining an accurate understanding of what the world truly is as well as of what God intends to do at the end-time.

Chapter Ten

Armageddon (1)

And I saw the heaven opened, and behold, a white horse, and one sitting on it, called Faithful and True, and he judges and makes war in righteousness. And his eyes are a flame of fire, and upon his head many diadems, having a name written which no one knows but himself; and he is clothed with a garment dipped in blood; and his name is called The Word of God. And the armies which are in the heaven followed him upon white horses, clad in white, pure, fine linen. And out of his mouth goes a sharp two-edged sword, that with it he might smite the nations; and he shall shepherd them with an iron rod; and he treads the wine-press of the fury of the wrath of God the Almighty. And he has upon his garment, and upon his thigh, a name written, King of kings, and Lord of lords.

And I saw an angel standing in the sun; and he cried with a loud voice, saying to all the birds that fly in mid-heaven, Come, gather yourselves to the great supper of God, that ye may eat flesh of kings, and flesh of chiliarchs, and flesh of strong men, and flesh of horses and of those that sit upon them, and flesh of all, both free and bond, and small and great.

And I saw the beast and the kings of the earth and their armies gathered together to make war against him that sat upon the horse, and against his army. And the beast was taken, and the false prophet that was with him, who wrought the signs before him by which he deceived them that received the mark of the beast, and those that worship his image. Alive were both cast into the lake of fire which burns with brimstone; and the rest were slain with the sword of him that sat upon the horse, which goes out of his mouth; and all the birds were filled with their flesh.

And I saw an angel descending from the heaven, having the key of the abyss, and a great chain in his hand. And he laid hold of the dragon, the ancient serpent who is the devil and Satan, and bound him a thousand years, and cast him into the abyss, and shut it and sealed it over him, that he should not any more deceive the nations until the thousand years were completed; after these things he must be loosed for a little time.

Revelation 19:11-20:3

We have been considering the testimony of Jesus in relation to the world for quite a long time and probably we must have one or two more sessions on that topic. And today I would like for us to concentrate ourselves on the last battle of this age—the conflict of Armageddon.

Many people believe that the world is getting better and wiser all the time. It is true that the world has made much progress in the physical realm, but it remains the same so far as its nature and character are concerned. The Bible tells us that the whole world lies in wickedness and under the wicked one (I John 5:19). As we now know Satan has usurped the rule over this world ever since the day he got hold of our forefather Adam. He has even been called in Scripture the god and ruler-prince of this world (II Corinthians 4:4a, John 12:31). And he has certainly stamped his character upon this world. Ever since the day when Adam surrendered himself and the world to Satan its nature and character have remained the same: a world filled with darkness and lies and falsehood and the continuing wickedness of sin and deceit.

We find in the book of Revelation that Satan has quite a few names. It is said that he is the great dragon, the ancient serpent, he who is called devil and Satan. He who deceived much of the heavenly realm and the entire world is also an accuser. When the Bible describes Satan as the great dragon, what impression does that convey to you? Does that not tell you that Satan is the fiercest and most powerful of creatures and that he is out to steal, kill and devour? (cf. John 10:10) He is called the *ancient* serpent for a very good reason, for it signifies that he, being a master of treachery and full of cleverness and craftiness, is not a new or fresh serpent to come onto the scene but is one who has been around for a very, very long time. This greatest of all fallen angels is also called the devil, meaning he is a dark, wicked, deceitful character who in a hidden way is always subtly at the back in perpetrating his unending nefarious works. His other name, that of Satan, conveys the idea of an adversary who is the archenemy of both God and man. He is also the great deceiver who goes forth to trick and deceive the entire world if he can. And, finally, he has been called the accuser who, with or without valid reason for doing so, never fails to accuse—especially the Son of man's brethren.

Now *that* is the nature of the present ruler of this world and he most certainly *has* stamped his character upon this world. For like him, the world is full of darkness, violence, deceit, treachery, devious schemes and tricks. Much of what is said or done in the world is what lies behind the scene, underneath, and is most subtle in its craftiness. Furthermore, we find everywhere in this world oppositions, deceptions, lies, accusations, and falsehoods of every kind. Such, then, is what much of the world has become. Like the nature and character of its present ruler, that is the very nature of this world.

Now if the nature of this world down through its many generations and centuries has never been altered for the better, can we expect its nature and character to be any different at its end? The Bible tells us that the world shall not come to an end marked by love, peace, glory, and so forth; rather, its end will ever be known both by its attitude and by its nature in the battle of Armageddon. That shall be how the world will come to an end. From Revelation we come to understand that at its end not only shall the nature of the world not have changed, even the *attitude* of the world shall not have changed. This latter observation probably needs a little explanation.

What is the attitude of the world today towards God and especially Jesus Christ? When God sent His Son to this world, its cry was: "We do not want this man born a king to reign over us (cf. Luke 19:14). We don't want him, away with him, crucify him!" (Luke 23:18, 21). Has the world's attitude towards Christ changed? No, the world is still crying forth that they do not want this man to be their king; and if that be true, and it is, then how can the kingdom of God be ushered in peacefully? It cannot, for we will find that the opposition shall become greater and greater as the end-time draws nearer and nearer.

What shall be the testimony of Jesus in relation to the world when the end of all things for this present age does finally draw near? That testimony shall be marked by a great battle—the battle of Armageddon. But before we consider this battle I think it would probably be profitable and helpful for us to review somewhat concerning what I believe has been God's strategy to regain the world for himself, because I feel that this is important for us to be aware of today.

We know that this world belongs to God by right of having created it. He is the only legal possessor of this world despite the fact that it today is in the hands of the enemy, and even though the enemy has had the audacity in the past to challenge the Lord Jesus, he having tempted Him out in the wilderness, saying: "If you bow down and worship me I will give you the world, for it is mine to give" (see Matthew 4:8-9). God had committed this world into the hands of man that man might rule the world for Him. Unfortunately, man surrendered himself—and the world which had been entrusted to him—to God's enemy, Satan. That is how the enemy got hold of this world, having usurped it and become its ruler. However, we know that God shall eventually regain the world for himself. But what is His strategy for doing so?

Let us bear in mind that God shall never regain this world by force. Doubtless He could easily step in and declare to Satan: "This is Mine, get out; I am going to reclaim it for myself"—He could readily do that. However, God's strategy shall not be physical but spiritual in nature. It would indeed be a simple feat for God to step in physically and force Satan out physically and materially; but He has chosen not to accomplish His recovery of the world to himself by that method but to reclaim it by means of a spiritual approach.

In fact, the way God intended to reclaim the world back to himself was by sending His Son here, for having been born for this purpose, Jesus was born a king. Yet, it became evident that this was not the time for Him to establish His kingship rule over the world but to come at the solution to the matter by other means. And as a result, oh how Jesus was misunderstood by the Jews at His coming. They were expecting their Messiah-King to be one who would assert His authority and declare to the Roman Caesar: "Go hence! I am now the One in charge of the world!" Such was what they were expecting Christ to do. That was unquestionably their concept and way for regaining the power and authority over this world. Instead, here came the lowly and humble Lord Jesus who, though indeed born a king, did not seize the world with force and assume control. Rather, Jesus was willing for himself to be seized and even to be crucified on a cross.

It becomes clear from God's word that the reason for this is the fact that His kingdom is different from man's concept of a kingdom. Though Jesus did come as a king, His approach was to be spiritual and not physical. By laying down His life on the cross the Lord had created for himself a new kingdom—and even having done so on enemy territory! By His approach He had surrounded himself with a new people, for as the Lord himself said to the Pharisees: "The kingdom of God is in the midst of you" (Luke 17:21b). Through the redemptive work of the cross He has gathered to himself a people with whom He has created His kingdom. And from that time forward and right up to the present moment the kingdom of God has been and is *continually* being established and strengthened even as I speak today.

Now I would say that the strategy of God in reclaiming the world is more geographical than chronological in nature. Satan, of course, is a very clever fallen angel, he being far more clever than we think. Not only is he very clever, he also has very much knowledge. For instance, he has known all along that the world does not belong to him, because he knows that he gained control over the world by trickery. And he also has known that the day shall come when God will reclaim and restore the world to His Son Jesus Christ. He knows all this, though he naturally is not willing to give up what he has gained by deceit; and hence, Satan's strategy is to play a delaying action in opposition to his Creator.

It bears repeating what has just been said, because it is essential to our understanding of what this fallen archangel's strategy has always been and continues to be in opposition to his Creator: Satan knows very well that God will not allow him to hold on to the world forever. Knowing also very well that it is not his and never will be, the only hope he has is for him to try to delay as long as possible the relinquishing of his grip on the world. Satan has therefore been playing a delaying action all through these past centuries. For him the strategy is time: by whatever means he can gain more time: by whatever evil means he can delay God's purpose to be fulfilled. Satan is therefore extremely interested in time, and we are told in the book of Revelation that he knows his time is running out (12:12c). And because he knows his time is growing short, he has "great rage" (12:12b). Indeed, because of this time factor, Satan has become furious, he now pulling out all stops—to the point that he sometimes even forgets himself, so pressed for time has he become.

So that is the strategy of Satan concerning the world, whereas the strategy of God is quite different. God is not at all troubled by time since He has all eternity at His disposal. What He is concerned with is geography, not time. To be most accurate, we may say that the world is physically encroached upon by the enemy today, it actually being what could be termed an occupied territory. So what concerns God is geographical territory. How, then, can He rescue and recover this territory? How can He reclaim the enemy's occupied territory? How is He going to achieve that? It has always been and shall continue to be by means of geography.

We will recall that after the Lord Jesus had accomplished the work of redemption on the cross, He began to gather that new people of His with whom He had surrounded himself prior to the cross, His resurrection and His ascension. So, first in Jerusalem, there were 120 of them praying together, and as they prayed together the Spirit of God united them into a body; and there in Jerusalem—in a tiny part of the enemy's territory—we find that God has established an embryonic beginning of His kingdom (Acts 1:15, 2:1-4; I Corinthians 12:13a). And then the gospel spread from Jerusalem to other places such as into all of Judea, to Samaria, to the uttermost part of the world (Acts 1:8), and even now to New York. In all these places God has been planting a foothold here, a foothold there, and other footholds elsewhere throughout the world. Thus, down through church history there have continued to be beachheads—both large and small—established in many parts of the world. And lest we forget, it must be repeated that for the Lord and for His people this world is enemy territory, and it is not yet the time of His return coming to the earth again. Nevertheless, it is as the Lord

Jesus has said, Wherever two or three of His people are gathered together in His name, there He shall be in their midst (Matthew 18:20). And such a gathering, no matter the size, constitutes an additional beachhead or foothold in the enemy's territory for God and His Christ.

Now *that* is God's strategy: the planting of His church, the planting of His people, the planting of the very essence of His kingdom and that which represents His kingdom. Briefly stated, God's strategy is spiritual in nature, and in planting those little or larger flocks of His people in different parts of the world, they stand here and there as footholds—as beachheads—for the coming of the kingdom of God.

Oh, God has planted brothers and sisters in the Lord in many places of the world, and why are they there? They are the embryonic representation of the coming kingdom of God and of His Christ—and they are standing valiantly on enemy territory! They are testifying that they have a king and that their king is Christ. And like them we too must bear testimony—testifying both with our lips and with our lives, and the impact must be felt by the world around us. In other words, we who are His people are here to undermine and undercut the power and influence of the enemy in his control over this world.

Do please realize that we are not here to engage in play. We are not here to live simply for 70, 80, or even a hundred years, and that is it. We are likewise not here to enjoy some comfort or to receive comfort from God. We are not even here for our personal spiritual benefit, although we experience that as a by-product. No, we are here specifically sent by God to occupy for the time being a strategic spot of enemy territory and as it were hold the fort for the Lord. That is primarily why we are here. This, then, is God's spiritual strategy, and when Christ has gained enough such footholds/beachheads which have matured into unshakable strongholds—when He has gained enough strategic locations throughout the world, the world will come back to the Lord again. So let us keep this in mind because this is very important.

Now when God has succeeded in gaining many beachheads and footholds throughout the world, which is to say that when the Lord has been successful in undermining all the power and influence of the enemy, that shall be the time when the final day will have come, which is what we have read together from Revelation chapter 19: And I saw the heaven opened and saw a white horse, and one sitting on it who is called Faithful and True. And there are many diadems upon his head, and his garment is dipped in blood; and his name is called The Word of God. And out of his mouth goes a sharp two-edged sword. Moreover, there shall be armies following Him from heaven and riding upon their own white horses, and they shall be clothed in white, pure, fine linen, etc., etc. And there is a name written upon the garment and thigh of the one called Faithful and True; and it shall read: King of kings, and Lord of lords.

The world shall be concluded by an incredibly great and horrific battle. It shall be a battle fought between Christ and His heavenly army and Satan and his worldly army. It will be of a magnitude which the world has never seen before; and whose nature shall be very different from all other battles fought prior to it. And with the appearing of Christ coming down upon the earth from heaven, that shall be the signal that this present world shall have come to an end.

But before we go on further I must remind ourselves of what we learned earlier from Scripture: that the coming of the Lord is not one event but *a series of events*. As explained previously, our English word coming in Greek is the word *parousia* and *parousia* conveys the concept of a period of time covering a series of events. It was therefore mentioned before that *parousia* begins with the rapture of the overcomers to the heavenly throne, and from there they, as it were, shall escort Christ downward to the air. His return coming shall occur as though coming forth like a thief because the world will not know Him. For the unbelieving world He shall come in a secret and hidden manner, but for His own people His coming should not be a secret event but it should be an open secret to them because they should be watchful, ready and waiting, and thus not be taken by surprise.

And then, as was also explained before, after the Lord Jesus shall come down from the throne to the air there will be great tribulation upon the earth, but at the end of that tribulation, at the sounding of the last trumpet, there will be a general harvest of souls, and that harvest of believers will be gathered to the air, and we shall all then meet the Lord in the air, there being present the entire church of God at the judgment seat of Christ which is set to occur right there in the cloud. But while the judgment of the saints is taking place, there shall be the great wrath of God falling down upon the earth: the pouring out of the contents of seven bowls upon the entire world.

And we will further recall that with the pouring out of the seventh bowl the fury of God is announced by a great voice from the heavenly temple declaring that God's fury is now completed and at an end. And that is when the heaven shall open and Christ shall come forth riding a white horse and shall make His appearance on the earth, accompanied by mighty angels and millions of overcomers. Thus, according to my understanding, *parousia* shall have begun with the taking away or catching up to heaven's throne of those who are ready, and *parousia* shall end with the open appearance of Christ on the earth. To the world of unbelief His appearing shall signify the final end of the world because when He shall appear this time on the earth, the Lamb of God will judge the world.

Now this review of some of what has been shared in several of the previous messages in this series is for the purpose of bringing us up-to-date for what I am about to say next. And as I have intimated previously on several occasions, it is perfectly all right if you should not agree to any or all of the above which is my best understanding of the relevant Scriptures.

Let us now read a few verses from II Thessalonians:

> ... at the revelation of the Lord Jesus from heaven, with the angels of his power, in flaming fire taking vengeance on those who know not God, and those who do not obey the glad tidings of our Lord Jesus Christ; who shall pay the penalty of everlasting destruction from the presence of the Lord, and from the glory of his might, when he shall have come to be glorified in his saints, and wondered at in all that have believed, (for our testimony to you has been believed,) in that day (1:7b-10).

Here we find both the revelation of the Lord Jesus from heaven and the appearance of the Lord Jesus from heaven. He shall come as a flaming fire with angels of His power and this shall be the time when He shall take vengeance upon whomever those are who do not know God and upon those who do not obey the gospel of Jesus Christ. Now be advised, friends, that this is speaking of Armageddon.

Dear friends, at the revelation of the Lord Jesus and at His appearing we find that there are those who do not know God and those who do not obey the glad tidings of the Lord Jesus Christ. The gospel demands not only faith but also obedience. If you do not know God and if you do not believe and obey the gospel at the appearing of the Lord, you shall be judged; and it will mean the penalty of everlasting destruction from the presence of the Lord and from His glory.

Is there anyone here today who does not yet know God? Who has not yet obeyed the gospel? If having read about it together with us just now but you have not yet obeyed, I would urge you to obey now because the time is very short and the day of recompense is coming.

Let us next notice something further concerning the glad tidings. It so happens that while on earth the first time Jesus had begun His preaching ministry by publicly reading in the synagogue at Nazareth on the sabbath day (Luke 4:16-19) from the 61st chapter of Isaiah which reads:

> The Spirit of the Lord Jehovah is upon me, because Jehovah hath anointed me to announce glad tidings unto the meek; he hath sent me to bind up the broken-hearted, to proclaim liberty to the captives, and opening of the prison to them that are bound; to proclaim the acceptable year of Jehovah ... (vv.1-2a)

And at that point Jesus rolled up the book of the Old Testament Scriptures and handed it back to the synagogue attendant and sat down.

Now it is clear that at Jesus' first coming to the earth He fulfilled what Isaiah the prophet had prophesied here concerning the Messiah's ministry of announcing the glad tidings to the meek, of binding up the broken-hearted, of proclaiming liberty to the captives, of opening the prisons of those that are bound, and proclaiming the jubilee year of the Lord. That is in fact a summary of what the Lord Jesus had done and is yet doing today, since this is still the Age of Grace and Mercy.

But this same prophecy of Isaiah concerning the Messiah actually did not end there; but Jesus, in quoting the prophet, closed the sacred scroll at that very point. Now why? Because what had been quoted and read by the Lord that day accurately characterized His ministry at His first coming to the earth; but the Lord Jesus has reserved the last part of Isaiah's prophetic words to the time of His second coming. For the next part of the Isaiah passage continues with these chilling words: "... and [to proclaim] the day of vengeance of our God" (v.2b).

Do we see the connection of this with the Thessalonian passage earlier quoted? Here we have the day of vengeance of God being mentioned. Whereas during Jesus' first coming and appearance on the earth He proclaimed the glad tidings to the people, at His return coming to the earth there will be the day of God's vengeance, in that the Lord will judge those who will not have obeyed the glad tidings which He had previously proclaimed to this world. And two chapters later in Isaiah one can find the same thought being expressed concerning the day of God's vengeance:

> Who is this that cometh from Edom, with deep red garments from Bozrah, this that is glorious in his apparel, travelling in the greatness of his strength?— I that speak in righteousness, mighty to save.— Wherefore art thou red in thine apparel, and thy garments like him that treadeth in the wine vat? I have trodden the winepress alone, and of the peoples not a man was with me; and I have trodden them in mine anger, and trampled them in my fury; and their blood is sprinkled upon my garments, and I have stained all mine apparel. For the day of vengeance was in my heart, and the year of my redeemed had come (63:1-4).

What we therefore have in Revelation chapter 19 is the apocalypse, revelation or appearance of the Lord Jesus Christ. And that revealing, disclosing or appearing of Him at the conclusion of this age shall lead immediately to the judgment of the world and shall mark its end. In short, Jesus' second appearing shall signify the judgment of the world. So let us not view the return appearing of Jesus to the earth as having to do with judgment for us Christians. For take note that Paul declared that there is a crown of righteousness laid up or reserved for him and for all those others who love and look forward to the Lord's appearing (II Timothy 4:8). And hence, for the Christian, the Lord's second appearing upon the earth shall have nothing to do with sin but with reward; whereas for the unbelieving world it shall mean the time of final judgment. The attitude of the Christian towards the Lord's appearing is to love and look forward to it as the time of reward.

Now the world will not be aware of the Lord's coming until he suddenly appears. As a matter of fact, the world is neither waiting for Him to come nor wanting Him to come. And His appearing shall therefore be a very sudden and surprising event. In this connection, let us recall again what Jesus had said to His disciples concerning His return coming to the earth which was in response to their question as to what would be the sign of His coming and the completion of the age: "As the lightning goes forth from the east and shines to the west, so shall be the coming of the Son of man" (Matthew 24:27). Thus, the sign of the Lord's return coming to the earth shall be like the striking of lightning in the skies from east to west so that the entire world shall know that He has come. So please be advised that that is surely a sign for the unbelieving world.

But as for us believers, that lightning sign is not given to us. We are not to look upon that sign as being for us a sign of the Lord's appearing upon the earth the second time, for He shall come *as a thief* to us believers, we not knowing at what hour He shall appear. And so we are told to watch and ready ourselves for that hour (Matthew 24:42-44, Luke 12:37-42, cf. Revelation 3:3b).

Interestingly enough, in relation to that exhortation made by the Lord Jesus to His disciples just prior to His arrest and crucifixion, the apostle John, under the inspiration of the Holy Spirit, inserted in a most striking way the very same exhortation. It is most striking because of the context within which the exhortation is to be found. But in order for us to grasp its meaning and significance some background and further explanation is essential, as follows. John inserts the exhortation when recording what he saw in the vision given him at the time when the angel of God shall pour out the sixth bowl's contents.

Here is how John described what he witnessed, within which the exhortation is to be found:

> And the sixth poured out his bowl on the great river Euphrates; and its water was dried up, that the way of the kings from the rising of the sun might be prepared. And I saw out of the mouth of the dragon, and out of the mouth of the beast, and out of the mouth of the false prophet, three unclean spirits, as frogs; for they are the spirits of demons, doing signs; which go out to the kings of the whole habitable world to gather them together to the war of that great day of God the Almighty. (Behold, I come as a thief. Blessed is he that watches and keeps his garments, that he may not walk naked, and that they may not see his shame.) And he gathered them together to the place called in Hebrew, Armagedon (16:12-16).

Unfortunately, all of this shall happen because the world of unbelievers shall have continually refused, right to the end, to listen to and obey the everlasting gospel when even at the last it shall have been proclaimed to them earlier by the angel whom John, in the vision given him, saw "flying in mid-heaven" and who would be sent by God "to announce to those settled on the earth, and to every nation and tribe and tongue and people, saying with a loud voice, Fear God and give him glory, for the hour of his judgment has come" (14:6-7a). Instead of that response from the world, however, we find that the people of the world, when they shall have even suffered under the hand of God's wrath and fury (the seven bowls), will not repent. And we learn further from John's prophetic record that the trinity of evil shall by magical influence gather all the kings of the world and their armies together "to the war"—the final battle of world history which shall occur on the plain of Har-Magedon (Megiddo). Such is what we are told in Revelation 16, earlier quoted.

But we now come to a consideration of the inserted exhortation which appears in the above-quoted passage from chapter 16. Is it not strange that we find, in the midst of John's preparatory record leading up to the mention of this present age's final battle, that he interjects in parenthetic fashion the by-now familiar exhortation of the Lord's: "Behold, I come as a thief, so be watchful and ready"? Why this parenthesis of John's when he is at the point of introducing to his readers the great and final battle of Armageddon? And why this particular exhortation taken directly from the Lord Jesus: Behold I shall come as a thief? Will He not come in the open, for two chapters later in Revelation John reports that the heaven will open and the Lord will come openly on a white horse for all the world to see. And yet, the exhortation of the Lord inserted by John says that He shall come as a thief. Let us understand that with respect to the world, the Son of man shall come openly at the time of the final battle. With regard to God's people, however, they should not be looking and preparing themselves for *that* aspect of His appearing but for His appearing which shall come upon them as would a thief appear on the scene—unexpectedly, which thus requires the Lord's people to be on the alert and continually watchful.

We know, of course, that Jesus can come at any time, at a time when we Christians do not expect it. If we are careless and asleep when we should be watchful and on guard, the Lord shall indeed come upon us as would a thief. So we must be watchful and on guard lest, as is stated in the inserted exhortation, we be stripped naked and put to shame before God and before our brethren in Christ.

Now we can infer, from this Holy Spirit-inspired recording of John's, that as he was writing all this down, he must have had one key element of the Jerusalem temple service in mind.

And as was mentioned in an earlier message in this series, there is a most sobering historical background to this parenthetic passage. During the last days of the temple's existence in Jerusalem various parts of it were especially to be guarded from outside intrusions. So different guards would be stationed in different locations of the temple to keep out any intruders during the nighttime. But periodically, and without any set time attached to the practice, the captain of the entire temple guard unit would go about the temple to observe whether or not these strategically-placed guards were being watchful and alert. And if he found any guard sleeping or even growing weary or listless, that one would immediately be stripped of his uniform garments and be compelled to shamefully walk about naked in the presence of his companions among the guards. That would be the punishment for his negligence.

What spiritually are we to derive from all this? What does it mean for us today? Before the dawn of the Age to Come, we are currently in the nighttime of world history, and the enemy of God is actively out and about seeking to wreak vengeance upon God's people, for he knows his time is growing shorter and shorter. And the testimony of Jesus, as symbolized by the temple of old's witness to the world, must be kept pure and intact throughout to the end. How, though, can that testimony be kept pure and intact? Throughout this closing long night of world history and in the midst of the enemy's ceaseless vengeful activity, God—by this time having strategically established numerous footholds and beachheads, even the local expressions of His church, everywhere in the world—has His people—His temple guards, if you will—as those who are to be watchful and praying that they may not fall into temptation and that the testimony of Jesus to the world may not suffer loss from the subtle assaults of the enemy.

If I may say so, you and I, dear brethren, are to be those guards, as it were. And the Captain of the guard—even the Lord Jesus—shall come at a time when we His guards do not expect it, for He will not sound any warning beforehand that He is coming. The Captain will not blow a trumpet but will come silently even like a thief; and if He should discover that you and I have not been watchful and made ourselves ready for His appearing, we shall be stripped not of life but of glory. And we shall thus be put to shame at His coming (cf. I John 2:28b).

Hence, even though our attention today may be focused on the final battle of this passing age, there is nonetheless a very sober warning for us in the midst of all that. Accordingly, let us be those who are ready and watchful; for, behold, in time the Lord Jesus shall indeed come—but as a thief. Blessed, therefore, are those who are watchful and ready for His coming.

Now if indeed we be ready, then we shall be privileged to be among those who, it says near the beginning of chapter 19, shall be blessed because we shall be called to the supper of the marriage of the Lamb of God. Having made ourselves ready as the wife of the Lamb, it shall be given to us to be clothed in fine linen, white and pure, which is the righteousnesses of the saints (vv.7-8).

So, first, there shall be the wedding and its feast, and then, those who shall be privileged to enter into that marriage and attend the supper feast of the Lamb shall be among the heavenly armies who shall follow the Lamb seated on His white horse in His return to the earth. They shall not need to fight, for the Lamb shall do all the fighting. They, being those who are clad in white, pure, fine linen, shall simply follow the Lamb into the battle on their own white horses (vv.9, 11, 14).

I believe we have covered enough today in our consideration together. May the Lord be able to bless us and use us because we make ourselves ready.

Chapter Eleven

Armageddon (2) and the Judgment of the Nations

And I saw the heaven opened, and behold, a white horse, and one sitting on it, called Faithful and True, and he judges and makes war in righteousness. And his eyes are a flame of fire, and upon his head many diadems, having a name written which no one knows but himself; and he is clothed with a garment dipped in blood; and his name is called The Word of God. And the armies which are in the heaven followed him upon white horses, clad in white, pure, fine linen. And out of his mouth goes a sharp two-edged sword, that with it he might smite the nations; and he shall shepherd them with an iron rod; and he treads the wine-press of the fury of the wrath of God the Almighty. And he has upon his garment, and upon his thigh, a name written, King of kings, and Lord of lords.

Revelation 19:11-16

But when the Son of man comes in his glory, and all the angels with him, then shall he sit down upon his throne of glory, and all the nations shall be gathered before him; and he shall separate them from one another, as the shepherd separates the sheep from the goats; and he will set the sheep on his right hand, and the goats on his left. Then shall the King say to those on his right hand, Come, blessed of my Father, inherit the kingdom prepared for you from the world's foundation: for I hungered, and ye gave

> me to eat; I thirsted, and ye gave me to drink; I was a stranger, and ye took me in; naked, and ye clothed me; I was ill, and ye visited me; I was in prison, and ye came to me. Then shall the righteous answer him saying, Lord, when saw we thee hungering, and nourished thee; or thirsting, and gave thee to drink? and when saw we thee a stranger, and took thee in; or naked, and clothed thee? and when saw we thee ill, or in prison, and came to thee? And the King answering shall say to them, Verily, I say to you, Inasmuch as ye have done it to one of the least of these my brethren, ye have done it to me. Then shall he say also to those on the left, Go from me, cursed, into eternal fire, prepared for the devil and his angels: for I hungered, and ye gave me not to eat; I thirsted, and ye gave me not to drink; I was a stranger, and ye took me not in; naked, and ye did not clothe me; ill, and in prison, and ye did not visit me. Then shall they also answer saying, Lord, when saw we thee hungering, or thirsting, or a stranger, or naked, or ill, or in prison, and have not ministered to thee? Then shall he answer them saying, Verily I say to you, Inasmuch as ye have not done it to one of these least, neither have ye done it to me. And these shall go away into eternal punishment, and the righteous into life eternal.
>
> Matthew 25:31-46

Our subject for discussion during these past weeks has been the testimony of Jesus in relation to the world, and I trust that this will be the last message on it. It was mentioned last time that the way God reclaims the world to himself is not by sheer force but by gathering people to himself and placing them in different strategic locations throughout the world. And when their testimony has exerted the desired impact upon the world, the Lord Jesus will then return to the earth. Today we shall proceed further.

Now it just happens that today is the very day this year on which much of the world is celebrating the birth of Christ. The people of the world this day have their thoughts focused upon the Lord Jesus as a baby in Bethlehem. To this tiny babe lying helpless in one's hands the people of the world can do whatever they like and can be sure that the babe can do nothing in return to defend himself. But the world forgets that this same Babe of Bethlehem—who became the Nazarene of Galilee and the Crucified One whom they came to despise and whose birth they nonetheless celebrate once every year—is the same One who shall one day return to the earth in glory and shall be acclaimed the King of kings and the Lord of lords and before whom everyone shall stand and give an accounting. It is therefore well and good for the world to be reminded of that.

We read in Revelation chapter 19 that the heaven shall open and one shall come forth sitting on a white horse. What does this citing of a horse represent? I would take that to be a symbolic description, for when one comes across the mentioning of horse in the Bible, that usually conveys the thought to the reader of swift action, therefore signifying that the Lord shall come back swiftly.

In this same passage the Lord is called the Word of God. This will doubtless bring one back immediately to the Gospel of John. For we read at the opening of that Gospel the following passage: "In the beginning was the Word, and the Word was with God, and the Word was God." The One who is coming back one day is the One who is from the beginning (1:1-2). Jesus is the Word of God—that is to say, He is the expression, the utterance of God. No one has ever seen God, but the Son, who is in the bosom of the Father, declares Him (John 1:18). As the Word the Son declares God, He expresses God to us and thus He makes God known to us. If a person wants to know God, that person must know God through the Lord Jesus Christ because He is the eternal Word—the *Logos*, the truth, even the changeless One. Indeed, by His word the world was created and the world shall be judged by His word. He speaks and it is done. He is the Word of God.

Jesus is not only called the Word of God in this passage, He is also called Faithful and True. I believe that in His being called Faithful and True it points more to His work. Jesus was faithful and true to the Father in His coming to the earth to do the Father's will, and He has been faithful and true in having accomplished all which the Father had entrusted to Him.

Let us notice, too, in this passage that the Lord Jesus also has a name that is unknown to anyone else but himself. It is axiomatic that we know other people by their name and our name tells others who we are. But the Lord Jesus has many names by which to know who He is. His name is the Word of God in relation to His person; His name is Faithful and True in relation to His work and service. And here we learn that the Lord Jesus has a name written upon His many crowns which no one knows but himself; and thus one could infer that Jesus is the great unknown, the great mystery, the great beyond, even the inexhaustible One. A person may learn to know the Son of man, and yet there is much more to be learned, and even throughout eternity we shall be unable to know Him completely. To repeat: the Lord Jesus is beyond and shall always be beyond and inexhaustible. And thus, there is that which is only known to Him and to His Father. That is our Lord.

I need, however, to say something further in relation to this unknown name of the Lord's. Is it not the case that when you make a new friend you begin to know him first by his name, and then gradually you know more about him until perhaps after a few months you know all about him. There is no wonder, no surprise, no amazement thereafter. With respect to Christ, however, it is a far different matter. Yes, you can come to know the Lord more and more, but the more you know Him the less you actually do know Him because you continually discover that there are more and more truths to know about Him, and there is always wonder and surprise awaiting you. What a Christ we do indeed have. If you cultivate a friendship with Him and have such a friend as He, He will make you wonder and be surprised and amazed all the time. Life is never flat or tasteless with Jesus, for it is continually full of wonder and surprise. To put it most succinctly, Jesus is the Great Beyond.

We learn further that there is yet another and very significant name which the Lord Jesus possesses. It is a name which is written upon His thigh and upon His garment: King of kings and Lord of lords. That is His official title. But let us notice that Jesus' garment is "dipped in blood"—signifying that in His coming again to the earth He shall judge the world.

But the Lord will not come alone. We are told that following Him will be heavenly armies and those ones in these armies will all be on white horses, too, and they shall be clad in white, pure, fine linen. Interestingly, that description is very similar to the description given in verse 8 of this same chapter 19: "it was given to her [the wife of the Lamb] that she should be clothed in fine linen, bright and pure; for the fine linen is the righteousnesses of the saints." Those people who shall follow the Lamb to the earth for engaging in the great battle of Armageddon are those who—as the wife of the Lamb—are privileged to attend the marriage feast of the Lamb. Those who have enjoyed that feast will be those who shall have followed the Lamb as King of kings in His coming back to the earth, and they are clothed with white, pure, fine linen. In the Scriptures, linen, and clothes in general, represent our conduct and behavior—the way we live—and it is described as *fine* linen as a way of referencing the righteousnesses of the saints.

Now when we first come to God through Christ and accept Jesus as our Savior, we are clothed with Christ as our righteousness (I Corinthians 1:30, cf. Jeremiah 33:16). But added to that robe of righteousness (Isaiah 61:10) there must be another garment: the righteousnesses of the saints (Revelation 19:8), with which we become clothed as we walk sensitively before the Lord in allowing the Spirit of God to so work in us that Christ is incorporated into our life. And as this ongoing work is accomplished in us, we in time become clothed with that other garment of righteousness. It is an actual righteousness in us, which then—in terms of our outward behavior and conduct—comes forth from us according to God; and thus it is pure and unmixed, not unlike white, fine linen.

Consequently, such a walk before the Lord during our lifetime on earth will enable us to enter into the marriage feast of the Lamb as well as enable us to participate with Christ the Lamb of God in following Him back to the earth as members of His immense army for engaging in what shall be the greatest conflict the world will ever have witnessed—the battle of Armageddon.

We will notice from chapter 16 that the sixth bowl was poured out upon the great river Euphrates, causing its water to dry up, which makes the way of the kings from the rising sun (i.e., from the East) to be ready to march with their armies westward. And there shall then come forth from the mouths of the trinity of evil (dragon/Satan, beast/Antichrist, and false prophet) three unclean spirits as frogs, which perform magical signs. These evil spirits go out to the kings of all the earth and entice them to gather together their armies to the place "called in Hebrew Har-Magedon" (v.16 ASV) for the purpose of going "to the war of that great day of God the Almighty" (vv.12-16).

The meaning in English of the Hebrew place name of Har-Magedon is the "hill" or "hill country" (Har) of Megiddo, the ancient town name from which the name of Magedon is derived. Several years ago I passed by this place, where there are hills, valleys and an extremely lengthy and very flat plain. Indeed, this plain has been the site of many crucial battles in world history, fought between or among Egypt, Israel, Assyria and Babylonia. And here, also, is where the last battle of world history shall be fought.

On the one hand Christ, accompanied by His armies of angels and overcomers, will come back to the earth to do battle against God's archenemy. On the other hand, Satan will gather all the nations of the world together to do battle against Christ. In fact, the apostle John records that he saw the beast (Antichrist) and the kings of the earth and their armies gathered together to make war against "him [Christ] that sat upon the horse and against his army" (19:19). From Revelation we do not know exactly how all these varied forces are gathered but by reading—in conjunction with Revelation—other portions of the Bible, especially the book of Daniel, we learn from his prophecies additional information. For instance, as was mentioned in a previous message, we learn that in the last days there shall appear "the little horn" (8:9ff.), also known as the beast or Antichrist, who in a sense shall control the entire world. We are told in Daniel that the little horn shall ultimately find his way into and occupy "the land of beauty," which is Palestine (8:9b; 11:16, 44). And while he is there he will hear rumors ("tidings") from the North and from the East which trouble and disturb him (11:44). I do not wish to be dogmatic here, because this is prophecy; but probably these rumors are concerned with the possibility of kings from the East and the North who are preparing to lead their armies into the land of beauty for whatever reason. And if so, the rumored kings from the East are most likely "the kings from the rising of the sun" mentioned in John's vision and referenced in Revelation chapter 16 (v.12b) who are going to be part of the kings, nations and armies who shall all ultimately be arrayed against Christ the Lamb and His overcomers. And these kings from the rising of the sun shall comprise a confederation of kings from the East who shall march their armies into "the Beautiful Land" of Israel.

But there shall also be a confederation of kings and their nations from the North whose armies shall likewise be marching towards Palestine. And perhaps this is the confederation of kings and armies which have been prophesied by the prophet Ezekiel; for in his book of prophecy, chapters 38 and 39, Ezekiel mentions a group of armies under their leaders Gog and Magog. And these armies belong to a confederation of kings from the North who shall lead their forces into the land of Israel.

Now we do not know for certain all the particulars, but the land of beauty shall be the goal towards which three world powers are going to make their way and invade. And hence, at the end of days of world history there shall be these three centers of power: one shall be headed by the little horn, the Antichrist; a second shall be a confederation of the kings and their armies coming from the rising of the sun—that is, from the East; and the third shall be the Northern confederation of nations headed by Gog and Magog.

Furthermore, we do not know for certain why these three groups of armies shall come into the land of beauty. Perhaps some of them have received information indicating that there is much spoil and wealth to be had in the land and ready for the taking (cf. Ezekiel 38:10-13). Several years ago scientists discovered an heretofore unknown wealth to be found in, of all places, the Dead Sea, a fabulous discovery. So it could be the attraction of wealth which may account for why all these kings and their armies shall gather and march towards Israel.

As they end up there, however, Satan, by means of his deceiving power, shall somehow turn these three centers of power from fighting one another into following him to fight against Christ and His overcomers. We know from man's past history that such a development has sometimes occurred. And such will happen again at the end of this present age. All these kings and leaders of the nations of the world shall be united under Satan and shall fight against Christ and His army. It shall be the final resistance by those who have never wanted the Lord Jesus to be their king.

But the Bible tells us that with the two-edged sword which comes out from the mouth of the One who sits upon the white horse all the armies of these nations shall be destroyed (cf. also 19:21a). He will destroy these nations by His words. Oh, how powerful is His word.

Also the beast and the false prophet shall be seized and thrown into the lake of fire alive (19:20), and Satan himself shall be bound in a great chain and cast into the bottomless pit for a thousand years (20:1-3).

Now we find described in chapter 19 a most chilling contrast between two end-time suppers. On the one hand, there shall be an angel standing in the sun who shall cry out in a loud voice to all the birds in the air: Come and gather yourselves to the great supper of God (v.17). On the other hand, there is another supper mentioned: the supper of the marriage of the Lamb. And for those who are called to this latter supper, the angel who shall announce it shall call those in attendance as "blessed" (vv.7-9). However, in dark and somber contrast to that joyful supper, the great supper of God shall be the result of the Lamb's victory in battle over all God's enemies: death to all; for all the birds shall be filled with the flesh "of kings, ... of chiliarchs [commanders of a thousand troops each], ... of strong men, ... of horses and of those that sit upon them, and flesh of all, both free and bond, and small and great" (vv.18, 21).

Chapter 14 of Revelation gives some idea of the huge loss of human life which because of the world's sin, wickedness and disobedience shall be the deadly consequence of this final battle. But first let us be reminded of a relevant passage in the description John records of the Lamb of God who shall be seated upon the white horse leading His heavenly armies down to the earth and into the battle of Armageddon. There we are told that He shall "tread the wine-press of the fury of the wrath of God the Almighty" (19:15c). And the horrific result of the Lord's treading is made known to us in chapter 14:

> ... the angel put his sickle to the earth, and gathered the vine of the earth, and cast the branches into the great wine-press of the fury of God; and the wine-press was trodden without the city, and blood went out of the wine-press [up] to the [height of the] bits of the horses for a thousand six hundred stadia (vv.19-20).

These 1600 stadia measure in length to approximately 200 miles; and thus the length and depth of blood of the enemy dead shall flow forth for 200 miles long and several feet deep from the ground up to the horses' mouths. Just this one datum alone is sufficient to indicate the magnitude of the carnage and destruction of life of this final conflict which shall take place at Armageddon. Most surely, the world shall conclude its history in immense bloodshed. The world shall not end up on a note of peace but war, conflict, and death. And why? Because of the devil-nature of the world whose very attitude since the fall of man has been one of opposition to God.

But then shall come the judgment of the nations. This is described in great detail in the lengthy passage of Scripture from Matthew 25 which we read together at the opening of our discussion today. The Lord shall "sit down upon his throne of glory" and shall judge all the nations which will have remained—that is to say, those nations which shall not have been present at the battle of Armageddon shall be gathered together before Christ's throne of glory and shall be judged. How will He judge those nations? Upon their being gathered together before Him, the Lord Jesus shall proceed to divide them into two groups: at His right hand He shall set the sheep nations and at His left shall be set the goat nations.

Then Jesus shall begin to tell those on His right hand, "You are blessed of My Father, for you are privileged to inherit the kingdom that has been prepared for you from the world's foundation." And how shall that be the case for those nations?

"Because," Jesus shall say to them, "when I hungered, you gave Me food. When I was thirsty, you gave Me drink. When I was naked, you clothed Me. When I was ill and when I was in prison, you visited Me." Those righteous nations shall reply: "Lord, when were You hungry that we fed You? When were You thirsty that we gave You drink? When were You naked that we clothed You? And when were You ill and in prison that we visited You? We have not done any of those things." And the Lord shall reply: "Inasmuch as you have done it to one of the least of My brethren, you have done it to Me. You may enter the kingdom and you can enter into eternal life."

After that, however, the Lord shall turn and speak to the goat nations on His left: "When I was hungry, you did not feed Me; When I was thirsty, you did not give Me drink; when I was naked, you did not clothe Me; when I was in prison, you did not visit Me." And these wicked nations shall reply this way: "Lord, when did we ever see You hungry? If we had known it, certainly we would have fed You. We have never seen You hungry, thirsty, in prison or ill. How, then, could we have had the opportunity to do such things for You?" And the Lord shall say in answer: "Inasmuch as you did not do it to one of the least of these, My brethren, you have failed to do it to Me. Go therefore from Me, you cursed ones, into eternal fire, the eternal punishment prepared for the devil and his angels."

Hell was never prepared for man but for the devil. But should you align yourself with the devil, you will be consigned to it, too. What God has prepared for us is His kingdom, and those nations on the right hand, the sheep, shall enter into eternal life, whereas those on the left shall enter into eternal fire. The judgment of the nations before Christ's throne of glory shall be very different from what we think. That judgment shall be based solely upon one thing: How have you treated Christ's little brother or sister? And who are these little brethren of Christ?

Let us recall our discussion together concerning the woman, the man-child, her other offspring, and Satan the dragon—all in Revelation chapter 12. The woman has conceived a child—the man-child—and as soon as he is born, he is caught up to heaven's throne. Therefore, the dragon can no longer reach the man-child, so Satan turns his anger upon the other seed of the woman, and who are they? And the passage states that they are those who during the Great Tribulation keep the commandments of God and have the testimony of Jesus. And it was also mentioned previously that during that time of tribulation Satan shall pour forth his anger upon the other seed of the woman (see again 12:1-6, 13-17). That is to say, he shall pour forth his fury upon two kinds of people.

First shall be those who keep the commandments of God. Well, now, who are those who have the commandments of God? Are they not the Jews? Not all the Jews, of course, only the pious ones. At the end of days there will be a remnant of faithful Jews who faithfully keep the commandments.

Interestingly, the other day a brother talked to me, and he told me that because he has been in contact with some Jews he discovered that many of them are atheists who no longer believe in God. However, though many Jews today are atheists, there will nonetheless be a faithful remnant. And because they shall have been faithful to God and shall have kept His commandments, they shall suffer during the Great Tribulation. And why? Because the beast who is the Antichrist shall insist that everybody worship him. But these faithful Jews shall refuse to worship his image and hence they shall be persecuted.

The second class of people upon whom during the Great Tribulation Satan the dragon shall pour forth his anger shall be those who have the testimony of Jesus. Now who are those ones? They are those who believe in the Lord Jesus. Only those who believe in the Lord have the testimony. Even during the Great Tribulation there shall be saints who have the testimony of Jesus, and because they testify that Jesus is Lord and none else, they shall suffer greatly.

These two kinds of people—the Jewish remnant and the faithful ones of Christ—shall suffer great persecution in the last days. They shall suffer hunger and thirst, for without the mark of the beast upon their hand or on their forehead, they cannot buy or sell (13:16-17). Now if anyone cannot buy or sell, such will have to suffer hunger and thirst. They will be naked, ill, be put into prison, and suffer greatly.

Hence, the identity of the least of the brethren of Christ shall probably be those who shall have been faithful to God and to Christ during this concluding troublous period of the world. And any nation who shall have treated them well shall be rewarded. Perhaps you may wonder, however, that if it is true that the beast shall be in control over the entire world at that time, how is it that a nation will be in a position to treat well those faithful ones among the Jews and suffering brethren of Christ? We must bear in mind that the beast shall control the world by force, lies, subterfuge; and, therefore, nothing is true concerning his rule. Accordingly, though those nations far distant from the beast's centralized control and hence not under his direct rule may *outwardly* go along with his control, they may not necessarily follow the beast *inwardly*. Consequently, there shall be some nations who shall be willing to feed and assist those being persecuted. And because they shall have done that, those nations shall be rewarded by the Lord Jesus, since He considers such sympathetic aid shown one of the least of His brethren as having been that shown to Him himself. In this very connection, let us recall this that Jesus once declared: If anyone shall give merely a cup of cold water to one of these little ones, these disciples of Mine that bear My name, they shall not lose their reward (Matthew 10:42; cf. Mark 9:41 ASV).

Thus, we see here the testimony of Jesus in relation to the world. It is that testimony which truly matters even when it comes to the matter of the judgment of the nations—it is based upon this: How do you treat even just the least of My brethren? And those nations that shall have treated them well, they shall enter into Christ's kingdom as sheep during the millennial age; but those who shall have ill-treated these little ones of Christ's shall go into eternal fire. And thus this world's present age shall come to an end.

Then comes the millennium, a thousand years in which righteousness shall be ushered in and shall rule; thus meaning that the kingdom of God shall be upon the earth with Christ ruling over it. For shall not great voices in heaven declare, after the sounding of the seventh trumpet: The kingdom of the world is become the kingdom of our Lord, and of His Christ? (see Revelation 11:15 ASV) That shall be the millennial kingdom upon the earth where there shall be peace everywhere. In fact, Isaiah has prophesied the following for this age of peace:

> The wolf also shall dwell with the lamb, and the leopard shall lie down with the kid, and the calf and the young lion and the fatted beast together, and a little child shall lead them. And the cow and the she-bear shall feed; their young ones shall lie down together; and the lion shall eat straw like the ox. And the sucking child shall play on the hole of the adder, and the weaned child shall put forth its hand to the viper's den. They shall not hurt nor destroy in all my holy mountain; for the earth shall be full of the knowledge of Jehovah, as the waters cover the sea (11:6-9).

Thus everything shall be in peace, for righteousness shall reign because the King of kings shall reign in righteousness and the Prince of Peace shall rule (cf. Isaiah 32:1a; 9:6c).

The question has been asked before, so I will take this opportunity to briefly help us to understand. When Christ shall come back to the earth and after the nations are judged, He will set up His kingdom upon the earth; and the nations represented by the sheep shall be relocated into the kingdom. They shall inherit the kingdom, by which is meant that they shall be the people—the subjects—of the millennial kingdom.

Recall again that Matthew 25 tells us that these sheep—even the righteous ones in the nations (vv.37a, 46b)—shall inherit the kingdom and shall enter into eternal life (vv.34, 46b). But their coming into possession of eternal life shall be different from the way we followers of Christ have received eternal life. We do so by believing in Jesus as our Lord and Savior and thus are born again of the Spirit of God (John 3:6), but they shall come into possession of eternal life by entering the millennial kingdom of God. In other words, the kingdom is a part of eternal life because life reigns during that age, and hence, by entering the kingdom, the people of the sheep nations inherit the age of eternal life, they enjoy eternal life, and they become the people of the age wherein eternal life reigns.*

Of course, Christ is the King of kings and the Lord of lords. But where are these other kings and lords? There shall be many of them in the kingdom, and they shall be those who shall have been faithful and true to Christ throughout this present Age of Grace. It shall not be enough to barely be saved, as though you have been plucked out of fire (I Corinthians 3:15). That is not God's thought; rather, His thought is that we may enter the kingdom richly and abundantly (II Peter 1:11) so that we may reign with Christ for a thousand years as kings and lords over the earth. If we are His faithful servants today, in that day to come the Lord shall say to us to enter into the joy of the Master (Matthew 25:21, 23). Because we today are faithful, the Lord shall say in that later day that we can be in authority over ten cities, and again, we can be placed in authority over five cities

* The use of the term eternal life in this passage from Matthew 25 is related to the time period and does not have reference to the life itself. It will still be possible for these righteous ones to die but death will no longer reign (cf. Isaiah 65:20). —*Publishers*

(Luke 19:17, 19). The kings and the lords during the kingdom age shall be those who are faithful to the Lord today and who go on with Him in following Him wheresoever He goes; they shall be those who have no reservations and are therefore utter for Him.

How often in the pursuit of ease and pleasure for a few hours we are willing to forfeit the joy and the glory of a thousand years. Is it worth it? Oh, that we may not live simply according to what we see. What we see shall soon pass away. Oh, that we may live with the kingdom ever in view. May the Lord be able to say to each one of us: "Well done, good and faithful servant, you can enter into the joy of your Lord." That anticipation should be an encouragement to us to press on towards the kingdom. For the kingdom's sake we should be more than willing to lay aside every hindrance because His kingdom is indeed coming. And such believers shall be made a nation of priests to God (Revelation 20:6b) and such a good state of affairs shall continue for a long, long while. Oh, that shall be the golden age: that shall be the realization at last of the elusive utopia which has been sought after by both saints and sinners down through all mankind's history, and the dream of well-nigh every philosopher who shall ever have lived. But it shall only be fulfilled by Christ and in Christ and by and in none else.

Be advised, however, that this is not the end yet. The whole earth and the whole heaven shall be burned up and pass away (II Peter 3:10) and God shall build a new heaven and a new earth, and a new Jerusalem shall be established on the earth (Revelation 21:1-2a), and the Lord God Almighty and the Lamb shall be its temple (Revelation 21:22). We are living at the end of this present age. The coming age—that of the millennial kingdom—is fast approaching. And after that coming age there will be eternity to come. Old things shall pass away (Revelation 21:4c). God shall make all things new (21:5a). There shall be no more tears (21:4a) because everything will be of God. Such, then, shall be the testimony of Jesus in relation to the world.

Part Four
The Testimony of Jesus: in Relation to the Jews

Chapter One

The Mystery of Israel (1)

The spirit of prophecy is the testimony of Jesus.

Revelation 19:10e

I say the truth in Christ, I lie not, my conscience bearing witness with me in the Holy Spirit, that I have great grief and uninterrupted pain in my heart, for I have wished, I myself, to be a curse from the Christ for my brethren, my kinsmen, according to flesh; who are Israelites; whose is the adoption, and the glory, and the covenants, and the law-giving, and the service, and the promises; whose are the fathers; and of whom, as according to flesh, is the Christ, who is over all, God blessed for ever. Amen. Not however as though the word of God had failed; for not all are Israel which are of Israel; nor because they are seed of Abraham are all children: but, In Isaac shall a seed be called to thee. That is, they that are the children of the flesh, these are not the children of God; but the children of the promise are reckoned as seed.

Romans 9:1-8

Brethren, the delight of my own heart and my supplication which I address to God for them is for salvation. For I bear them witness that they have zeal for God, but not according to knowledge. For they, being ignorant of God's righteousness, and seeking to establish their own righteousness, have not submitted to the righteousness of God. For Christ is the end of law for righteousness to every one that believes.

Romans 10:1-4

I say then, Has God cast away his people? Far be the thought. For I also am an Israelite, of the seed of Abraham, of the tribe of Benjamin. God has not cast away his people whom he foreknew. Know ye not what the scripture says in the history of Elias, how he pleads with God against Israel? Lord, they have killed thy prophets, they have dug down thine altars; and I have been left alone, and they seek my life. But what says the divine answer to him? I have left to myself seven thousand men, who have not bowed knee to Baal. Thus, then, in the present time also there has been a remnant according to election of grace. But if by grace, no longer of works: since otherwise grace is no more grace.

... I say then, Have they stumbled in order that they might fall? Far be the thought: but by their fall there is salvation to the nations to provoke them to jealousy. But if their fall be the world's wealth, and their loss the wealth of the nations, how much rather their fulness? For I speak to you, the nations, inasmuch as I am apostle of nations, I glorify my ministry; if by any means I shall provoke to jealousy them which are my flesh, and shall save some from among them. For if their casting away be the world's reconciliation, what their reception but life from among the dead?

... For I do not wish you to be ignorant, brethren, of this mystery, that ye may not be wise in your own conceits, that blindness in part is happened to Israel, until the fulness of the nations be come in; and so all Israel shall be saved.

Romans 11:1-6, 11-15, 25-26a

We have spent a great deal of time on this most important subject, the testimony of Jesus. And we have considered and seen the testimony of Jesus in relation to the church as well as in relation to the world. But this cannot be complete without seeing the testimony of Jesus in relation to the Jews or Israel. Christ is the universal man. He is related to all mankind, inasmuch as God so loved *the world* that He gave His only Son (John 3:16a).

Now according to the Bible all mankind in the world is divided into three groupings of people: the Jews, the Gentiles, and the church. In I Corinthians chapter 10 verse 32 Paul wrote that he would not be a stumbling block to anyone, whether to the Jews or the Greeks (Gentiles) or to the assembly (church) of God; but that he might please everyone in all things. So Biblically speaking, the world is divided into those three categories. And Christ is related to all of them. Whether you are a Jew or a Gentile, you cannot escape being involved with Christ, since He is related to you both; and, of course, we know that being a member of the church you are united to Christ.

I do not know how you feel, but as I read from Matthew onward and come to the book of Revelation, immediately I sense myself entering into the now quite familiar atmosphere of the Old Testament. By that I mean that as I read the book of Revelation my mind begins to revert back to the book of Daniel, to the book of Ezekiel, to the books of Joel and Zechariah; and this is because the very atmosphere of Revelation is quite similar to the atmosphere to be found in those prophets' books.

Furthermore, the very name of God appearing in the book of Revelation brings me back to the time of the patriarchs of the Old Testament. God is the Almighty One, and that reminds me of Abraham, Isaac, Jacob, and the other patriarchs of the Jewish people. They knew God as the Almighty One, and thus again and again in Revelation I meet up with Israel—a nation whose people have not been forgotten but a people remembered by God. And hence, I believe that if we want to understand this book of Revelation fully, we must see the testimony of Jesus in relation to the church, in relation to the Gentile world, *and* in relation to the Jews—all three. But if we miss or overlook the testimony of Jesus in relation to Israel, then our understanding of the book of Revelation will be restricted and our seeing the testimony of Jesus in fullness will be lacking and will therefore be incomplete.

I must confess that I hesitated very much before the Lord, waiting for weeks before Him as to whether I should continue on with this aspect of Revelation or whether I should go on to other Biblical subjects; but somehow I could not avoid the sense in my spirit that I should continue along this line. And hence, I hope and pray that our consideration together of the testimony of Jesus concerning the Jews may be spiritually profitable to us. Let none of us say to himself/herself that because I am not a Jew, what does this further discussion have to do with me. No, I wish for us all to understand that though you and I may not be Jews, nevertheless, the testimony of Jesus has much to do with us. Therefore, let none of us who are non-Jews insist on adhering to a restricted understanding of the testimony of Jesus, but let us come to see how glorious that testimony is in its complete realization.

Now in order for us to come into that more complete understanding which must include Israel, we cannot go immediately to the book of Revelation; instead, I believe there is a need first for some preparatory groundwork to be laid. This is because I do not know how much we who are present here know about the Jewish people or about God's thought concerning Israel or whether or not your concept of the Jews is scriptural. Accordingly, it was my sense that we shall need to prepare ourselves with some background before delving into Revelation itself. And the best preparation I could think of was for us to compare our concept regarding the Jews and Israel with what we find in chapters 9 to 11 of Paul's Letter to the Romans. So let us see how far we can go or how much we can cover today of what there is to be discovered in those chapters, some passages of which have already been read aloud for our consideration.

The testimony of Jesus in relation to the Jews begins with Abraham. We know that immediately after the fall of man God promised that the seed, the offspring, of the woman Eve shall at some point in future come forth and shall crush the head of the serpent (Genesis 3:15b). And we know that this seed of the woman ultimately pointed to Christ. He is that seed of the woman and through Him the power of the enemy shall be broken, and we shall be released and saved from sin. Christ being the seed of the woman is thus related to the whole world—to mankind as a whole—because at that time mankind was not divided yet. Christ therefore stands as the Universal Man. He is the salvific offspring of the woman for all mankind. Salvation is in Him and salvation is for the whole world.

So as man's history unfolded and reached the time of Abraham, God called him and gave him a promise: that in his seed all the nations would be blessed (Genesis 22:18). Now let us bear in mind that the seed of Abraham is the seed of the woman. But whereas the seed of the woman is related to all of mankind, the seed of Abraham is especially related to Abraham; which is to say that Abraham's seed is related to the Jews. Paul wrote in Galatians 3 that the promises of God were addressed to Abraham "and to his seed" and not "to seeds, as of many; but as of one, And to thy seed, which is Christ" (v.16 ASV). So we know from Paul that Christ is the ultimate seed of Abraham, and in *that* seed all nations shall be blessed.

Interestingly enough, in opening up the New Testament to the very first chapter of the very first book therein, we find the genealogy of Christ listed from generation to generation; and the very first verse of the New Testament thus reads this way: "Book of the generation of Jesus Christ, Son of David, Son of Abraham" (Matthew 1:1). That is how the Lord Jesus is presented—as the Seed and Son of Abraham. And thus He is the promised seed of Abraham. All the promises of God made to Abraham are focused upon Him, and therefore we may rightly say that all the promises of God made to Abraham shall be realized in Christ and only through Christ who is the Son of Abraham.

He is not only the Son of Abraham, he is also the Son of David. Let us recall that after David had ascended to the throne of Israel and had a heart to build God a temple, God sent the prophet Nathan to him and through Nathan said: "I will set up thy seed after thee, which shall be of thy sons; ... It is he who shall build me a house, and I will establish his throne forever. I will be his father, and he shall be my son" (I Chronicles 17:11b-13a). Now, of course, we know that this was partially fulfilled in Solomon but is fully fulfilled in "a greater than Solomon" (Matthew 12:42c)—even a greater son of David, and that is Christ, because Solomon's throne did not continue forever. So we see here that God promised David that a son-seed shall be given to him and that his throne-dominion shall know no end and that his kingdom shall be forever and that God will be a father to him and he will be a son to God; and all this is fulfilled in Christ. So the Gospel of Matthew begins with the generation of Jesus Christ, the son of David and the son of Abraham.

The Gospel of Matthew has especially the Jews and Israel in view. Yet let us not make the mistake in thinking that this

Gospel is a Jewish Gospel, meaning that it is exclusively concerned with and is for the Jews and thus has nothing to do with us. I know some people take it that way, but if you do, you will miss a great deal. On the other hand, let us not go to the other extreme and claim that the church is the total concern of the Gospel of Matthew because God has abandoned His former people the Jews. Not at all. The Jews are still before God, that there is yet a place for them, and that most certainly the Gospel of Matthew especially (though not exclusively) has the Jews in view.

We must not forget the historical background here, that when Christ came into the world, He was first presented to the Jews. And how or in what capacity? As the son of David and as the son of Abraham. That is the testimony of Jesus in relation to the Jews, that Jesus is the son of Abraham. In other words, all the promises of God towards Abraham and to his descendants will be fulfilled in Christ and can only be fulfilled through Christ. He is the promised Seed of Abraham and He is also the son of David—the ultimate King who is promised to Israel, even the Christ. And when He shall come, He shall rule over His own kingdom.

Moreover, these two promises include all the other things which we find in the Old Testament. Moses recorded in his book of Deuteronomy that from among the Jewish brethren Jehovah God would raise up a prophet-servant like unto Moses himself who must be listened to; and that if the people would not listen to him, it would be required of them, for God's word would be with that servant-prophet (18:15-19). And we all remember Isaiah's great prophesies concerning the Messiah—the Christ—the Sent One of God: that a child would be born, a son shall be given, and upon whose shoulders the government shall rest; but that this one shall also be a suffering though in the end a most glorious servant of Jehovah God (9:6-7, 53:2-12). And then there is the psalmist who wrote much concerning one who shall come and through whom all the covenants of God shall be fulfilled (Psalm 89:3-4, 19-29, 34-37). We also cannot forget the prophecies of Zechariah (3:8, 6:12-13, 9:9, 11:4-13, 12:10, 13:7). And Malachi prophesied that the Lord, even the messenger of the covenant, shall suddenly come as a refiner and purifier (3:1-3).

Now as we go through the entire Old Testament we find promise after promise and prophecy after prophecy, and all these promises and all these prophecies are centered upon but one person, whatever his identity or title: the son, the seed, the servant, the prophet, the king, the priest, the messenger. Every promise and every prophecy is focused upon that one person, and we can gather them together and they all signify but one person: the Messiah, the Christ of God. Moreover, the entirety of Old Testament promises and the entirety of Old Testament prophecies—whether they touch upon the servant, the son, the prophet, the king, the priest, the seed, the Lord, the angel (messenger), or the covenant—all can be gathered together under two rubrics: the son of David and the son of Abraham. And these two again tell us of but one person: the Messiah, even the Christ of God. He is the One whom God has anointed as King, anointed as Priest, anointed as Prophet, anointed as the One in whom all the promises of God shall be realized. Therefore, the testimony of Jesus in relation to the Jews can be summed up in one short statement: the Anointed One of God is the Messiah.

And most certainly the Jews clearly understand that the Messiah is the One who shall be the realization of all the prophecies and promises of God. God prepared a people two thousand years before the time of Christ. First He called Abraham out of the nations, and then through Abraham He established a family, and from that family there was established a people and nation, and during that long period God was preparing a people and nation—for what? Why was Abraham called? Why was the nation of Israel established? Why did God deal with them in the way He did for those two long millennia?

Why, too, did He give them the law and the oracles of God? Why did He send prophet after prophet to them? What is the reason Jehovah God chose this people and prepared and prepared and prepared them for two thousand years? For what purpose? There is only one answer: God prepared this people for the coming of the Messiah. Oh, for two millennia God was preparing these people in order that the Messiah might eventually come forth; that in the fullness of time the Messiah, the Lamb of God might appear at last (Galatians 4:4).

Now in Romans 9 Paul provides for his readers in a nutshell what that preparation by God consisted of: "who are [called] Israelites; whose is the adoption, and the glory, and the covenants, and the law-giving, and the service, and the promises; ..." (v.4). Let us briefly consider each of these elements comprising God's preparation of a people out of whom would come forth the Messiah.

"*Who are [called] Israelites.*" At a certain point in their history this people came to be called *Israelites*, and we know that the name Israel was given by God himself to Jacob, who among the patriarchs came to be known as the supplanter, the deceiver, the grasper—for that is what his name, translated into English, meant (Genesis 25:26). And after God had so dealt with Jacob that he came to the end of himself, he held onto God so tightly in their wrestling with each other at Peniel, and saying to the Lord, "I will not let You go unless You bless me," that God did indeed bless Jacob: He gave him the new name of Israel—which means prince of God (Genesis 32:24-31). Jacob in essence had reached the lowest point in his life, wherein he realized he could not live a moment any longer without God, he confessing inwardly that the Jacob in him was finished and that he would henceforth have to depend on God. And thus, in God's eyes this chosen people of His are princes and not strangers, outsiders or commoners. They are Israelites.

"*Whose is the adoption.*" That is a great word. Oh, God adopted the Jewish people. We may recall that when God sent Moses to Egypt to lead His people out from there and into the Promised Land, Moses had declared before Pharaoh: "Thus saith Jehovah: Israel is my son, my firstborn. And I say to thee, Let my son go, that he may serve me" (Exodus 4:22b-23a). Thus, God had adopted these people and made them His son, his firstborn. What a privilege has been given to the Jewish people.

"*And the glory.*" We know that throughout Israel's history the glory of the Lord rested upon the ark of the covenant. The glory of the Lord filled the temple. The glory of the eternal presence of God was with these people, and what a glory it was.

"*And the covenants.*" God made a covenant with the Jews. First in Abraham; then in Isaac, in Jacob, in Moses, in Aaron, in Phinehas. God covenanted again and again with His people. Oh! In tracing out the numerous covenants of God with His chosen people Israel one discovers what a full well of blessing God's covenantal relationship with Israel has been.

"*And the law-giving.*" The Lord gave the Israelites the basic laws on Mt. Sinai—the Ten Commandments and all the precepts and statutes which were to be observed by His people as their moral and ethical guardrails for righteous living before God and their fellow human beings.

"*And the service.*" This refers to the temple service and the priesthood for conducting all aspects of the service in the sanctuary. What a full and rich typology it all served to be in pointing to the Messiah and His priestly and spiritual ministry.

"*And the promises.*" All the many promises given by God concerning the Land of Promise, concerning the multitude, concerning a coming King, and concerning the coming kingdom of peace and righteousness. All these glorious promises.

Now having briefly reviewed all these various elements constituting God's preparation for introducing to the world the

Messiah, let us pause to contemplate for a moment what an extraordinarily full and complete preparation it was! Here was a people chosen by God out of all the nations of the world, and a truly privileged people they were. God had covenanted with them, given them promises on how to serve Him with a vast system of temple service, etc. etc., and all these were theirs. And this was the people whom God had set apart and prepared for being the historic corporate human vessel through whom, in the fullness of time, the Messiah-King could make His appearance as the Redeemer and true Lord of the universe.

Let us now go back in history. After the last prophet Malachi prophesied that the Lord, the Angel of the covenant, shall suddenly come and shall purify God's people, then, for 400 years God was silent towards Israel. For 400 years God said not a word to His people. The Scriptures became totally silent. And after those 400 silent years what was the situation in Israel? The scene was as follows. The Jewish nation was under the dominion of the Gentiles. The Roman Empire had taken hold of the Jewish nation and now ruled over it. And because of this, the Israelites were not a free people. Yes, on the one hand, it could be said that they were free to do many things, but on the other hand, they were not really free. They were under the yoke of the Romans. The temple was still there, the service therein was going on, but the glory of the Lord was not there. In fact, the service was a dead thing. The law was still there and a special group had arisen whose role was to interpret the law; nonetheless, the spirit behind the law was not evident. Legalism had developed, and that enslaved all the people. It could be said that outwardly everything seemed to proceed as usual, but actually everything was wrong. The great majority of the Jews were not really waiting for the coming of the Messiah. So, outwardly they were crying for the Messiah, but inwardly they were not waiting and preparing themselves.

How do we know that this was the true state of affairs in Israel? Well, when the wise men came to Jerusalem and asked where is He who is born King of the Jews, King Herod had to call the experts in the law and Scripture, the scribes and Pharisees; and Herod inquired, Now tell me where the Christ should be born; and immediately they said that it was in Bethlehem of Judah, because it was prophesied by the prophet Micah (Matthew 2:1-6, quoting Micah 5:2). But the news of the newly-born King troubled not only Herod but also all the people of Jerusalem (Matthew 2:3). In other words, with their lips they cry out for the coming of the Messiah, but in their hearts they do not want Him to come; they were troubled by the news of it. Do notice the condition of these people. After two thousand years of preparation—the law in their hand, the temple in their midst, the priesthood functioning, and so on and so forth—and yet we learn that when Christ did come, the whole nation was sleeping. They were not ready. They were not waiting for the coming of the Messiah.

And yet, everything connected with God's preparation was bound up with the Messiah. How will this people be adopted? Through the Messiah. How will the glory of God be with them? In the Messiah. How can the covenants be fulfilled? In the Messiah. How will the law be fulfilled? In and through the Messiah. And all those temple services and all those promises are likewise to be realized in the Messiah. In other words, the whole destiny of this people Israel is bound up with the Messiah. With the Messiah they have everything; without the Messiah they have nothing. The entire history of Israel is bound up with the Messiah, and the Israelites know this. Yes, in one sense they know it. But do they actually know it? They do not know it. Yet, in another sense they do know. They do know that their destiny is bound up with the Messiah.

Today in Jerusalem there is part of a wall still standing which dates from the second temple of old. It is called the wailing wall, and Jews will go there and pray and weep there. And why? They weep and weep, saying, Lord, send the Messiah—send the Messiah! On the one hand, they are waiting for the Messiah; but on the other hand, they are not. Because when Jesus the Messiah did come, the whole nation was sleeping. There was only a small remnant among the Jews who were truly waiting for the Messiah. *They* were prepared and ready to receive Him but the rest of the people were not. The great majority of the Jews went their own way, they wanting things their own way; in fact, they were afraid that when the Messiah should at last come He might interfere with their plans and their ideas. They were not ready.

Now who were some of those few among the faithful remnant who were waiting and ready to receive the Messiah? Well, among the priesthood there was Zacharias, and his wife Elizabeth (Luke 1:5ff.). Among the royal family (that is, of King David) there were, of course, Joseph and Mary (Luke 2:4-5). The royal family had been reduced to poverty living in Nazareth and taking the trade of a carpenter (Matthew 13:55a). The faithful among the other tribes were Simeon and Anna, who were looking for the consolation and redemption of Israel (Luke 2:23-35, 36-38). And then, too, there were the lowly shepherds outside Bethlehem who were also waiting for the Messiah (Luke 2:8ff.); and there were a few others. So, out of the whole nation there was only a small remnant (Luke 2:38b) who were truly waiting and looking for the consolation and redemption of Israel (Luke 2:25b, 38b). For two thousand years God had been preparing this people for the coming of the Messiah, and yet, when He came, what did He find? Only a small faithful remnant who were waiting and ready for Him. Nevertheless, the sentiment of that remnant could be summed up in what the just and pious Simeon had uttered upon receiving the child Jesus into his arms and blessing God at the temple in Jerusalem: "Now lettest thou thy bondservant depart, Lord, according to thy word, in peace; for mine eyes have seen thy salvation, which thou hast prepared before the face of all peoples" (Luke 2:28-31 ASV).

When Christ came to the world He first came among the Jews. He could not go elsewhere because the other people in the world had not been prepared as the Jews had been. But when Christ Jesus did come, what was the response? At first the Jewish people were happy to receive Him, but before long an opposition began to arise. A spirit of hostility became prominent, especially among the ruling class: the priests, the Pharisees, the Sadducees, scribes and lawyers. And the ruling class held the people and nation in their hand. Their opposition to Christ grew greater and greater all the time. Why was this? Did they not realize that their whole hope and destiny was bound up with the Messiah? They should be most happy to see that the Messiah had finally come. They could breathe a thankful prayer of rest. Why, then, did they oppose Christ?

The reason is given by Paul in Romans, who explains there that his kinsmen in the flesh were partially blinded (11:25b, cf. vv.7b-10). They have been partially blinded and their hearts made obdurate. By what? These people were blinded and hearts became hardened by their materialistic and physical concept of the Messiah and His kingship. They expected that the Messiah who was to come was to come from the palace. They expected a Messiah who in appearing on the scene would break the power of the Roman Empire and restore Israel as the first among the nations. In the one instance when their Messianic expectation was realized in the miraculous feeding of the five thousand with the five loaves and two fishes, they immediately wanted to take Jesus by force and make Him their king (John 6:15) because that was the kind of Messiah-King they had expected—that their Messiah would provide all they needed, expected and wanted: food, prosperity, health, rank and position (on the part of the ruling class), and making Israel the head of all nations.

But the Messiah of God came in a manger, was raised in the obscure, backwater village of Nazareth. Furthermore, His kingdom was not like the kingdoms of this world, for He said blessed are the poor in spirit, for theirs is the kingdom of God;

blessed are those who hunger and thirst after righteousness; blessed are those who mourn and weep; blessed are the meek; blessed are the pure in heart; blessed are the peacemakers; and blessed are those who are persecuted (Matthew 5:2-12). Jesus the Messiah brought to the earth a concept of mind and heart which was totally different from the earthly worldly concept of the Jews. The Jewish ruling classes opposed Christ because they were followers of Moses. They would rather have him than Jesus, for in their estimation Moses gave more. As the apostle Paul wrote: "they, being ignorant of God's righteousness, sought to establish a righteousness of their own" (see Romans 10:3). They truly did not know themselves (v.2).

Let us not forget that when Christ came, He came by way of John the Baptist, whose message was one of repentance (Matthew 3:1). Spiritually, that means that one has to know Christ through repentance. If you think highly of yourself, if you think you can in and of yourself keep the entire law, if you think you can faithfully follow Moses in all respects of the Mosaic law, you obviously will not come to Christ and receive Him as your Messiah because you are trying to establish a righteousness of your own. Even so, the righteousness supposedly gained according to the law is like filthy rags in the eyes of God (Isaiah 64:6b). We must come to see that we are sinful, wicked, rebellious, that there is nothing good in us; and that if we repent of our sins and sinful nature, then we shall truly see Christ as the Messiah of God. Had the Jewish people—both rulers and ruled—sought after the righteousness of God, they would have been saved. Instead, the Jews stumbled over this matter of repentance in their not submitting to the righteousness of God (Romans 10:3c). They insisted on establishing their own righteousness by holding onto and elevating Moses; and so, they refused to follow Christ.

Before closing our discussion for today, I need to add something further which I believe is very important for us to understand. As indicated earlier, God had chosen and elected

Israel out of all the nations and peoples of the world. Israel was and still is His chosen people. He had given them numerous covenants and promises and blessings. But does that mean that each and every Israelite shall automatically inherit the promises of God? And be under the good of the covenants? Not so, according to Scripture. For God never does anything mechanical; that is not God's operating principle.

Yes, it is quite true that God has chosen Israel and given her people many covenants and promises. Nevertheless, let us remind ourselves of the passage in Romans 9 which was read aloud at the beginning of the message for today. There Paul wrote that not all the seeds—the descendants—of Abraham are regarded as the sons of promise; they are not all Israel who are descended from Israel (vv.6-7). Let us recall that Abraham had many sons. First he had Ishmael. Then he had Isaac. Then he had other sons through Katurah, his wife after Sarah's death (Genesis 25:1). Abraham therefore had more than one son; and yet, only in Isaac shall all the nations be blessed (Genesis 21:12c, 22:15-18 with 26:3-4). So here we see how the Spirit of God used that declaration in Scripture to show and instruct us of this one fact: that not all who were born of Abraham automatically became sons of the promise—only Isaac. So Isaac was the only son of Abraham who came through a promise, namely, that he would inherit all the covenants and the promises of God made to his father.

Let us therefore cease making the mistake at times of thinking that whoever is born a Jew, and no matter how that one lives, that that Jewish person shall inherit God's promises. That is simply not the true state of affairs in God's relationship with His chosen people Israel. God never operates in an automatic or mechanical manner. With Him there must be a spiritual and moral component to the working out of His will and purpose. This is true not only with respect to the Jewish people but also with respect to the Gentiles, and not only with respect to the Gentiles but with respect to the church as well.

Hence, it is hoped that we have come to learn that though God had chosen all Israel, only a faithful remnant of the Jews actually came into the good of God's promises to His people. And this was equally true at the time of Christ while He was on earth the first time, and this was likewise true when Paul was writing his Letter to the Romans; but even at the present time on earth there is a faithful remnant from among the Jewish people according to the election of grace.

Moreover, this shall be true as well at Messiah's second coming at the end of days. We must never go to the one extreme of thinking that all who are descended from Israel are Israel, which thinking posits the notion that all Israel shall inherit God's promises and covenants. No, there must be, and there shall be, a faithful remnant according to the election of grace in the end-time. But neither must we ever go to the other extreme of thinking that God has now forsaken Israel and the church has thus been substituted for Israel. That, too, is not true. The nation of Israel still has her place in God's end-time purpose.

Meanwhile, more than likely we shall delve into this matter further at our next gathering. But for now, I have simply tried to present some background as a help to our understanding, and I hope that next time I may finish presenting the rest of the background which I feel is necessary for us to understand—and to more fully enter into—the testimony of Jesus in relation to the Jews.

May God help us to understand more clearly this very important matter.

Chapter Two

The Mystery of Israel (2) and the Church's Ministry to the Jews

Brethren, the delight of my own heart and my supplication which I address to God for them is for salvation. For I bear them witness that they have zeal for God, but not according to knowledge. For they, being ignorant of God's righteousness, and seeking to establish their own righteousness, have not submitted to the righteousness of God. For Christ is the end of law for righteousness to every one that believes.

For Moses lays down in writing the righteousness which is of the law, The man who has practised those things shall live by them [quoting Leviticus 18:5 here]. But the righteousness of faith speaks thus: Do not say in thine heart, Who shall ascend to the heavens? that is, to bring Christ down; or, Who shall descend into the abyss? that is, to bring up Christ from among the dead. But what says it? The word is near thee, in thy mouth and in thy heart [quoting Deuteronomy 30:12-14]: that is, the word of faith, which we preach: that if thou shalt confess with thy mouth Jesus as Lord, and shalt believe in thine heart that God has raised him from among the dead, thou shalt be saved. For with the heart is believed to righteousness; and with the mouth confession made to salvation. For the scripture says, No one believing on him shall be ashamed. For there is no difference of Jew and Greek; for the same Lord of all is rich towards all that call upon him. For every one whosoever, who shall call on the name of the Lord, shall be saved.

Romans 10:1-13

I say then, Have they stumbled in order that they might fall? Far be the thought: but by their fall there is salvation to the nations to provoke them to jealousy. But if their fall be the world's wealth, and their loss the wealth of the nations, how much rather their fulness?

For if their casting away be the world's reconciliation, what their reception but life from among the dead?

For I do not wish you to be ignorant, brethren, of this mystery, that ye may not be wise in your own conceits, that blindness in part is happened to Israel, until the fulness of the nations be come in; and so all Israel shall be saved. According as it is written, The deliverer shall come out of Zion; he shall turn away ungodliness from Jacob. And this is the covenant from me to them, when I shall have taken away their sins. As regards the glad tidings, they are enemies on your account; but as regards election, beloved on account of the fathers. For the gifts and the calling of God are not subject to repentance. For as indeed ye also once have not believed in God, but now have been objects of mercy through the unbelief of these; so these also have now not believed in your mercy, in order that they also may be objects of mercy. For God hath shut up together all in unbelief, in order that he might shew mercy to all. O depth of riches both of the wisdom and knowledge of God! how unsearchable his

> judgments, and untraceable his ways! For who has known the mind of the Lord, or who has been his counsellor? or who has first given to him, and it shall be rendered to him? For of him, and through him, and for him are all things: to him be glory for ever. Amen.
>
> Romans 11:11-12, 15, 25-36

I today wish to continue presenting some general background concerning the testimony of Jesus in relation to the Jews and to the nation of Israel before we look into the book of Revelation itself. And from our consideration together last time we learned that the Israelites have been the most privileged people in the world because Christ himself—the Messiah of God—came forth from that people according to the flesh.

But privilege must be accompanied by responsibility. And if the privilege be great—which in this case it was with the Israelites—then the responsibility must correspondingly be great as well. However, as we saw last time, when the Messiah did come, the Jewish people for the most part refused to receive Him as their Messiah-King, even though over a period of two millennia God had been preparing this people most thoroughly for the coming of His Son and their King. He had prepared them through His promises and covenants, through His sent prophets, through the giving of the law, and through the temple service—all of which pointed to the coming of the Messiah. And yet, when the Messiah did come, most of the nation refused to receive Him (John 1:11). Except for a remnant of the election of grace the rest of the nation rejected their Messiah. What a failure of responsibility!

But thank God that when the Messiah came, there was a remnant from among the Jewish people who became the promised children of Abraham. They entered into the good of all God's promises and covenants which He had made to

His chosen people over that two-thousand-year period of preparation for Messiah's coming.

We also saw last time what the main reason was for Israel's rejection of Christ as their Messiah except for that remnant of the election of grace. And we learned from the apostle Paul's letter to the Romans chapters 9 and 10 what the Spirit of God has given us as being the primary reason for that rejection: that Israel wished to establish her own righteousness according to law and refused to accept the righteousness of faith which can only be found in Christ Jesus. And I would like today to expand further on this refusal by most of the Jewish people; and in doing so, I wish to continue to base my observations and explanation on Paul's Holy Spirit-inspired words in Romans.

Now at one point in his Romans epistle Paul declared that his kinsmen in the flesh had great zeal. But their zeal was not according to knowledge. At the time of Jesus' first coming the Jews were most zealous in observing the law of Moses. The temple service was still being carried on exactly and correctly as before. Moreover, by the same time there had arisen the sect of the Pharisees who specialized in studying and interpreting the Scriptures, and they had become so zealous that over time they had added precept upon precept, interpretation upon interpretation, until they had developed a huge amount of tradition. And they did their best to keep to all these traditions. But this was not an easy undertaking for them.

Now we must not entertain any prejudiced notion concerning the Pharisees or look upon them as being bad people whenever mention is made of the Pharisees. That should not be our attitude at all. They were the elite of Jewish society at that time. They were a class of people looked up to because they specialized in the very law of God. They bound themselves to this established tradition of theirs so tightly and so intensely that it was not an easy life for them; in fact, it was a highly disciplined life. Furthermore, these Pharisees were so zealous for God that they were willing and ready to kill anybody if they thought anybody was exhibiting what they considered to be blasphemous conduct. If somebody's actions were blasphemous against God, they became extremely zealous for God.

However, in their zeal for God they became partially blinded spiritually, as Paul, a former Pharisee himself, informs us (11:25b). Oh, how zealous they were for the law of God by keeping the law of Moses. They were all out to do whatever God had said, and in their zealousness they were blinded—blinded to the fact that it was impossible for the flesh to keep the divine law of God. They, and the people of Israel in general, thought they had kept the law. For instance, we will recall that rich young ruler who came to Jesus asking what he must do to inherit eternal life, and Jesus said, Keep the Ten Commandments. And that young man replied that he had kept those from his childhood (Luke 18:18-23). He was blinded. The Jews were blinded then and they are still being blinded by their zeal for the law.

Here we see that the Jews did not know or recognize the weakness of their flesh and at the same time they did not understand the true meaning of the law. They did not realize that the law is not an end but is only a means to an end. Paul explains to us in his Galatians epistle that the law was meant to serve as a schoolmaster or tutor to lead people to Jesus the Messiah, for He is the end of the law. It being just a means, the law, as it were, shuts people under sin in order that they may acknowledge their inability to live up to the law of God and therefore look for and receive the mercy of God in Christ Jesus (3:22-24).

Now God had given the Israelites the law, the Ten Commandments and all the other precepts, statutes and commandments—in order to open their eyes to see how weak their flesh was, how impossible it was for them to please God with their own strength. But instead of having their eyes opened the Israelites blinded their eyes with their pride. They thought that they were keeping the law and thus establishing the righteousness according to law. In their minds and hearts they were essentially saying: We can do it, we can keep the law of God, we can be perfect, we can please God, and we are able to save ourselves by building up a righteousness of our own; and hence, they believed and mused, God cannot but accept us because we are righteous. Consequently, they became so self-righteous that they became blinded and most obdurate and stubborn in their hearts.

Oh, such was the tragedy of the Jews. Yet not because they wanted to do something bad but because they wanted to do something good. And not because they were cold in heart but because they were too warm of heart—that is, they were too zealous, and somehow the enemy succeeded in blinding their eyes and fostered a great misunderstanding in their minds as to the basic purpose of the law. The Jewish people rejected Christ because they were too zealous for the law of Moses. They thought Moses was enough for them. After all, thought these Israelites, who could be greater than Moses? In the end they would rather have Moses than have Christ; and, therefore, in a very profound sense, if you insist on having Moses rather than Christ, that means that you insist on having yourself instead of having God. In other words, you have become self-confident and self-righteous: you want to depend upon yourself, establish your own righteousness; and thus, you refuse to accept the mercy of God. In fact, you do not want mercy nor do you need mercy.

This attitude is reminiscent of one of the two men in Jesus' parable who entered the temple to pray (Luke 18:10-14). Now the first one, said the Lord, was a Pharisee; and he went forward to the very front of the sanctuary, and there he stood with eyes uplifted and began to pray: "Oh, God, I have been faithful to You and have been so good in not having done any bad things; moreover, I have kept the law: I fast twice weekly and give you a tithe of all my goods." And upon completing his self-serving report he returns home *not* justified in God's eyes. This is a picture, is it not, of the blindness of the entire nation of Israel: she does not need mercy because she is righteous in her own eyes.

But let us now recall the other man in Jesus' parable, who was an acknowledged sinner, in fact, a corrupted tax collector. Like the first man, he enters the temple to pray, yet he dare not go to the front but remains way at the back. Indeed, he does not want to be seen, and there he bows his head and beats his breast and has nothing to report. This man can only pray a very short prayer to God: Oh God, be merciful to me a sinner. Kindly be advised that that phrase, be merciful, in the original Greek means—Let me be atoned for—because this sinner's eyes were looking at the sacrificial lamb which was at that moment burning on the brazen altar. In other words, this man was saying: That is my only hope; I need mercy, and mercy comes from the lamb that is offered for me by You, oh God, through Christ Your Lamb provision. Consequently, declared Jesus, when this man returned home, he was justified in God's eyes.

Now this parable in its totality can serve as a picture of Israel at that very time. As typified by the Pharisee the nation as a whole had become so self-righteous and had so held on to Moses that they did not desire the righteousness of faith which is through Christ Jesus (Romans 10:6-7). On the other hand, the remnant of the election of grace is typified by the sinner who knew he needed and required mercy, and obtained it.

Even Moses tells us the difference between man's righteousness and that of the law. This we find in Leviticus chapter 18 where Jehovah is quoted as saying: "ye shall observe my statutes and my judgments, by which the man that doeth them shall live" (v.5). Which is to say that the man who does all those things shall live, shall have life. Such is the righteousness of the law. How, then, can you be righteous according to the law? Not occasionally but continuously you must observe, practice, and keep obediently practicing all the things written in the law, and only then shall you have life. The question is, however, Is there anyone on earth who has attained to this righteousness of the law? If you are able to achieve this on a continuing basis, you shall live, you shall have life—indeed, you will be righteous, you will have attained to the righteousness of the law. But the question remains, Who among all of mankind is able to do this?—for if anyone violates just one of the things written in the law of God, that person shall have violated all of them (James 2:10). That, in fact, is the reason there is no one among us who can become righteous under, or according to, the law. It is an impossibility.

Nevertheless, there *is* one who can, and who has attained that righteousness, and that One is Christ. According to God's law Christ is righteous, because He has practiced all the things written in the law of God. He has kept all the commandments of God. He is the only person in the history of the world who has obtained the righteousness which is according to law, and because of that, He is entitled to live. As a matter of fact, He is the end of the law; He is the only person who has fulfilled all the requirements of the law. However, in fulfilling all the requirements of the law Christ ought to live, and yet He gives himself up to die. And that is the gospel. By virtue of having kept all the commandments of God throughout His walk on the earth and by virtue of having been righteous according to the law, Jesus proved himself to have been qualified to redeem us: the Sinless One for the sinful one, He having died for us sinners. Let us thank and praise God, Christ Jesus not only fulfilled all the requirements of the law in himself but he also received all the penalty of the law in His body on the cross; and because of that sacrificial act He opens the way to having another kind of righteousness—even the righteousness of faith.

Now what is the righteousness of faith? In giving answer to this, Paul quotes the Old Testament again. This which Paul does is most interesting. In mentioning previously the righteousness of law (in Romans 10:5) he quotes from

Leviticus 18, and then immediately thereafter he writes of the righteousness of faith (10:6a). Now you will perhaps exclaim, surely you will not find that in the Old Testament! But Paul says, Oh, yes you will. And he proceeds to quote a lengthy passage from Moses' book of Deuteronomy. And before quoting from Moses, the apostle first writes this: "But the righteousness of faith speaks thus." And then he proceeds to quote Moses' words to the Israelites and gives those words a distinctly Christian flavor: "Do not say in thy heart, Who shall ascend into the heavens? that is, to bring Christ down; or, Who shall descend into Hades? that is, to bring up Christ from among the dead. But what says it? The word is near you, in your mouth and in your heart: that is, the word of faith, which we preach" (see Romans 10:6-8, quoting in paraphrase Deuteronomy 30:12-14).

Now, let us notice that in ferreting out the Deuteronomy passage we discover that there is something rather different in the way Paul handled it, which is why, incidentally, the word of God is living. And in order to notice this difference it will be necessary to begin first, not with verse 12 but with verse 11 of Deuteronomy 30. There Moses said that the commandment which on that day he commanded the Israelites to observe was "not too hard" for them to obey nor was it "far off" (v.11 ASV). Moses then proceeded to explain why this was so: because the word—the commandment—was very near to them, in their mouth and in their heart. Indeed, they did not need to go up to heaven to bring the commandment down that they might know it and obey it. Nor did they need to go over the seas to bring the commandment to them to make them hear it and keep it. No, it was so close to the people, because it was in their mouths and in their hearts. And here is the difference of which I spoke moments ago: that in Deuteronomy the term Moses used is *commandment* whereas in Romans the apostle used the word *Christ*. Did Paul misquote here and do something wrong? Not at all. It is the Spirit of God who imparted Deuteronomy to us, and it is the same Spirit who inspired Paul to write as he did in Romans. We may therefore say that according to the Spirit of God the commandment in Deuteronomy 30 is Christ.

Oh how wonderful that we do not need to go up to heaven to draw Christ down from there that He may come to this world to save us. He has already come. We do not need to go over the seas or down into Hades to draw Christ out that He may be raised from among the dead in order for Him to complete our salvation. He has already been raised from the dead. Christ has already come down from heaven, has died on the cross, has been buried and raised from the dead. It is all done. Now, then, where is Christ today? If you believe in Him, He shall be as close to you as though in your mouth and in your heart. If, as Paul declared, you believe Him with your heart and confess Him as Lord with your mouth, you shall be saved. And consequently, you shall have a righteousness which is of faith (see Romans 10:6a again).

Perhaps, however, you may be inclined to say that in his old age Moses must have unknowingly contradicted himself. For in Leviticus 18 he had declared that anyone who without exception shall observe and practice all the law of God shall live; whereas much later, in Deuteronomy 30, we find him saying that the commandments of God’s law are in a person’s heart and mouth, the righteousness of the law now having been given the person who without effort of any kind just takes and receives. Moses would therefore appear to be contradicting himself. But does he in fact do so? Not at all. Let us look into this matter more closely.

If we read God’s word carefully, we shall find that Moses’ words in Leviticus 18 are based upon the covenant of God with Israel which had been announced on Mt. Sinai. According to that covenant whoever practices without fail all the things of the law shall live; but after the failing experience of the wilderness the Israelites ought to know themselves better—that they were incapable—in themselves—to keep the law. So that by the time of the conclusion of the 40-year wilderness wandering experience the Israelites had been led to the frontier border of the Promised Land of Canaan. They were now stationed on the east bank of the river Jordan in the land of Moab. And before God would, through Joshua, lead them across the Jordan into the Promised Land, God entered into a new covenant with His chosen people.

Thus, we must bear in mind that Israel did not enter the Promised Land on the ground and basis of the Mosaic law of Mt. Sinai but on the basis of that new covenant established by God with Israel in the land of Moab just opposite Canaan. Furthermore, we must understand that the book of Deuteronomy is not only a restating of the laws of God for His people but is also, by the time of this book's last few chapters, an introduction to that new covenant which would serve as God's replacement provision for the failure of God's people in faithfully following God's law under the previous covenant enunciated decades earlier at Mt. Sinai.

We therefore read in the latter part of Deuteronomy 29 and the first part of 30 that God through Moses prophesied that the Israelites shall forsake the Lord and worship idols. And because of that, the curse of the law shall come upon them and the chosen people will be scattered to all the nations. But if their hearts turn back to the Lord, He will turn back to them; and in His mercy God will bless them once more. Thus, what we find here is that in Moab God has come to His people again, yet this time not with the law but on the basis of mercy. And hence, in the mercy of God the Israelites are now going to be able to enter the Promised Land.

Accordingly, these two periods of covenantal history between God and His chosen people explain how it is that neither Moses nor Paul have contradicted themselves in their respective books of Scripture. Under the older and previous Mosaic covenant there is the righteousness according to law, whereas when the people failed to live up to the requirement of the covenant of law, God replaces that covenant with the new covenant of mercy and grace. And His provision of mercy is Jesus Christ—the Messiah of God. He, in fact, is the commandment of God.

Oh, may God's people no longer say that it is very difficult to keep His commandment; rather, let mankind agree with Moses, who long ago declared, under the inspiration of the Spirit of God, that the commandment—even Christ himself—is in men's hearts and in their mouths. He is so very near that if a person only opens the heart to Christ and confesses Him as the Lord with the mouth, Christ shall indeed come into that person, bringing forgiveness and cleansing from all one's sins and become life to that one. Such, then, is the righteousness of faith by grace plus nothing more. And how blessed that can be!

Now when Jesus the Messiah came to the earth, the Israelites as a nation rejected Him. And why? Because they were so proud of themselves that they refused the mercy of God. Even today this principle holds true with God's chosen people Israel. Oh, there are so many of them who do not enter into the joy of the kingdom of God. The only obstacle standing in the way is their self-righteousness. They are too proud to humble themselves and receive the mercy of God. Even today Israel still does not understand that Christ is the end of the law which they so proudly seek to uphold—but in vain. Christ is not only the fulfillment of the law, He is the purpose and goal of the law. Indeed, it is only in Christ that the law finds its fulfillment and finds its focus, and when it is found by the humble seeking heart, it shall be fullness in Christ, for His righteousness shall be freely given to all those who come to Him—both Jews as well as Gentiles; and there is in fact a remnant among the Jews today who do believe in the Lord Jesus.

This, then, is the primary reason given by the Scriptures for why, when Christ came to the nation of Israel, the nation for the most part rejected him. Thank God, however, that there was a remnant according to the election of grace.

But we must hurry on in our further consideration together in the time remaining today. Now because the nation of Israel rejected Christ as their Messiah, some people may therefore mistakenly believe that God has rejected her. Perhaps you have heard that belief expressed—that God has cast Israel aside and has forever forsaken her because she has fallen; and that as a consequence He has turned His attention to another nation—the church—with the church being His substitute for Israel now and forever. Indeed, as part of that erroneous thinking, all the promises of God to Israel are henceforth to be enjoyed by the church: Israel is now finished and the church has come into the good of those promises instead of Israel. Such thinking is not at all correct.

Let me declare as forcefully as I can that none of that is the truth. It *is* true, of course, that because God's chosen people were blinded by the enemy into refusing to accept the Messiah whom He had sent to them, with only a remnant having received Christ, therefore God has temporarily set Israel aside. That word temporarily needs to be emphasized and remembered. God has laid His chosen nation aside temporarily and thus the gospel is preached to the Gentile nations. And, yes, it is likewise true that during this present age God's preeminent concern is centered upon the church. And that explains why, in chapters 2 and 3 of Revelation, it is the seven local churches of Asia Minor that are mentioned and not Israel.

Nevertheless, let none of us forget this fact, that God has only laid Israel aside as a *temporary* measure, and not permanently. This is because God's calling and election never change (Romans 11:29). But let us take note of the fact that due to this temporary measure the gospel has been preached, and continues to be preached, all over the world and that out of every tribe, nation, people and tongue God has been gathering together in Christ a people and new nation—the church, if you will—which has become the body of Christ. And most certainly this is the primary concern of God today.

But, again, I would caution all of us not to succumb to the notion that because God's interest today is centered upon the church, this must mean that no Jews will be saved and included in the church—that the church is composed mainly of Gentiles, with only the believing Jews of the early church era having been included in the body of Christ. Again I say, that is not true. Yes, God's interest during this current age in man's history is centered upon the church, which is composed of people redeemed out of all the world's nations—including the nation of Israel.

Moreover, at the beginning of the church, she originally consisted of people who were ethnically Jewish and of those people who were non-Jewish—the Gentile people—because salvation comes upon the chosen among the chosen people of God (Israel) and upon the chosen among the non-chosen people of the world (Gentiles). And so, back then, God brought together people from everywhere throughout the world and gathered them together and made them one. And God has continued to do the same thing ever since the era of the early church.

So where are the nations today? They are still out there in the world. And where is Israel today? She, too, is currently there, but she is situated, as it were, on the sideline. So what is the church today? She is that which is composed of both Jews and non-Jews—the church of Jesus Christ. She is composed of believing Jews and believing Gentiles. And yet, in the church there is neither Jew nor Gentile but all are one in Christ, a transformation having taken place, in that spiritually speaking, they have become new creations in Christ (II Corinthians 5:17a). True, whenever someone today is called out of Israel, that one is a Jew; and whenever someone is called out of the nations, that one is a Gentile. But in being called of God through His salvation in Christ, you and I are transformed. We are no longer either a Jew or a Gentile but are now members of the body of Christ. Can I therefore be called a Jewish Christian or therefore a Gentile Christian? There is no such person. Yes, at one time I was a Gentile but now I am a Christian. And, yes, I was a Jew but today I am a Christian. Therefore, spiritually speaking, according to their life experience in Christ Jesus they are no longer either Jew or Gentile but are members of the body of Christ.

Do please thus understand that in Christ and in the church, neither Israel nor the nations enter through New Jerusalem's gates but both are barred outside her gates. Hence, let us remember that though the nations remain and Israel has remained, God has nonetheless created a new nation, His church; and it is formed by God bringing together those who come both from Israel and from the rest of the nations; and yet, the result is entirely different from what went before: the church thus formed is something new, she now being neither Jew nor Gentile but all those in her are one in Christ Jesus (I Corinthians 12:12-13, Colossians 3:10-11). Oh, do let us get beyond the Jewish and Gentile distinctions when it concerns the church of God, and let us instead realize and enter into the reality of all of us being members of the body of Christ. That is something far better.

Allow me, if I may, to add a further few words on this matter of what happens when we become members of the body of Christ, regardless whether we be Jews or Gentiles. Because of this change of life from the old creation to the new, neither Jews nor Gentiles have the right to bring into the church their old concepts and traditions, for if so, the testimony of the church will be spoiled. For instance, you may be born a Jew, and so far as the world is concerned you are still a Jew, but with respect to your new birth, you are no longer a Jew; and hence, you cannot bring into the church your Jewish traditions and concepts, for if you do, the church's testimony shall be spoiled if not totally destroyed.

As we have come to realize, the church is a new creation with all things new; therefore, all the old things—including both the bad *and* even the good—are to pass away. Yet, how willing we are to let the bad old things pass away but how tenaciously we hold on to and bring into New Jerusalem the *good* old things. However, the Bible makes clear that all those things, as mentioned earlier, must be left outside the gates (II Corinthians 5:17, Revelation 21:27, 22:14). This must be a reality in our daily experience of life in Christ. Even so, let us not be lulled into thinking that this can be done easily, for how the old holds on tenaciously. It actually requires the work of the cross to bring the old down into death (Galatians 2:20).

So let us acknowledge that in the church all racial, cultural, and background differences that exist in the world must be left outside the church. Whenever by the grace of God we come willingly into the church as believers in Christ and thus become members of the body of Christ, everything of the old life is left outside and all things in the church are to be on the ground of resurrection.

Moreover, all this which has been said about the Jew is to be equally applied to everybody—not only to the believing Jew but also to the believing Gentile, because there is no partiality in God's dealings with all of mankind. This means that if you were born, let us say, a Chinese or an American or a Nigerian or a German, you cannot bring your particular national or ethnic culture, background, concept, or tradition into the church; otherwise, the church shall end up being a Chinese, an American, a Nigerian, or a German institution and not be the living body of Christ. Indeed, the testimony of the church will have been destroyed. After believing in the Lord Jesus and coming into the church you are no longer a Chinese or an American or a Nigerian or a German but you are simply a Christian who is now a living member of Christ's body. Praise the Lord!

But let us also be aware of the fact, as we learn also from Paul in Romans, that the fall of Israel has meant that God's salvation has come to the nations. Nevertheless, is that the end?

It is not the end; rather, a chain reaction has set in, and God is its greatest catalyst. And Paul recognized this chain reaction of God's; for as the apostle pointed out in his Romans epistle, the fact that as people from the Gentile nations are gathered in—as the church comes into existence and develops into maturity—Israel is provoked to jealousy (11:11). This chain reaction eventually leads into the fulfillment of the mystery of Israel:

> For I do not wish you to be ignorant, brethren, of this mystery ... that blindness in part is happened to Israel, until the fulness of the [gentiles] be come in; and so all Israel shall be saved (11:25-26a).

Now I believe that this is the primary mission and ministry of the church to the Jews, in that because we enjoy Christ so much and if our enjoyment of Him becomes so manifest, the Jews can and will be provoked to jealousy. By which is meant that a Jewish person would perhaps normally say to himself/herself: Christ is one of us, he was born a Jew; how then is it that you Christians enjoy him so much? And after some little while and continuing to observe this joy exhibited over Christ among the people of the church, this Jewish person will end up acknowledging: I want Christ also. That, I believe is the primary mission of the church towards the Jews.

I believe it can never be that Christians will succeed in thrusting the gospel down the throats of the Jewish people. That attempt will only end in failure. The one and only way by which the Jews shall be made jealous for Christ for themselves is for us who are in the church to so live such a life of enjoying Christ that they shall want Him also. How the church has failed in this kind of ministry to our Jewish friends. She has failed in her ministry to the Jews because she as the body of Christ fails to manifest her enjoyment of the Lord Jesus to the watching world. The people of the church do not make Christ attractive and lovable enough to cause the Jews to be filled with jealousy to the point that they openly acknowledge and declare that Jesus is their kinsman who belongs to them as well. That should be the ministry of the church to the Jews.

Chapter Three

The Fig Tree

And he spoke this parable: A certain [man] had a fig-tree planted in his vineyard, and he came seeking fruit upon it and did not find any. And he said to the vinedresser, Behold, these three years I come seeking fruit on this fig-tree and find none: cut it down; why does it also render the ground useless? But he answering says to him, Sir, let it alone for this year also, until I shall dig about it and put dung, and if it shall bear fruit—but if not, after that thou shalt cut it down.

Luke 13:6-9

But early in the morning, as he came back into the city, he hungered. And seeing one fig-tree in the way, he came to it and found on it nothing but leaves only. And he says to it, Let there be never more fruit of thee for ever. And the fig-tree was immediately dried up.

Matthew 21:18-19

But learn the parable from the fig-tree: When already its branch becomes tender and produces leaves, ye know that the summer is near. Thus also ye, when ye see all these things, know that it [i.e., he] is near, at the doors.

Matthew 24:32-33

Today, I am happy to say, will be our final session together in providing some final and necessary preparation for us before looking into the book of Revelation to learn what it can tell us concerning the testimony of Jesus in relation to the Jews. And I would like to make the matter clearer, if possible, by the use of an illustration from the Bible. It is my hope that by doing so, we may better understand how God deals with the Jewish people and nation. And from the Scriptures which have just now been read aloud I believe we all can probably guess that the fig tree shall be serving as the illustration to be used throughout the message for today.

To begin with, I would ask this of us: Where in the Bible do we first meet up with the fig tree? We find that the fig tree is the third tree that is mentioned by name in the Bible. The first one is the tree of life, the second one is the tree of the knowledge of good and evil, and the third tree to be mentioned by name is the fig. After the fall of man Adam and Eve turned for covering of their nakedness to a fig tree and made aprons with its leaves (Genesis 3:7b). But sad to say, this first human manufacture did not cover their nakedness nor protect them from the cold wind. It was a futile work. But this is the first mentioning of the fig. Now, of course, the first mentioning in Scripture of anything is usually meant to lay down a spiritual principle to be followed, and I will explain about that later.

The fig tree is also related in a very special way to the Jews. When God brought the Israelites to the border of the Promised Land, they sent 12 spies into the land. And in order to prove what they had seen they cut down a branch of the grape vine from the Eshcol Valley because the grapes were in such abundance; so much so, that that vine branch with just one cluster had to be carried by two men. Even today in Palestine they still have very sweet grapes; this I know because I tasted them when I was there. Not only did these spies cut down a branch with the one cluster of grapes but in addition they brought something else: both pomegranates and figs (Numbers 13:23).

There is another interesting fact about the fig tree to be gleaned from Scripture. Whenever in the history of the Jewish people the Bible wishes to convey the thought that at any given time the Jews were living in prosperity and security, God's word has employed the descriptive declaration that each Israelite could be found dwelling under his vine and fig tree. For example, it was said that during all the days of King Solomon's reign over Judah and Israel—the golden age of the Jewish nation—all people "dwelt safely" and "every man [dwelt] under his vine and under his fig-tree" (I Kings 4:25). In a very special way the fig tree is related to the Jew.

Another very informative detail regarding the relationship between the fig and the people of Israel can be found in Jeremiah chapter 24. Here is explained that Jehovah God showed the prophet a vision of two baskets, with one filled with very good first-ripe figs and the other full of very bad figs due to their rottenness. And the interpretation given by the Spirit of God was that these two baskets of figs represented the Jewish people who would be dwelling in two different places of the world: those Jews who had been captured by Babylonia's King Nebuchadnezzar during the reign of King Jehoiakim of Judah and carried off into captivity were represented by the basket of good figs, whereas those Jews who would remain in Judah and those currently dwelling in Egypt were all represented by the basket of bad figs (vv.1-5, 8). From this we see again that the fruit of the fig tree is a symbol for the Jews.

Moreover, the prophets, when foretelling the coming of distress upon the Jewish people, would sometimes employ the fig tree to describe it. For instance, the prophet Habakkuk described the approaching dire situation for the people by declaring that the fig tree would not blossom and therefore not bear fruit, nor would the grapevine produce any fruit (3:16a-17a). On the other hand, when foretelling the future recovery of the Jewish people—Zechariah comes to mind here—the figurative language employed to describe the favorable and prosperous environment was once again the fig tree and the vine, but this time the prophet would declare that they would be bearing fruit and both would be increasing (3:10), thus serving as a description of the nation's recovery. Hence, in a very special way the fig and/or its tree has always been emblematic of the people and nation of Israel. That has continually been the Old Testament interpretation of Scripture's use of the fig and its tree in a symbolic or illustrative manner.

This is further borne out in the various ways the Lord Jesus employed the fig tree in His multi-faceted ministry while on the earth the first time. Let us first recall the occasion in which Jesus called his disciple Philip, who then sought out his friend Nathanael and told him that he had found the Messiah: He is Jesus, the son of Joseph of Nazareth. To which Nathanael replied that nothing good can come out of Nazareth. Philip, unable to argue with his friend, simply said for Nathanael to come and see for himself. Now when Nathanael came to the Lord, Jesus said of him, Look, a true Israelite in whom is no guile! To which Nathanael wondered aloud to Jesus, How do you know me? And the Lord replied: Before Philip had called you, I saw you seated beneath the fig tree. Immediately Nathanael, overcome with amazement, declared: Rabbi, You are the Son of God and King of Israel! (John 1:43-49)

Let us pause here for a moment. Jesus had described Nathanael as being a true Israelite, and He knew what this new disciple of His was doing while sitting under that fig tree: he was dreaming of the day which the prophets of old had prophesied concerning the coming of the Messiah and when Israel shall be the head of all nations. In essence, Jesus was saying to Nathanael that beneath that fig tree he had been dreaming about the coming glory of Israel in the days of Messiah. And that caused Nathanael to say without hesitation that Jesus is the Son of God, the Messiah-King of Israel.

However, the Lord in response instantly said to His newly-won disciple: Did you believe who I am because I said to you that in My spirit I saw you under the fig tree? Nathanael, you shall see greater things than these. Yes, you shall see glory; but do not be limited by your national spirit, because I am going to do far greater things. For you shall see the Son of man as the ladder that joins heaven to earth and earth to heaven and upon whom the angels shall ascend and descend (vv. 50-51). Moreover, the Son of man is the One who has come down to earth from heaven and shall depart the earth and bring many from earth up to heaven (cf. John 3:13). Indeed, the Son of man is the way, and no one can come to the Father but by Him (John 14:6). So here we see again that in a sense the fig tree represents the Jewish people and nation.

Let us next consider Jesus' use of the fig tree in His teaching ministry when speaking in parables. And the parable of the fig tree recorded in Luke 13, which we read together at the beginning of our time here today, is a prime instance of this. But in order for us to understand the thrust and basic meaning of it, a little background will probably be helpful.

We will recall that Jesus was about 30 years old when He began His public ministry to the nation (Luke 3:23a), and for some three to four years He walked up and down the land of Judah and Galilee visiting city after city and out in the countryside. One could find the Lord everywhere—on the hillsides, in the valleys and on the plains. And for over three years He preached the glad tidings, and in so doing He had offered himself to the Jews as their Messiah and had offered to them the kingdom of God. But after some three years and towards the end of His public ministry we learn from the Gospels that the Lord Jesus was being opposed and rejected; nevertheless, a remnant followed Him. The nation as represented by the elite class of priests, scribes, lawyers, Pharisees, Sadducees, and rulers rejected the Lord. So it was after some three years of ministry that Jesus had occasion to speak forth the Luke 13 parable of the fig tree which needs now to be reviewed against the aforementioned background.

A man planted a fig tree in his vineyard. But after three years he still could find no fruit on it; so the owner of the vineyard ordered the vinedresser to cut the tree down, for, he asserted, what is the use of having this fruitless tree continuing to waste this ground by its presence? The vinedresser, however, pleaded with the owner, saying: Sir, leave it for another year and I shall dig around it and pour in fertilizer; and if it should bring forth fruit, good—but if it should not bear fruit after my further work on it, then you shall be free to cut it down.

Is not this parable a true picture of the relationship between and among God the Father, the Son of God, and the nation of Israel as represented by the vineyard owner, the vinedresser, and the fig tree? After three years of constant ministry to His people in Israel, Jesus their Messiah-King could find no spiritual fruit coming forth from the nation which could satisfy the Father's heart. (Keep in mind that the fig tree here is representative of the Israelite nation as a whole, not of individual Israelites, though there was in fact a remnant of individual Jews who did bear satisfying fruit.) And because God could not find any fruit satisfying to His heart after three years, He finally ordered that Israel be cut off. Jesus, as symbolized by the vinedresser, pleaded with His Father, however, to give the nation a little more time and give himself more time to labor among the people of Israel a bit longer.

Here we see the mercy and love of the Son of God towards His people. Jesus, like the vinedresser with the fig tree, loves the nation so much. I personally have a few flower plants in my home, and some of them produce flowers while others do not; and yet I have come to love those plants regardless the outcome. And like this vinedresser with the fig tree, who had already labored very much on and around it for three entire years and had shown it so much love and was most reluctant to have to cut it down, the Son of God beseeched the Father to grant more time: Allow Me, Father, to give the people another chance, for I am very reluctant to see them destroyed. Grant Me more time and I shall minister even more than before among the people, and if they should bear fruit, all well and good. That was the hope and expectation of the Messiah, thus revealing the Lord's heart of love for His people. He would do something more.

Nevertheless, the Lord Jesus' final period of ministry, which extended into a fourth year, proved to be a most difficult one. For in carefully reading the record of the four Gospels we discover that He, having already been rejected and opposed by the aforementioned ruling class, felt He had to retreat to the other side of the river Jordan in the land known as Peraea. But from time to time Jesus would cross back over the river with the hope that there might blossom forth from "the fig-tree nation" some satisfying fruit. But as we shall see, that was not to be.

Now the above parable has a distinct connection with an incident surrounding an actual fig tree with which Jesus and His disciples had a most amazing encounter. We will remember that during the last week in the earthly life of the Lord Jesus, He had spent the daytime hours in Jerusalem but would lodge overnight in the nearby Olivet village of Bethany only about two miles east of Jerusalem (John 11:18, 12:1; Mark 11:11, 12a, 15a, 19; Matthew 21:17, 37). Recall, too, that most likely on one of these final days in His life He had seated himself on the Olivet hillside overlooking the entire Jewish capital. And while there He began to weep over the city, saying:

> Jerusalem, Jerusalem, the city that kills the prophets and stones those that are sent unto her, how often would I have gathered thy children together, as a hen her brood under her wings, and ye would not. Behold, your house is left unto you [desolate]; and I say unto you, that ye shall not see me until it come that ye say, Blessed is he that comes in the name of the Lord (Luke 13:34-5; cf. 19:41).

On another day during Jesus' final week before His arrest, and fairly early in the morning, the Lord and the Twelve left Bethany bound for Jerusalem (Matthew 21:17-18; Luke 21:38). It is believed, of course, that Jesus most likely lodged during this week in the home of Lazarus and his two sisters, Martha and Mary (John 12:1, Matthew 21:17, Luke 21:37). And it is not believable that, knowing Martha as well as we do, she would not have prepared breakfast for the Lord before His setting out on foot for Jerusalem. And hence, I am confident that Jesus and His party must have had breakfast that morning no matter how early the hour was. Even so, as Jesus approached the city, for some reason He became hungry; and it is my belief that His hunger was not caused by any physical reason since He had been served a full and very good breakfast by Martha. I believe, therefore, that His hunger was spiritually caused. Sometimes in the midst of deep spiritual conflict a person can go without food and forget one's hunger; but at other times a person can become quite hungry due to spiritual reasons, and that is what I believe occurred here: Jesus became hungry when He saw the city lying before Him.

And as the Lord and His disciples made their way towards the city Jesus became extremely hungry; and seeing just ahead a fig tree rich in foliage with many leaves, the Lord walked up to it looking for some figs to satisfy His great hunger, but He could find none (Matthew 21:18-19a). And in Mark's account of this incident we are told that it was not the season for figs, at least not for the sweet, tasty figs (11:13b).

Now when Jesus found no figs, He cursed that tree and immediately it withered and dried up, He having said to it, Let there never be anymore fruit from you (Matthew 21:19b). Never once had Jesus ever cursed either man or thing till now; instead of cursing, He had always blessed. This was the only time during His life on earth that He ever cursed anything or anyone.

Now some have questioned how it was that Jesus could have perpetrated such action in having cursed a tree which, it not being the season of harvest, had only leaves and no fruit. It seemed so unreasonable. They therefore could not understand Jesus' conduct here. In their minds, it would seem to have been done out of selfishness on the Lord's part because His hunger had not been satisfied. Yet, because this that Jesus did was so much out of character, we must search out a different reason than petty selfishness to account for this incident's outcome. What, then, was that reason?

At the outset of offering an explanation, we need to be aware that Palestine had two harvest or crop seasons in a given year for figs. The first crop harvest is in June and the second occurs in August. In Palestine's hilly regions the fig tree will shed all its leaves in December and remain barren until the winter is past. Then, when spring arrives in March the fig tree begins to bring forth branches and tender leaves; but during this branching forth period tiny figs will appear on the trees. These tiny figs will grow amid the leaves until they each assume the size of a cherry. And when a strong-enough wind blows, most of these tiny figs will fall to the ground. They are called unripe figs; nevertheless, people will gather them off the ground or from the tree and eat them.

Now most fig trees in Palestine lose all their tiny figs by May; but there are some other and better species of fig trees on which their tiny figs will remain (and not fall to the ground) and ripen by June and are harvested as the first crop of those good species of tree (see Isaiah 28:4, Hoseah 9:10, Joel 2:22, Nahum 3:12). So, when Jesus and His disciples approached the city and came upon this fig tree, it was the time of Passover; which means that this encounter with the fig tree occurred in April, and was thus the time for this tree's branches to have been full of leaves and accompanied by the presence of these tiny figs. If, however, this tree should lack those tiny figs, it would mean that the tree could never bear any fruit. And hence, the presence or absence of these tiny figs determine whether a tree is a fruitful or unfruitful one.

Accordingly, when Jesus caught sight of this tree full of leaves, He quite naturally expected there to be some tiny figs present on the tree. But if in April He could not find any tiny figs even well prior to the June harvest season, then their total absence would prove, as it did prove, that this particular fig tree could never ever bear fruit. It therefore being totally barren and not able to bear fruit in future, what was the use of this tree standing there? Far from it being unreasonable for the Lord to have acted the way He did towards this tree, it was quite reasonable for Him to have expected to find figs on it, but finding none He cursed the tree for being unfruitful.

Now it was intimated at the beginning of our session today what principle might be meant by the first mention of fig leaves in Scripture: what would these leaves symbolize or represent? And, of course, we recall the very first mention of fig leaves occurred in the Genesis narrative which recorded our original ancestors in the Edenic garden—Adam and Eve—as having made aprons from the leaves of the fig tree for covering their nakedness which they discovered after they fell into sin. Consequently, these ancestors of ours had attempted unsuccessfully to cover themselves with a natural righteousness without there being any shedding of blood. They had sewed these aprons with the leaves from the fig tree, but this first human manufactured item was ineffective as an acceptable covering in God's eyes, for He subsequently provided them with animal skin—most likely a lamb's—and obviously, that cannot be obtained without the shedding of blood.

Permit me to pause here for a moment and apply this principle to all of mankind in general before doing so more directly to the Jewish people of yesteryears and today, as well as to the church. If anyone falls into sin of whatever sort, how natural for that person to cover himself/herself with that one's work, merits, and/or deeds in an attempt to cover oneself with a righteousness made by man's hands without there being the necessity to do so through the offering up of a blood sacrifice pleasing to God above. Having fallen into sin, man's one and only recourse to cover one's nakedness before God is the faith application of the shed blood of God's precious Lamb, for Christ himself is our righteousness (I Corinthians 1:30). Whoever believes in the Lamb of God—even Jesus Christ—shall have the righteousness of God.

Now we have mentioned several times already that the past and continuing problem with the Jewish people as a nation has been simply this: they have wanted to establish their own righteousness, which is a righteousness according to the law; and for that reason they reject the righteousness of faith which is in their Messiah, Jesus Christ. God can only be satisfied with nothing but Christ. Oh, at the time of Jesus the Messiah on earth the Jewish nation, symbolically speaking, was full of leaves in abundance: the temple, the priests, the temple service, the synagogue system, the Pharisees, the scribes and lawyers. The nation had all these things as outward leaves of self-righteousness. They even had the word of God, but the people as a whole lacked the inward fruit of the spirit which can truly satisfy the heart of God.

As is well known, God does not regard outward appearance but looks upon the condition of the heart (I Samuel 16:7b). Yes, the nation's outward appearance seemed quite good, but the heart of the nation's people was bad and thus did not satisfy God's heart. For this reason, so far as God's dealing with the nation is concerned, He has had to set her aside temporarily; and meanwhile, for the past two millennia He has been creating, building and developing another nation which can produce satisfying fruit, and that nation has been the church of Jesus Christ.

Let us be most clear, however, that the principle which God has applied to the Jewish people and to the individual unbeliever He also insists on applying to us who comprise His church. If God has worked so long and has bestowed so much upon the Jewish nation and the result has been nothing but leaves and no fruit and for that reason she has dried up, are we who are the church in any better position and condition? Are we not to believe that because we have been chosen by God, we have been privileged and are expected today to bear fruit?

What, then, is God looking for in the church today? Is He looking for leaves sewn together as an apron for the purpose of manifesting self-righteousness, self-dependency? No, the Lord Jesus is not looking for these in the church but is looking for the result of His life being developed in us and then being expressed out from us—even the ripening of Christ's life in us who are the church, and that alone can satisfy God's heart. That alone will be the inward reality which satisfies and not the outward appearance of things.

So, the fundamental question before us all is, What will Christ find in us? Are we, as that new nation of God, in any better condition than what God had found in the nation of Israel? Is the church today a fruitful nation? Will the church render satisfying fruits to God? Or must He be disappointed once again? Oh, do let us not think that the basic principle of the apron of fig leaves does not concern us. That same principle very much does.

Now if the parable of the fig tree were to end with a conclusion like the tree which withered and dried up, it would be very tragic and sad. But God does not believe in tragedy for His people. Yes, temporarily for a time Israel, like the actual fig tree which Jesus encountered, has remained dried up spiritually in terms of fruit-bearing. However, Jesus held out great hope for the nation. For in His Olivet discourse on the dramatic end-time events He instructed His disciples to learn from the fig tree the import of its parable, thus taking up the imagery of the fig tree one final time. And that great hope is bound up with His coming back to the earth a second time. For the Lord said to His disciples to consider the fig tree once more. Yes, indeed, at the end-time God shall again take up the Jewish people as a nation. For Jesus instructed the Twelve in the following manner, focusing once more on the parable of the fig tree that in its every appearance is symbolic of the Israelite people and nation: When you see the fig tree beginning to bear branches and produce many leaves, you will know that the summer is near. And when noticing all the various end-time events beginning to occur, you will know that He, the Son of man, is very near, even at the doors.

I do not know how you yourselves view this tree, but it is nothing short of extraordinary how God has orchestrated the ongoing history of the Jewish people. One day the Prussian King Frederick asked one of his assistants if he could offer him one proof of the truth of the Bible. To which the attendant replied, Yes—the Jews. And he was right. No philosopher, no historian, no academic scholar, no political leader can quite explain fully the Jews' continued existence. For thousands of years, and without a homeland or government of their own, and scattered all over the world as prophesied by the Bible they would be—and yet, there they still remain in existence as a distinctive people who, unlike other beaten-down, persecuted and dispersed ethnic peoples throughout world history, have never disappeared from the earth.

In this regard, let me highlight one or two signposts of just 20th-century history which are illustrative of the extraordinary history of this people. Although there are many versions to explain the cause for World War I (1914-1918), that war ended on a prophetic note, the world being reminded by some of its leaders that the Bible declares that the Jews shall soon commence returning to their homeland. That was one of the results of the first world conflict. Next, what was the result of World War II (1939-1945); who gained from it? Again it can be said that the Jews gained tremendously from the war. For one of the remarkable outcomes of that world conflagration was the establishment at last of the State of Israel, which was created on 14 May 1948. One could therefore say that the fig tree had not only developed branches but had also produced leaves. The miracle of miracles had occurred: the State of Israel had been able to be carved out of Palestine against the intense opposition of most of the Arab nations surrounding this new State.

If you have never visited Palestine, your impression of this event will probably not have much depth to it; but should you have had the opportunity to go there and observe the situation on the spot, you could never forget the uncertain and tense environment the Israelis face daily. Surrounded by enemy territory, as it were, this tiny new country has learned ever since her creation that there can probably never be any reconciliation between Israel and the hostile Arab states. It has been a longstanding enmity which seems hopeless for there to be reconciliation. I have been there and have witnessed the deep hostility which exists between the Israelites and the Ishmaelites, with little if any hope of its cessation. Nevertheless, given this highly unfavorable environment, there is the further miracle surrounding this little new state: she having not only been established but having also continued to exist ever since its founding in 1948.

Of course, it must immediately be acknowledged that the recovery of the Israeli homeland is only a political reality, it is not a religious one—yet. Even so, according to the constitutional law of the State of Israel, the question of who shall be considered a Jew has been fairly well settled: not only must a person have been born of Jewish parents but the person must have embraced Judaism. If a person is born a Jew but has embraced another religion besides Judaism, that one is not considered a Jew according to State law. And although the Orthodox segment of the Jewish population is only a minority, they nonetheless have an influential voice in the affairs of the state and is therefore heard. Moreover, the Orthodox community wishes to see the law of Moses become the law of the Israeli state. And in certain areas of Israel today where the

Orthodox Jews live in majority presence, if on the Sabbath a person were to drive a car, the car would literally be smashed by them!

Hence, as the Lord Jesus himself explained in His later and more hopeful Olivet version of the fig tree parable, when you see all these things happening, you will know that the Son of man is very near, at the very doors. Do let us notice that the word door here is cast in the plural. In order for us to grasp what that means, we must understand the way Oriental homes were designed back in the days of the Lord Jesus and which are still similarly designed among other Asian populations today.

Here in America, if a visitor is at the door of one's house, when that door is opened to the visitor, he is already, as it were, in the house; but not in the Orient. There, when a visitor is at the *doors* (plural), he is at the outer gate of the courtyard, and if it is a very wealthy family or a royal family, a visitor may need to pass through *several* courtyards before he arrives at and gains entrance into the actual residence. So this is the figure of speech being used here—"at the doors"—in reference to the timing of Jesus' return to the earth. Perhaps He is at the front gate of the *first* courtyard or at that of the *second* because there are several doors to cross before a person arrives at the actual entrance of the residence. But if Jesus is merely at the doors, His arrival is nonetheless near enough for a person to be concerned if that one has not been watchful; for the Lord cannot be miles away.

Chapter Four

The 144,000 Remnant

And after this I saw four angels standing upon the four corners of the earth, holding fast the four winds of the earth, that no wind might blow upon the earth, nor upon the sea, nor upon any tree. And I saw another angel ascending from the sunrising, having the seal of the living God; and he cried with a loud voice to the four angels to whom it had been given to hurt the earth and the sea, saying, Hurt not the earth, nor the sea, nor the trees, until we shall have sealed the bondmen of our God upon their foreheads. And I heard the number of the sealed, a hundred and forty-four thousand, sealed out of every tribe of the sons of Israel: out of the tribe of Juda, twelve thousand sealed; out of the tribe of Reuben, twelve thousand; out of the tribe of Gad, twelve thousand; out of the tribe of Aser, twelve thousand; out of the tribe of Nepthalim, twelve thousand; out of the tribe of Manasseh, twelve thousand; out of the tribe of Simeon, twelve thousand; out of the tribe of Levi, twelve thousand; out of the tribe of Issachar, twelve thousand; out of the tribe of Zabulun, twelve thousand; out of the tribe of Joseph, twelve thousand; out of the tribe of Benjamin, twelve thousand sealed.

Revelation 7:1-8

> At the beginning of thy supplications the word went forth, and I am come to declare it; for thou art one greatly beloved. Therefore consider the word, and have understanding in the vision: Seventy weeks are apportioned out upon thy people and upon thy holy city, to close the transgression, and to make an end of sins, and to make expiation for iniquity, and to bring in the righteousness of the ages, and to seal the vision and prophet, and to anoint the holy of holies. Know therefore and understand: From the going forth of the word to restore and to build Jerusalem unto Messiah, the Prince, are seven weeks, and sixty-two weeks. The street and the moat shall be built again, even in troublous times. And after the sixty-two weeks shall Messiah be cut off, and shall have nothing; and the people of the prince that shall come shall destroy the city and the sanctuary; and the end thereof shall be with an overflow, and unto the end, war,—the desolations determined. And he shall confirm a covenant with the many for one week; and in the midst of the week he shall cause the sacrifice and the oblation to cease, and because of the protection of abominations there shall be a desolator, even until that the consumption and what is determined shall be poured out upon the desolate.
>
> Daniel 9:23-27

We are still considering together that most important subject, the testimony of Jesus; and it is a matter which is related to everyone. It is of course related to the church, it is also related to the world—the Gentiles, and it is also related to the Jews; and we are currently considering together its relationship to the Jews. And today we finally shall look into the book of Revelation together. Interestingly enough, some people have found right in the book's opening chapter, in verse 7 that the Jews have been brought into view once again. For we read this: "Behold, he comes with the clouds, and every eye shall see him, and they which have pierced him, and all the tribes of the land shall wail because of him. Yea. Amen." So it has been pointed out that this verse actually is the fulfillment of a prophecy, because in the Old Testament prophecy of Zechariah, chapter 12 from verse 10, there are these quite similar words: "And I will pour upon the house of David and upon the inhabitants of Jerusalem the spirit of grace and of supplications; and they shall look upon me whom they pierced, and they shall mourn for him..."

So some people think that this Revelation passage is the fulfillment of the Zechariah prophetic passage. We cannot be certain whether this Revelation passage should have reference just to the Jews or whether this has a larger application. Certainly the Jews are included, but probably there are more of mankind meant to be included in the fulfillment to be found in this Revelation verse. Be that as it may, we can nonetheless observe that from the very beginning of Revelation God has brought the Jews back into view.

And then they are brought into view again in chapter 5. It is the conclusion to the ascension of the Lord Jesus, and the text says that the lion of the tribe of Judah and the root of David has overcome and is ready to take the book from the hand of one who sits on the throne, and to open it and its seven seals (v.5b). We know that this is a reference to Christ the Lord who ascended up to the heaven and received from the Father's hand the sealed book which is the title deed to the universe. He is the one who is worthy to take the book and open its seals and bring all to pass in taking back the earth to God.

Now this person is described as being the lion of the tribe of Judah. The first mention in the Bible of the word lion is found in Genesis 49:9. Obviously lions existed before being first mentioned in Scripture, for certainly the lion was one of the living creatures created by God at the very beginning of creation as recorded in the Genesis creation account. And when lion is mentioned for the first time, it is related to Judah. In fact, it is a part of the prophecy pronounced by Jacob concerning his twelve sons. And as for his son Judah, he described him as being like a young lion. But besides the lion of the tribe of Judah being mentioned in Revelation 5, there is also the mention of this person as being the root of David. So He who is to inherit the universe is the lion of the tribe of Judah and is the root of King David. All this is reflective, therefore, of Messiah-Jesus' relationship to Israel and the Jewish people, because if He is called the lion of the tribe of Judah and the root of David, He is definitely related to them; and if He is thus related when He shall inherit the universe, then most certainly He cannot leave the Jews behind and forget about them.

Let us further notice that the truly open-mentioning of the Jews is clearly to be found in Revelation 7. For after the opening of the sixth seal but before the opening of the seventh there appears upon this scene which John beheld the 144,000 bondmen or servants of God who shall be sealed with the seal of God on their foreheads. John continued with his description of the unfolding scene:

> I saw another angel ascending from the sun rising, having the seal of the living God; and he cried with a loud voice to the four angels to whom it had been given to hurt the earth and the sea, saying, Hurt not the earth, nor the sea, nor the trees, until we shall have sealed the bondmen of our God upon their foreheads. And I heard the number of the sealed, a hundred and forty-four thousand, sealed out of every tribe of the sons of Israel.

So these 144,000 who shall be sealed are from the twelve tribes of Israel. Now I do not believe we can spiritualize this Scripture portion. I certainly believe that when it is said here that the ones to be sealed are of the twelve tribes of Israel, with all the names of those tribes being identified, it means exactly what is being said. And I do not believe that there is anyone clever enough to be able to legitimately spiritualize away all these tribes as denoting something else. I think it would require a great intellect to do that, and I do not possess the intellectual ability to do that. Hence, once more, we see the Jews are again being brought into view.

All this signifies that God has remembered his covenant with Abraham, and as the end-time approaches He shall bring them back into His direct dealing. These 144,000 sealed on their foreheads shall constitute the remnant of the Jews at the end-time. I cannot imagine, and it certainly is not possible, that these 144,000 shall include all the Jews then existing in the world. Of course not, since in New York city alone there are more Jews than that living there. So I believe that these 144,000 are representative of the faithful remnant among the Jews who shall witness for the Lord on the earth during the end-days or, as described by Jeremiah, during "the time of Jacob's trouble" (30:7b). Now these were called the servants or the bondmen of God and the seal of God shall be placed upon their foreheads.

Now if you put a seal on certain other places of the body it can be hidden, but if a seal has been placed on one's forehead, then everyone can see it. In other words, these bondmen of God shall be openly witnessing for Him during the end-time. They shall not be hidden ones but they shall be open in their witness. Everybody shall know that, and thus we can conclude that they shall not be afraid to bear open, public testimony for God.

This may perhaps remind us of the great apostasy which had occurred in the nation of Israel during the time of Elijah and who seemed to have been the only one who had remained faithful to God and who was at that time standing for the testimony of God. And during a weak moment he had complained to God, saying: Oh God, the whole nation has left You, and I am the only one left; and those who oppose You want to kill me, and that will be the end of Your testimony in Israel. But God reminded Elijah with these words: "I have left myself 7,000 who have never bowed their knees to Baal" (see I Kings 19:14, 18).

Now these 7,000 were apparently hidden. But these 144,000 here mentioned in Revelation 7 cannot be considered to be hidden. They shall not be secret Jews but shall be those who openly testify for God and for His Christ.

It can further be said that these 144,000 are the wise ones prophesied about by Daniel, for in this prophet's book, chapter 12, we are told that during the great distress in the end-time these shall be the wise ones who shall shine as the brightness of the firmament and who shall shine as stars forever for turning many to righteousness (vv.1, 3). Which is to say that these 144,000 shall be used by God to maintain His testimony at the most difficult time in world history.

In reading this portion of God's word in Revelation 7 we may be reminded of another scene in the Old Testament which is quite similar in some respects to this one in Revelation 7. We may recall that Ezekiel had beheld a vision of the glory of the God of Israel gradually leaving the Jerusalem temple, but before that had occurred he saw the messengers of God with slaughter weapons waiting there; and there was also one who was clothed in linen who was holding a scribal ink-horn (writing kit or case) at his side. And the Lord had commanded this man to go through all of Jerusalem and seal the foreheads with the seal of God upon all the ones who were His and who had grieved and lamented over all the abominations which were being committed in the midst of the city. And after the sealing was finished, then the word came to God's messengers to slaughter everyone who had not the seal and mark of God upon their foreheads, beginning at the temple and moving outward from there throughout the city. And Ezekiel found himself spared, and so he prayed: Oh Lord, will you also wipe out the remnant of Israel by pouring out your wrath on Jerusalem? Certainly not, indicated the Lord (9:1-11).

So what is the meaning of being sealed? It means that whoever is sealed with another's seal, that one belongs to the one who does the sealing. Which means that in this case, the 144,000 who shall be sealed on their foreheads are those who truly belong to God. God has claimed them to be His own; consequently, because they belong to God they are protected by Him and He will not allow anyone to touch them. Indeed, "the firm foundation of God stands, having this seal, The Lord knows those who are his" (II Timothy 2:19a). And those who belong to the Lord at the end-time must be sealed on the forehead.

So here we find a group of people numbered at 144,000. In comparison with all the people of the Jews at the end-time, this number shall be but a remnant of the election of grace. But some have wondered whether this is an exact number or is a symbolic number. I do not know. We cannot be dogmatic here, though it is possible for it to be an exact number, for God is able to do that. On the other hand, it could be symbolic, because 144,000 is the result of the multiples of twelve, and the number twelve in the Scriptures stands for perfection. Which is to say that the Lord shall gather to himself a perfect number of people who shall jointly testify for God and for His Christ just before the return of the Lord. Furthermore, let us realize that this is to be more than an individual testimony but a corporate one. They shall testify together as one for God and for His Christ.

However, a question arises: How is it that this remnant of the Jews shall be observed testifying for God and *for His Christ*? What will have brought them to this point of bearing testimony not only for God but also for Christ? In order for us to understand that, we will need to consult the Old Testament, especially the prophecy of Daniel. Hence, I would like for us to spend a little time considering the special prophecy of Daniel, which in turn shall bring us to what we have here in Revelation chapter 7 concerning the 144,000.

Now when Daniel became aware—from reading several books of prophecy, and especially God's word to Jeremiah—that the end of the seventy-year Babylonian captivity was approaching, he gave himself to fasting and prayer; for he noticed that God had promised Israel that after the seventy years of captivity He would remember His people once again and would bring them back to their homeland and restore them. Daniel therefore sought the Lord's face about this matter. The prophet did not simply read about this and then concluded that this was a very good thing which God would soon begin to fulfill, and let the matter go. Many others would dismiss the matter as of no concern to them, but not Daniel. Upon reading about this in Jeremiah, he began being exercised by it and sought God's face and asked him to fulfill His word. Thus Daniel was one who read the word of God with an active, not a passive, attitude.

I believe this is an important principle for God's people to follow. As we read His word, what is our attitude? Is it a passive one? Yes, we may be better than the unbeliever who does not believe God's word, for we do believe it when reading it. But is that all we should do with His word, saying to ourselves that, well, this word is definitely from God and He will perform it, and let it go at that? Or do we read Scripture with a very active attitude? If so, like Daniel, we would be those who set our face towards the Lord, seek Him, and definitely pray about the matter and inquire of Him as to how it should be fulfilled. If so, then we are expressing the right attitude in the reading of God's word. And consequently, we shall receive revelation about the matter. The reason why many believers read God's word but never obtain revelation is because their attitude is passive and not active. If we read His word with an active attitude, God will reveal himself to us and we shall receive even greater revelation.

So Daniel was waiting upon the Lord and seeking His face. And from the very beginning of his supplications the word of God came forth, and a messenger was sent to Daniel to declare it to him as one greatly beloved of God. And the word was this: "Seventy weeks have been decreed for your people, Daniel, and for your holy city." We must understand that this seventy weeks is meant to convey the idea of seventy units of seven, for in the original language the word for weeks is literally to be translated as seven; and, therefore, in the strictest sense, the seventy weeks phrase should be read as seventy sevens. And the Jewish people of that day were quite familiar with the idea of sevens. For example, the sabbath day is the seventh day of the week, and the sabbatical year is the seventh of years being spoken about. Furthermore, when Daniel read Jeremiah, he noticed that that prophet of God had used the word seventy in reporting God's word to him as to what would be the foretold length of years for which the captivity would last (25:11-12, 29:10). Accordingly, when the Lord revealed His mind to Daniel, it was on the basis of seven, yet not seventy but seventy sevens.

Now in God's prophetic words to Daniel via His messenger Gabriel, this seventy sevens of years were as it were set apart or singled out from time—and for what purpose? These years, said the Lord to Daniel, are being specifically identified concerning your people and your holy city. In other words, God is here informing Daniel that the object of singling out this portion of years from time is definitely related to Daniel's people the Jews and to Daniel's holy city of Jerusalem. We know, of course, that the existence of time began after the eternity past and it shall end before the eternity to come; and in between these two eternities is time, and that parallel to time is history because events have been happening in time from time's beginning.

And hence, within this time frame God, in prophetically speaking to Daniel, set apart or singled out a portion of time—

the seventy sevens—for a specific purpose concerning a specific people and city, and that people is the Jews and that city, Jerusalem. God's prophetic word to Daniel was not meant to convey the thought that during this singled-out portion or block of time only the Jews and the city of Jerusalem are there and nothing else in world history would be happening. No, those other events would in fact be occurring within that set-apart portion of time, but this portion of time is especially singled out in God's dealing for the Jews and the holy city Jerusalem. I trust you all understand, but if not, it may become clearer as we proceed in our discussion together.

Now since that portion of time—the seventy sevens—has been singled out specifically for the Jews and their holy city Jerusalem, what is God's purpose in doing this? What does He intend to accomplish during that portion of time? God never wastes any time. If God sets apart a time He will fill up that period of time with His doings. Hence, what will God do during these seventy sevens? Well, in His word to Daniel through His messenger Gabriel, God has told us, and there are six specific actions He has intended to take: close the transgression, make an end of sins, make expiation for iniquity, bring in everlasting righteousness, seal up vision and prophecy, and anoint the holy of holies.

It is believed that these six actions can be divided into three pairs. The first pair is to close the transgression and make an end of sins. In this regard, we know that God's people have certainly sinned against Him. In fact, Daniel while on his knees was confessing the sins of his people: how they had sinned over and over again—how they had sinned against God in the wilderness—how they had sinned against God in the Promised Land—how they had even sinned against Him in the land of captivity. The people of God had transgressed and transgressed His laws, but God now said: "I am going to close the transgression and make an end of sins. One day My people shall no longer transgress and sin against Me. I will close the transgression and I will make an end of sin."

And consequently, that pair is logically followed by the second pair—make an expiation for iniquity and bring in the righteousness of the ages. That pair of actions is a step further, for it is not only that the people of God shall no longer sin but all their sins shall be expiated; which is to say, that people are going to be atoned for—their past sins shall be atoned and the righteousness of the ages shall be brought in. And we know what the righteousness of the ages is: it is the righteousness of God—even Christ, who is our righteousness (I Corinthians 1:30; cf. II Corinthians 5:21). This shall be brought in to the people.

And then the third pair: seal up the vision of the prophets and anoint the holy of holies. What does this pair mean? It means, first, that there will be no more vision and no more prophecy. Shall that be a good thing? Yes, because vision shall become reality and prophecy shall become fact. And hence, both vision and prophecy shall pass away because they have been closed and sealed up; and there is now no more use of it; it is put away because the reality shall in effect have now come in. And, second, there shall be the anointing of the holy of holies. There has been a great difference in how this action is to be interpreted. This is because in the original Hebrew the phrase, the holy of holies, can mean a person as well as a place or site. If it has reference to a place, then, of course, we know it specifically means the holy of holies in the house of God or temple, which was one of its compartments or spaces. However, we naturally would most likely enlarge the scope of its meaning in the end-time because New Jerusalem, as presented in Revelation, shall in its entirety be the holy of holies (Revelation 21:3, 22-23). For there shall not be, as was true in the Jerusalem temple of old, any division between the holy place and the most holy place. And in that case this phrase, the holy of holies, would include the whole temple or house of God. On the other hand, the phrase may refer to a person, and if so, that person would be the Lord Jesus, who shall be openly anointed among His people even as David had been anointed King of Israel and Judah by all twelve Jewish tribes.

Accordingly, we see here that God, having long ago chosen the Jews as His people out of all the nations of the world, has never forgotten them but in His word to Daniel has cut out of time a certain period of years for the sake of bringing His people to fullness in order that Christ may be the Head of that people. What a blessing shall be the effect of those six actions. But for God to accomplish those six objectives He will need to carve out of time seventy sevens of years. And these seventy sevens of years are divided up into three segments of years of varying lengths: seven sevens, sixty-two sevens, and one seven. Let us take up these segments in some detail.

"From the going forth of the word to restore and to build Jerusalem unto Messiah, the Prince, are seven weeks, and sixty-two weeks. The street and the moat [or wall] shall be built again, even in troublous times." Here we see that the first seven sevens and the sixty-two sevens are joined together in their description; nevertheless, though they are joined together, the one continues after the other. It is continuous, in that the seven sevens is followed by the sixty-two sevens; and thus these sixty-nine sevens have their beginning from the word which comes forth for the restoring and the rebuilding of Jerusalem and have their ending with the coming of Messiah, the Prince.

I need to pause here for a few moments of explanation, which is, that there is no room for imagination when it comes to this prophetic word which has been so clearly defined. For if we can find in the Bible a similarly clearly-defined passage about the rebuilding of Jerusalem and its street and moat, then we shall know to what this prophetic word in Daniel means and to what it has reference. And sure enough, we find this explicitly described in the Bible. But first, an observation needs to be made as to which decree by which Babylonian ruler concerning the future of Jerusalem is the relevant one. Most likely the decree issued for the rebuilding of the holy city was not that of King Cyrus. His decree had authorized those in captivity who wished to rebuild the temple in Jerusalem to return to their homeland for that purpose. But the decree issued authorizing the rebuilding of the city itself is actually found in the book of Nehemiah, chapter 2, in which is recorded the decree of King Artaxerxes in the twentieth year of his reign. Nehemiah and those of the Jews with him were granted permission to leave their captivity in Babylon and go and rebuild the wall of Jerusalem; and obviously, to rebuild the wall of a destroyed city is for the purpose of rebuilding the city itself. And Nehemiah was certainly used of God to rebuild Jerusalem and its wall in very troublous times, for we know from his Old Testament book how much trouble he and his fellow builders of the wall encountered from various enemies who tried to frustrate God's servant in attempts to obstruct the wall's rebuilding.

Now God's prophetic word to Daniel indicated that from the building of the wall to the coming of Messiah the Prince would be seven sevens and sixty-two sevens. Why is it, though, that these sixty-nine sevens (7 sevens + 62 sevens = 69 sevens) were divided into two segments of years? Most likely these seven sevens are described by these words which appear in God's prophetic utterance to Daniel through Gabriel: "The street and the moat shall be built again, even in troublous times." And thus these words serve as a summary of what happened during this segment of years: the seven sevens. But what happened with the Jewish people during the much longer segment of years, the sixty-two sevens? Well, God had prophesied that "after sixty-two sevens shall Messiah be cut off and shall have nothing." Therefore, these sixty-two sevens of years would cover the unfolding of all the events involving the Jewish people and which would bring the people down to the coming of Messiah the Prince.

What, then, is the number of years covered by the entire sweep of the seven sevens and the sixty-two sevens combined? Well, though we can trace back in history, we cannot be precise down to the very last year. And why? It is because our calendar with respect to B.C. and A.D. is questionable as to its accuracy—even as to the way we state the years after the birth of Christ. For there can be a difference of as much as four years and perhaps slightly more. And that is the reason we should not go into so much detail in trying to fix the exact year and month and even day and hour. We simply should not do that.

However, there is one thing we *can* do legitimately, which is that we can compute *approximately* the number of years which span the period from the rebuilding of Jerusalem's wall up to the coming of Messiah based on the sixty-nine sevens marked out in Daniel chapter 9: it is about 490 years. But with the coming of Jesus the Messiah to His people, His own received Him not (John 1:11) except for a remnant of the election of grace. We find that the nation of Israel rejected Jesus the Messiah, and because of that, the Jews were widely dispersed throughout the world. But let us proceed further.

We read in Daniel 9 that "after the sixty-two weeks shall Messiah be cut off, and shall have nothing"; and in the Hebrew original the phrase, cut off, conveys the thought of a *violent* end and not a natural end. Thus, this prophecy was literally fulfilled in Christ because He met a violent death in crucifixion. Moreover, not only did Jesus the Messiah's life end violently, but also afterwards He had nothing: all His disciples had scattered; so that it would appear as if Messiah indeed had nothing left to Him, all having been lost, although He and His disciples did meet once again following His resurrection.

Let us remind ourselves again that the complete number of the units of seven which in God's prophetic word to Daniel were "apportioned out" upon God's chosen people was seventy sevens (9:24a). And then the prophecy mentioned the seven sevens and sixty-two sevens (v.25a); and these two segments of years were understood to be continuous, the second larger segment following immediately after the smaller segment. This thus left the final one seven out of the seventy sevens to be considered. In other words, the seven sevens and sixty-two sevens were joined together because they were continuous in their unfolding of Jewish history, whereas the one final seven stood alone in the prophecy. And why? It is because there would be an interval of time, between the end of the sixty-nine sevens and the beginning of the final one seven, during which certain events pertaining to the Jewish people were to occur. What were these events to be?

First, the Messiah would be violently cut off. Second, the people of another prince and not of the Messianic Prince shall come and shall destroy Jerusalem and its sanctuary, the temple. The title of prince here has reference to head or ruler. And Jesus the Messiah, as we know, is God's Anointed Head to His people, the Jews. But, as we also know, they did not want Him as ruler over them. Consequently, if they did not wish to have God's Anointed Head, they would get another head, another prince, who would certainly not be God's choice. His prophetic word to Daniel indicated that after messiah Prince would be cut off, there would come anther prince whose people would destroy the Jewish capital.

To what in Jewish history, you may ask, does that have reference? It is now well known that in 70 A.D. the city of Jerusalem was laid siege to by none other than the military forces of the Roman Empire under the command of General Titus. And this Roman army ruthlessly and cruelly destroyed the entire holy city of the Jews and the entire temple (except for one section of the temple wall which is still preserved today by the Jewish people and now known as the Wailing Wall). Hence, during the interval between the conclusion of the sixty-nine sevens and the beginning of the one remaining seven of seventy sevens, that is what the second event consisted of as happening.

However, God's prophecy continued to inform Daniel of what would thereafter ensue during the unfolding of this lengthy interval period of years. The prophecy predicted that the end of this interval shall come in like a flood (the "overflow") and shall continue till the very end and be marked by war, war, and more war: small wars, great wars, world wars, with desolations being decreed and everywhere determined. In fact, looking back from where we stand today, that is what has happened and has continued to happen even up to this very day.

But, of course, there has also been a bright aspect to this interval: God in Christ called the church into being commencing on the day of Pentecost after the risen Messiah's ascension back to His Father. Indeed, during this interval the Jewish people of God have been temporarily set aside, as God has moved in raising up another people of His own, the church, to be His witness during this entire interval of years, centuries, and even millennia. Obviously, this bright side was not recorded as part of the prophecy which came from God to His Old Testament prophet Daniel, for back then people knew nothing about the church.

Now, though, we must next consider the concluding one seven as has been briefly described in Daniel 9. That last seven shall begin with the following, with the identity of the pronoun "he" in this descriptive passage pointing to the second prince:

> He shall confirm a covenant with the many for one week [or, for one seven]; and in the midst of the week he shall cause the sacrifice and the oblation to cease, and because of the protection of abominations there shall be a desolator, even until that the consumption and what is determined shall be poured out upon the desolate.

Let us be clear that the day is approaching when the prince spoken of here—who is the continuation of the aforementioned second prince, "the prince that shall come"—shall make a covenant with the many for one week: that is, for a period of seven years. This prince actually points to the Antichrist, because in the preceding verse, "the prince that shall come" is a phrase foreshadowing the Antichrist, who is the other head—the false head—of the world empire which shall emerge under his control at the end of the ages.

So, the Antichrist shall make a covenant with the many for one seven-year period. Let us notice that the word many is preceded by the definite article, the: the many. And since the Jews are the people in view in this entire prophetic utterance of God to Daniel here, therefore, the phrase, the many, refers to the many Jews who shall be dwelling at the end-time in Jerusalem and Israel.

Now when the Antichrist shall come, he will assume rule over the world and place it under his will. Being so powerful, he shall appear to be able to provide so much to people everywhere. In fact, the Antichrist will announce, If you come under my protective wing, you shall enjoy peace, prosperity, and security; but if you refuse to do so, then war and extermination shall be your end.

How will the Jewish people in the State of Israel—a nation that in 1948 was born in the midst of great opposition and hostility by her neighboring Arab states—respond to this sinister invitation by Antichrist? They shall find themselves in a quandary as to what they should do. On the one hand, they shall be frightened by the thought that the Antichrist could come and destroy their nation again as he had done through Titus and the Romans way back in 70 A.D. On the other hand, the Jews came to believe that if they agreed to come under Antichrist's wing of protection, they could experience the advantages of peace and security which they so greatly desire to have. Hence, they shall be frightened but also attracted to Antichrist's overtures. In the end they will enter into a pact or covenant with the second prince. It shall be a decision based on human wisdom, it being a political move of expediency instead of exercising a dependency upon the Almighty God of Abraham, Isaac and Jacob.

Therefore, despite the fact that the 144,000 Jews who will be faithful to God shall oppose this decision, the great majority of the Jewish people—"the many"—shall make a pact with the false head, the Antichrist, for a term of seven years. Viewed by the Jewish majority as a covenant of peace, in reality it shall end up being a covenant of death, even as prophesied in the book of Isaiah, chapter 28:

> Therefore hear the word of Jehovah, ye scornful men, that rule this people which is in Jerusalem. For ye have said, We have made a covenant with death, and with Sheol have we made an agreement; when the overflowing scourge shall pass through, it shall not come unto us; for we have made lies our refuge, and under falsehood have we hid ourselves (vv.14-15).

In accordance with this prophetic word of Isaiah's, the great majority of the Jews in Israel shall think that by making a covenant with the false head, Antichrist, thus making lies and falsehood their refuge and hiding place, they will believe that when the overflowing scourge shall make its way in the earth, it will not come to them. Because the Jews shall have joined themselves to the prince of their choice and not God's, they will believe that they shall be spared of the scourge, and thus be protected from all harm.

However, they shall be proven to have been fools to have relied upon the word of Antichrist. For Isaiah's prophetic word from the Lord Jehovah continues:

> Therefore thus saith the Lord Jehovah: Behold, I lay for foundation in Zion a stone, a tried stone, a precious corner-stone, a sure foundation: he that

> trusteth shall not make haste. And I will appoint judgment for a line, and righteousness for a plummet; and the hail shall sweep away the refuge of lies, and the waters shall overflow the hiding-place. And your covenant with death shall be annulled, and your agreement with Sheol shall not stand; when the overflowing scourge shall pass through, ye shall be trodden down by it (vv.16-18).

The Lord Jehovah thus declares here that their "covenant with death" "shall not stand" and the Jewish people shall be trodden underfoot by the overflowing scourge which shall indeed come to them. Oh, how many have been those who have been wise in themselves but God declares them to be fools who shall be victims of their own foolishness.

Now after having concluded their negotiations with the world empire's false head, the Jewish nation shall begin to experience what she will initially believe to be a seven-year period of peace, prosperity, and security. And in fact that is what it shall be like at the beginning, with everything appearing to be quite fine and promising. However, in the middle of this pact's period of years—that is, after three and a half years of their initial season of promised peace and security—suddenly Antichrist shall break his covenant. Oh, have we not all heard or even witnessed this conduct among nations in the world's history? We should never put much stock in agreements on paper.

Antichrist will have cunningly used this covenant to extend his influence and accomplish his nefarious purpose; but once he has obtained what he desires, he shall break the agreement in the middle of its term of years. What, then, will he have desired to obtain? We are told in Daniel 9 what his objective shall be: believing himself to be safe and secure now, the false head shall reveal his true face: he shall break the covenant by causing the regular sacrifices and grain offerings to the one true God to cease because he has now got the entire world under his wing. In other words, self-assured that all is under his control, Antichrist shall put an end to all religions but his own: I am now the god of Israel, he shall proclaim—meaning that no one can worship any god but him. And to reinforce this declaration, Antichrist shall set up his image in the temple at Jerusalem (cf. II Thessalonians 2:3b-4), this being what the prophecies of Daniel 9 and elsewhere in Daniel and in still other Scriptures call "the abomination of desolation" (9:27b Darby mgn; 9:27b ASV mgn; see also Daniel 11:31c, 12:11b; Matthew 24:15; Mark 13:14a).

But, then, there shall arise tribulation which shall last throughout the final half of years of the one seven—a tribulation of three and a half years. To the Jews this is what God's prophetic word in Jeremiah has termed "the time of Jacob's trouble" (30:7). In fact, this is what the Lord Jesus alluded to in His lengthy prophetic Olivet Discourse to His disciples: "When therefore ye shall see the abomination of desolation, which is spoken of through Daniel the prophet, standing in what is a holy place, … then let those who are in Judaea flee …" (Matthew 24:15; Mark 13:14). And why flee? Because the Great Tribulation will have come!

Thus, as was observed earlier, all this which we have considered together today from Daniel 9 has now led us to what, at the very beginning, was read aloud from Revelation 7 concerning the 144,000 whose foreheads shall be sealed with "the seal of the living God." Let us thank God that though the Antichrist shall set himself up as the only one to be worshiped—and, oh, how many shall be caught unaware—there shall nonetheless be 144,000 of the election of grace from among the Jewish people who at the end-time shall not bow their knees to this false head.

Now because the 144,000 will have the seal of God on their foreheads, these faithful ones of the remnant of the Jews shall be open targets to be cruelly treated by the enemy, but they shall stand firm for the testimony of God and of His Christ. They shall refuse to acknowledge that the world belongs to Antichrist; instead, they shall testify that it belongs to God and to Christ, and to none other. This 144,000 remnant of the election of grace may have to lose their lives, but the testimony of God and of His Christ shall be protected and sustained.

We do therefore praise and thank the Lord that He knows who are His.

Chapter Five

The Two Witnesses

And there was given to me a reed like a staff, saying, Rise, and measure the temple of God, and the altar, and them that worship in it. And the court which is without the temple cast out, and measure it not; because it has been given up to the nations, and the holy city shall they tread under foot forty-two months. And I will give power to my two witnesses, and they shall prophesy a thousand two hundred and sixty days, clothed in sackcloth. These are the two olive trees and the two lamps which stand before the Lord of the earth; and if any one wills to injure them, fire goes out of their mouth, and devours their enemies. And if any one wills to injure them, thus must he be killed. These have power to shut the heaven that no rain may fall during the days of their prophecy; and they have power over the waters to turn them into blood, and to smite the earth as often as they will with every plague. And when they shall have completed their testimony, the beast who comes up out of the abyss shall make war with them, and shall conquer them, and shall kill them: and their body shall be on the street of the great city, which is called spiritually Sodom and Egypt, where also their Lord was crucified. And men of the peoples and tribes and tongues and nations see their body three days and a half, and they do not suffer their bodies to be put into a sepulchre. And they that dwell upon the earth rejoice over them, and are full of delight, and shall send gifts one to another, because these, the two prophets, tormented them that dwell upon the earth. And after the three days and a half the spirit of life from God came into them, and they stood upon their feet; and great fear fell upon those beholding them. And I heard a great voice out of the heaven saying to them, Come up here; and they went up to the heaven in the cloud, and their enemies beheld them. And in that hour there was a great earthquake, and the tenth of the city fell, and seven thousand names of men were slain in the earthquake. And the remnant were filled with fear, and gave glory to the God of the heaven.

Revelation 11:1-13

In reading the book of Revelation one very quickly discovers that from its chapter 4 onward it is divided into roughly two parts. The first part gives us the prophecies found from chapter 4 through chapter 10, and the second part begins with chapter 11. In the first part there are prophecies given and which end in chapter 10 showing an angel holding in his hand a little open book and the apostle John being commanded to go to that angel, take the book, and eat it, and after he has eaten it he was to prophesy again.

We do not know whether this little open book is the same book spoken of shortly after the beginning of Revelation. Recall that in the hand of the one who sits on the heavenly throne there was a book or scroll written both within and without and was sealed with seven seals. Recall, too, that when the Lamb of God shall have stepped forward and taken that book from the hand of God, He shall have begun to open its seals; and that as the seals shall be opened, things shall begin to happen on the earth. But since, in John's vision, this little book is described as open, we do not know whether or not this little book is the same as the earlier mentioned book. I personally feel that probably it is not because its description here is that it is both little and open.

However, there is one thing we do know, which is that in this little open book there are more words of prophecy written for John to resume prophesying again. In other words, the second part of Revelation is the adding to those prophecies which have already been given in Revelation's first part. Another way to look at Revelation is to see that in its first part we are given to see the broad outline of prophecy and are given to see in its second part the filling in of the details of those prophecies. And, of course, for the past several weeks we have been focused in on the second part of Revelation.

There is another observation which needs to be made; namely, that in the first part of Revelation the throne seems to be the governing factor. It is as if all things come from the throne and thus are governed by the throne. In the second part of Revelation, however, the temple comes into prominence and would appear as though it governs all things. Nevertheless, the temple can be seen in the first part, too, and the throne can be seen in the second part as well. But it does seem to be that in the first part the throne is more prominent while in the second part the temple takes on more prominence.

I will try to offer an explanation for this circumstance. You do not need to accept my explanation if you do not agree. My explanation would be that because the place of the throne seems, at least to me, to be in relation to the world more, therefore, one finds that in Revelation's first part the things being prophesied are those concerning the world; and, in fact, all those things are shown as coming from the throne. And hence, the throne is the governing factor and is accordingly more prominent in the first part. In the second part, however, it would appear that the Jewish people come into view far more than in the first part. And because the temple is related to the Jews more than to the world, therefore, the temple takes on a more prominent role in the second part than does the throne.

We know, of course, that the temple of Jerusalem was situated on Mt. Moriah (II Chronicles 3:1) whereas the temple or tabernacle of David was located on Mt. Zion (I Chronicles 15:1, II Chronicles 5:2). These are adjoining peaks or hills within the vicinity of the holy city; nevertheless, spiritually speaking, because the throne of God is in His house, therefore, these two governing centers—temple and throne—are actually together as one. I only mention this as a way, possibly, to help those of us who may wish to study the book of Revelation further.

Now we come to chapter 11 of Revelation. We mentioned before that Israel will be revived after thousands of years of the Jews having been scattered throughout the world. Towards the end of this age Israel will be restored and this we have already come to see; for on 14 May 1948 the State of Israel was established, whose reviving in and of itself was considered a miracle. Actually a prior miracle had occurred, as was pointed out earlier; for consider this: The Jews have been a people who have existed for thousands of years without ever having been totally exterminated or ever having died out naturally as a distinct group of people. In fact, this may be the only people group in world history about whom this could be said. Indeed, one could therefore deem this outcome to have been a great miracle of God's grace and mercy, perhaps surpassing even the miracle which saw the restoration of the nation of Israel in 1948. No statesman in this world could explain this development. It did not seem possible that a people dispersed throughout the world, a people greatly persecuted, a people without land and a government could ever see a nation for themselves reestablished, and yet such an event became a reality in 1948. What a wonder this was to the world's statesmen and political leaders.

Even so, let us realize as well that the very continuance of this State of Israel is likewise a great miracle. This is because this small nation is surrounded by enemies on three sides, and the other side is the sea. And it is the determined will of these enemies to destroy that nation and push her into the sea. As was pointed out last time, the enmity between the adjoining nations and Israel is so great that there seems to be no solution. Many statesmen of the world have energetically attempted to solve the problem, but this vexing problem has remained unresolved to this very day. When I visited that area for the first time I was struck by the hatred and enmity which was there. There seemed to be no solution, and yet that small nation continues to exist despite the constant threat from her neighbors. In fact, a state of war still exists there. If one visits old Jerusalem and then steps into new Jerusalem on the Israeli side, one finds that in between there is a piece of land which the United Nations had to establish in order to keep the peace.* So in spite of all these difficulties and troubles, that little nation prospers and continues to exist. It is truly a miracle.

But as we learned last time, towards the end of world history there will arise a world ruler in the person of Antichrist, and his power shall become greater and greater. Moreover, the little State of Israel will begin to feel its force, and as prophesied by Daniel, "the many" of that nation (9:27)—meaning, the great majority of Israel—shall in time feel it expedient to draw up an agreement or pact with this powerful ruler at the end of the ages. Most Jews in Israel will think that because they have signed such a pact they will be left alone and that they will obtain all the benefits from this world power in what will be the last days. And as we also saw last time, a remnant of the election of grace among the Israelites shall oppose the pact; but inasmuch as they shall be only a remnant, the majority shall carry the day in the making of this nation's decision.

Now during the first three and a half years of this pact's seven-year term—and just as the Bible had prophesied—

* This message was given sometime in the 1950s. By the time of this publication those specifics had changed somewhat, but the enmity between the adjoining nations and Israel still remains. —*Publishers*

everything will go very well for Israel. Antichrist will keep the promise he made in confirming the covenant with Israel, with this little nation allowed to grow and peacefully prosper as if under his wing of protection. Indeed, all will seem to be peaceful, prosperous, and secure; but in the middle of this seven-year pact this world ruler will break the agreement and do worse: he will set up an image—an idol—of himself in the temple of God and demand, under penalty of persecution and perhaps death, that all worship it.

Let us recall again what the Lord Jesus had prophesied to His disciples about this very thing:

> When therefore ye shall see the abomination of desolation, which is spoken of through Daniel the prophet, standing in what is a holy place, ... then let those who are in Judaea flee to the mountains; let not him that is on the house [top] come down to take the things out of his house; and let not him that is in the field turn back to take his garment. ... For then shall there be great tribulation, such as has not been from the beginning of the world until now, nor ever shall be ... (Matthew 24:15-18, 21).

Jesus was saying here that the moment you become aware of the setting up of the abominable image in the temple of God, you must flee! In fact, if you shall be on the housetop, you shall not go down and into your house but just run away. Get away and flee. Let us take note that in Jerusalem and elsewhere in Israel the housetop is reached by a stairway located outside the house. And it is usually the place in the house to where the people go to meditate and enjoy quietness. And so, if you are on the housetop and want to go into the house you must descend the stairway outside the house and then walk into the house. So the word of the Lord here indicated that when you see the abomination of desolation standing in the holy place you who are on the housetop must instantly descend the stairs and flee away. Do not go into the house for the purpose of gathering together some goods and carrying them with you, because you shall not have the time to do that. And if you should be out in the field working, do not go back to your house: instead, immediately leave everything behind and flee, because the time of the Great Tribulation will have arrived—such that the world has never ever witnessed before.

So this will be the time at the end of the first three and a half years of the covenant when the Antichrist shall show his true face. Having heretofore worn a mask, he will now uncover his mask and show his real face. Antichrist shall proceed to wipe out all religions and proclaim himself as the god of the world and command everyone to worship him and him alone. It will be because of this action by him that the pact is broken; and when this pact is broken, immediately persecution will be inflicted upon God's chosen people, the Israelites. Not only the remnant of the election of grace shall suffer persecution but also the whole nation, because no matter what, Israel stands for the belief in the one true God. They worship Jehovah God. Hence, a great persecution will break forth upon the Israelites. Many will be killed during the Great Tribulation, which among the Jewish people is known as the time of Jacob's trouble (Jeremiah 30:7).

But thank God, who knows the frailty of human beings. He shall therefore send two witnesses to the Israelites to strengthen their hands, especially the hands of the remnant—the 144,000 who are mentioned in Revelation chapter 7. They are those who shall prove to be faithful to God and to His Christ. To these two witnesses God shall not only give words to prophesy but also give abilities by which to back up their words. Thus, they shall be able to shut up the heavens, that there be no rain and shall be able to call fire down from heaven and even turn water into blood. They shall therefore be able to bring forth many plagues by which to plague the land; and should anyone desire to hurt them that person will be killed. Notice that if someone shall merely have the *desire* to hurt these two, that person is to be killed. Thus, God shall send two powerful witnesses to the earth, for the purpose on the one hand to withstand the enemy and on the other hand to strengthen the hands of those who shall be faithful to Him.

Is it not true that this is very much like God? He will not only do that for the faithful remnant of Israel, but throughout the generations and ages past, whenever the Lord's people have been in great distress, our God has always provided some help to strengthen and to encourage. Our God is very much like that.

Now these two witnesses are described as being the two olive trees and the two lamps which stand before the Lord of the earth (cf. Zechariah 4:3, 11, 14). We know that olive trees give oil, and oil in the Scriptures often symbolizes the Holy Spirit. The Spirit of God is like oil. So these two olive trees are "the two sons of oil" mentioned in the prophetic book of Zechariah (4:14)—that is, the two sons of the Spirit of God. In other words, these two witnesses shall be filled with the Spirit of God, because unless they are filled with the Spirit of God they shall not be able witnesses in the midst of such circumstances as shall obtain during the Great Tribulation. So these two witnesses shall be filled with the Holy Spirit and thus are able and most powerful. They are not only described as two olive trees but also two lamps. Lamps in Scripture stand for testimony because lamps give light. So here we find two men who shall be filled with the Holy Spirit and who shall shine when the world is in its period of pitch darkness and who shall stand before the Lord of the whole earth. At the end-time it will seem as though the Antichrist is the lord of the earth because it shall seem as though he has everything under his control; but with the coming of these two witnesses who shall stand before the true Lord of the earth and bear their testimony, the world will have to take into account these two able and very powerful men.

Now, then, who shall these two witnesses be? Different commentators have given different interpretations. But, personally, I believe these two witnesses whom God shall send to Israel during the Great Tribulation or the time of Jacob's trouble are Moses and Elijah. And here are my reasons for believing them to be those great Old Testament figures.

Let us first turn to the last book of the Old Testament, which, as you know, is the book of Malachi. As a matter of fact, Malachi is the last Old Testament book of prophecy. And its last few verses can certainly give us a clue regarding what will happen in the New Testament era. Here is how those verses of chapter 4 read:

> Remember the law of Moses my servant, which I commanded unto him in Horeb for all Israel, the statutes and ordinances. Behold, I send unto you Elijah the prophet, before the coming of the great and terrible day of Jehovah. And he shall turn the heart of the fathers to the children, and the heart of the children to their fathers, lest I come and smite the earth with a curse (vv.4-6).

Here at the close of the entire Old Testament are verses which especially mention two outstanding persons whom God greatly used in the past. And everybody easily connects Elijah with the coming of the Lord because it is stated here in no uncertain language that he shall come before the great and terrible day of Jehovah and shall turn the heart of the fathers to the children and the heart of the children to their fathers. But we tend to forget that Moses is equally included here, for these two persons are mentioned together as God as it were concludes the Old Testament. In fact, Moses and Elijah not only conclude the Old Testament prophecy, these same two—if my personal belief is correct—shall conclude the New Testament prophecy as well.

Another reason for believing that the two God-sent witnesses shall be Moses and Elijah is because of their appearing with Jesus on the Mount of Transfiguration. We will recall that as the Lord was transfigured and the Shekinah glory enveloped Him, there suddenly appeared on the scene Moses and Elijah, who began talking with Jesus about His soon-approaching departure from the earth—that is to say, about His crucifixion. Moses and Elijah were there.

A third reason for my belief stems from the kinds of works of power and miracles which these two witnesses shall perform during the time of Jacob's trouble. For it turns out that these are the works which Moses and Elijah had been used by God to perform in their past ministry as His servants: Moses, for example, had turned the waters of Egypt into blood (Exodus 7:20), and Elijah had shut up the heavens from rain (James 5:17; Luke 4:25; I Kings 17:1, 18:1). So according to Revelation 11, we find that in the course of these two witnesses prophesying during the Great Tribulation, the works of miracles which they shall perform shall simply be a repetition of what Moses and Elijah had done previously.

There is a fourth reason. I do not know how you feel when reading the life of Elijah as recorded in the Old Testament. But I have always felt that his life seemed to have suddenly been cut off prematurely—that for some reason God took Elijah away before his work was finished. That is something which God normally never does but which He seems to have done in the case of Elijah. Now why, I asked myself. I believe the answer is to be found in Revelation 11: God was going to send Elijah back to the earth again to finish the work which He had given him to do.

There is yet a fifth reason, and in this instance it has to do with the dead body of Moses. According to the Old Testament book of Deuteronomy Moses died atop Mount Nebo on the eastern side of the Dead Sea in the land of Moab and opposite Jericho (32:49). And God buried Moses in the valley in the land of Moab, with no one having discovered his burial site (34:6). However, according to the New Testament book of Jude, before God buried Moses, the archangel Lucifer—having become the devil and Satan—contended with God's archangel Michael for the body of Moses.

Now why? For if a man's work for God is done and he dies with his body about to be buried, that should be the end of his earthly life's story. There is no use to be made of *that* body anymore because in resurrection it shall become a spiritual body and shall no longer be a fleshly body. Consequently, why was it that two mighty archangels would fight for control of that body? Indeed, what use is desired to be made of that body by God? There certainly must be a good reason for it. It must be because God will make use of that body once more: Moses' fleshly body shall be raised up from the dead, and the same Moses and the same Elijah shall together be the two witnesses whom God shall send to the Jewish people.

Let us not forget that these two men of the Old Testament era represent, respectively, the law and the prophets—which together stand for everything worthwhile to the Jews. And hence, if this people could have Moses and Elijah, they would obtain the best help possible in the time of Jacob's trouble. So from Revelation 11 we learn that God shall provide for His chosen people the greatest help He could afford them in the person of these two servants of His. They together shall be a great strengthening and comfort for them, especially for the remnant of the election of grace—the 144,000—at the end-time.

Hence, Moses and Elijah shall be sent and bear testimony to the one true God during the three and a half years of the Great Tribulation. And after their work is finally done on the earth, the beast, who is the Antichrist, shall rise up out of the Abyss and war against these two witnesses, overcome them, and slay them. Then, their bodies shall be laid out upon the street of Jerusalem. Their bodies shall thus be put on display for people to visit and look at. And meanwhile, the whole world shall be rejoicing because of the death of God's two witnesses.

Then, after their bodies shall have been exhibited in this manner for three and a half days, the breath of God shall come into them and these two dead men shall rise up, causing great fear to fall upon those who shall observe this happening. But next, a great voice from heaven shall be heard saying to these two witnesses to come up to heaven, and they do indeed rise up to heaven in a cloud while their enemies on earth shall be watching with great wonder.

Next, at that very hour a great earthquake shall strike, causing a tenth of the city to collapse and the lives of "seven thousand names of men" to be snuffed out. These are very peculiar words used to refer to these slain men, which most likely have reference to those people in the world who at that time shall be very important. In fact, Revelation 11 tells us that men—probably these seven thousand—from every people, tribe, tongue and nation shall gather in Jerusalem to celebrate the killing of these two witnesses, but those men shall themselves be destroyed by the earthquake. And thus this prophecy of John's concerning the two witnesses of God now brings us to a consideration of "the coming of the great and terrible day of Jehovah" prophesied by the prophet Malachi in that closing passage of the entire Old Testament which was quoted earlier, and which day, declared Malachi, shall come after the sending by God of His servant Elijah. But I must leave this consideration of that day till the next time we gather.

However, before concluding our discussion together today, a most important question needs to be asked and answered. What shall be the testimony which these two witnesses shall bear? We know that the law and the prophets both testify of the Lord Jesus, for He himself had declared that the law and the prophets spoke of Him (Luke 24:25-27, 44). Moses, for example, while he was leading the people of Israel, prophesied concerning the Lord Jesus that there would be One raised up from among the Israelites, that everyone must hear Him, and that if anyone did not hearken to Him, it would be required of that person (Deuteronomy 18:15, 18-19). Moses also testified regarding the Lord through his law, his statutes, the tabernacle, and the priestly services. Everything which God used Moses to issue as law, statute, or priestly service spoke of or betokened the coming Christ. But so too was that true of the prophets. Sometimes they may have prophesied about things which were of immediate concern before them; nevertheless, many times those same prophecies went beyond the immediate or present concern by having application or relevance as well regarding the future; and all their prophecies focused upon but one Person, the coming Messiah, even Christ Jesus.

Hence, we find that in representing the law and the prophets, Moses and Elijah, during their earlier earthly ministry, had testified concerning the coming of the Messiah. And then, again, when appearing on the Mount of Transfiguration as representatives of law and prophets, they were talking with Jesus the Messiah regarding His approaching exit from the earth via Calvary and His resurrection and ascension. In other words, the One about whom they had prophesied had at last come to the earth and was going to accomplish the work of redemption by going to the cross. And so they are talking with Messiah about these very matters. And finally, what will these two witnesses testify and prophesy about when they shall come again to prepare the way for the Lord's return? Will their testimony be limited just to the oneness and supremacy of God? Or will they—in their capacity as joint representatives together of the law and the prophets—look back over the entire span of Jewish history and testify to the world that the Messiah, about whom all the law and all the prophets had spoken, not only had come but also had accomplished His redemptive work? Will they not likewise testify that the supremacy of the one true God is now to be seen in the Christ? that the glory of God is now to be seen in the face of Jesus Christ? (II Corinthians 4:6; cf. v4b).

Personally, therefore, I believe their testimony cannot be limited just to foretelling something that shall come to pass; rather, their testimony must be very full at that critical time because the One whom they have testified about in the past has already come, and has already been anointed by God to be Christ and Lord of the whole universe. A very full testimony is required because these two witnesses shall be contending with the enemy over the issue of who is to be worshiped, God or Satan, Christ or the beast. And thus they shall stand for the testimony that Jesus Christ is Lord (Philippians 2:11a), that God is in Jesus Christ (II Corinthians 5:19a), and that the glory of God is in the face of Jesus Christ (II Corinthians 4:6b).

Again, I say, I believe this must be their testimony and it must be a full one; for they shall be offering up this testimony when the whole world shall be under the power of the Antichrist and when he shall proclaim himself to be the god of the universe who must be worshiped by everyone. And given those critical circumstances, the response by these two witnesses in their capacity as representatives of the law and the prophets and even of the prophetic psalms (cf. Luke 24:44) must be a strong and full one, causing these two to stand up in resolute opposition to the beast and say, No! —for God, they shall proclaim, has set His Son as King upon His holy hill of Zion (Psalm 2:6-7 ASV) and everyone must worship Him.

Thus, I believe, shall be the force of their testimony, and because of their testimony, the 144,000 shall be able to overcome the beast. For their victory is confirmed by another vision which the apostle John was given to see and which is found in Revelation chapter 15:

> And I saw as [it were] a glass sea, mingled with fire, and those that had gained the victory over the beast and over its image, and over the number of its name, standing upon the glass sea, having harps of God. And

> they sing the song of Moses bondman of God, and the song of the Lamb ... (vv.1-3a).

Those who overcome the beast shall be standing on the glass sea singing the song of Moses and the song of the Lamb. Let us remind ourselves that the church will sing the song of the Lamb but not the song of Moses. These people, however, shall sing both songs—the song of Moses and the song of the Lamb. Hence, these must be the faithful Jewish remnant of the election of grace. By the strengthening of their hands through the strong and full testimony of those two witnesses they are able to stand to the end.

Whether these Jews shall bear their faithful testimony by life or by death, we do not know. But one thing we do know, they shall overcome the beast. Most certain is it towards the end that this faithful remnant—the 144,000—shall be given revelation to see that the Messiah for whom they have been waiting is Jesus Christ. They shall believe Him. It is known, of course, that it is only when the Lord appears on earth again that the whole Israelite nation shall be saved; but even before then, there shall be this faithful remnant who shall put their trust in the Lord Jesus, and they shall testify to the world that Jesus Christ is Lord.

Now if this shall be the case with the faithful remnant of the Jews at the end-time, how much more should it be true with us today. We who are believers in Christ are here for the testimony of Jesus. And our testimony must ever be that Jesus is Lord. No matter what happens on this earth, we know for certain of one basic truth—because it has been revealed to us—that God has declared that Jesus is the Christ and is the Lord over all. Let us realize that it shall not be easy for those two witnesses to bear their testimony, but because they were described as being the two olive trees, they were filled with the Spirit of God. If we want our testimony to be effective, too, we must be filled with the Spirit of God. Before we can manifest life we must have more of His Spirit. If we are not filled with the Holy Spirit then we cannot testify to the world of the supremacy of Christ.

Let us therefore acknowledge that though we are considering the Jews at this moment, the principle is the same. God wants us to be faithful witnesses for Him at all times, but how are we going to be faithful? We must seek to be filled with the Holy Spirit. He is in us, for when we believed in the Lord Jesus, the Spirit of God came to take up His dwelling place in us. And He shall never leave us nor forsake us—that is true. But that does not mean that because the Spirit dwells in us, He fills us. He dwells in us in order to fill us, but very often we do not allow Him to fill us. Instead, we fill our hearts with many other things. Consequently, what is necessary is for us to empty ourselves in order that we may give room to the Spirit of God who dwells in us so that He may fill us.

So how can we be filled with His Spirit? The answer is very simple. Let us prepare to become empty vessels. If we each become an empty vessel, then the oil of the Spirit of God will flow forth into us, but whenever we as vessels cease being emptied of ourselves and of the things of this world, then the oil of the Spirit shall cease flowing. Therefore, we need to be emptied all the time. We not only need to be emptied of the world, we need to be emptied of ourselves. And how are we to be emptied of self? Through the cross. The cross is the means for self-emptying. The Holy Spirit will apply the cross to our lives in order that we may be emptied; and to the extent that we are emptied will be the extent of our being filled. And when we are filled with the Holy Spirit there is godly power and effectiveness. We can testify to the world that Jesus is Lord.

Let us always bear in mind, however, that our testimony is not to be only a testimony in word. Our testimony must be the result of our life. Unless we live a life with the Lord, and unless in our life Jesus is truly Lord, we cannot bear a proper testimony to the world in telling them that Jesus is Lord, because it will not be effective. May we all therefore be very much before the Lord that He may be allowed to examine us and be given the rightful place that has heretofore been occupied by other things. As we come to Him He will surely shine upon us and reveal to us; and as He reveals to us, let us accept the cross and be emptied until there will only be room for the Spirit of God to fill us to overflowing, and then our testimony will be a strong, powerful and effective one.

Chapter Six

The Day of the Lord

And the sixth poured out his bowl on the great river Euphrates; and its water was dried up, that the way of the kings from the rising of the sun might be prepared. And I saw out of the mouth of the dragon, and out of the mouth of the beast, and out of the mouth of the false prophet, three unclean spirits, as frogs; for they are the spirits of demons, doing signs; which go out to the kings of the whole habitable world to gather them together to the war of that great day of God the Almighty. (Behold, I come as a thief. Blessed is he that watches and keeps his garments, that he may not walk naked, and that they may not see his shame.) And he gathered them together to the place called in Hebrew, Armagedon.

Revelation 16:12-16

And I saw the heaven opened, and behold, a white horse, and one sitting on it, called Faithful and True, and he judges and makes war in righteousness. And his eyes are a flame of fire, and upon his head many diadems, having a name written which no one knows but himself; and he is clothed with a garment dipped in blood; and his name is called The Word of God. And the armies which are in the heaven followed him upon white horses, clad in white, pure, fine linen. And out of his mouth goes a sharp two-edged sword, that with it he might smite the nations; and he shall shepherd them with an iron rod; and he treads the wine-press of the fury of the wrath of God the Almighty. And he has upon his garment, and upon his thigh, a name written, King of kings, and Lord of lords

Revelation 19:11-16

And as he was sitting upon the mount of Olives the disciples came to him privately, saying, Tell us, when shall these things be, and what is the sign of thy coming and the completion of the age? ...

For as the lightning goes forth from the east and shines to the west, so shall be the coming of the Son of man. For wherever the carcase is, there will be gathered the eagles. But immediately after the tribulation of those days the sun shall be darkened, and the moon not give her light, and the stars shall fall from heaven, and the powers of the heavens shall be shaken. And then shall appear the sign of the Son of man in heaven; and then shall all the tribes of the land lament, and they shall see the Son of man coming on the clouds of heaven with power and great glory. And he shall send his angels with a great sound of trumpet, and they shall gather together his elect from the four winds, from the one extremity of the heavens to the other extremity of them.

Matthew 24:3, 27-31

This today will be the concluding message on the testimony of Jesus in relation to the church, the world, and the Jews. In our many discussions together during these past months we have come quite far—even to the end of this age. And last time we described in some detail the Great Tribulation which will be coming upon the earth. And we mentioned last week that during the Great Tribulation, which is also called the time of Jacob's trouble, God will send two witnesses and they shall strengthen the hand of the faithful remnant of the Jews "who keep the commandments of God and have the testimony of Jesus" (Revelation 12:17b).

After the Great Tribulation of three and a half years the end will come. This end is very often described as "the day of the Lord," "the day of Jehovah," or "the great and terrible day of the Lord." This is a very specific and special term. It is a term related to Israel because many prophets of old used that term: the day of Jehovah, the day of the Lord, the great and terrible day, that day. What did they mean when using this term the day of the Lord?

The day of the Lord is a very different term from *the Lord's day*. We should not mix up these two terms. In the first chapter of Revelation we read that John was "in the Spirit on the Lord's day" (v.10a). That is a reference to the first day of the week. But the day of the Lord has a very different meaning attached to it. The first mentioning of that term is to be found in the book of Isaiah: "there shall be a day of Jehovah of hosts upon everything proud and lofty, and upon everything lifted up, and it shall be brought low" (2:12).

Usually, when anything is mentioned the first time in the Bible, it gives us a clue about something to which it has made reference or, as in this instance, a clue as to the meaning of the term introduced. And on this first occasion of this term's use, Isaiah was prophesying concerning Judah and Jerusalem. This therefore shows us that the term, the day of the Lord, is especially related to the Jews. He was prophesying about the future of the Jews when the Lord shall return to His people and His people shall return to Him.

Moreover, from this first mentioning of the day of the Lord we learn that He will judge everyone, for it is the day in which the Lord shall bring the proud and the lofty low. It is the day in which the Lord shall come in and take up the world and its responsibility upon himself. It is the day in which He shall judge His people as well as the nations.

But the day of the Lord is not only a day of judgment but also a day of vengeance: "it is the day of Jehovah's vengeance, the year of recompenses for the controversy of Zion" (Isaiah 34:8). Not only Isaiah but also the prophet Jeremiah spoke of this day of the Lord as being a day of vengeance:

> This is the day of the Lord Jehovah of hosts, a day of vengeance, that he may be avenged of his adversaries; and the sword shall devour, and it shall be sated and made drunk with their blood; for the Lord Jehovah of hosts hath a sacrifice in the north country, by the river Euphrates (46:10).

Of course, there are many other verses which we could read but I think these are sufficient in giving us a right impression of what that day is. Furthermore, in bringing together all the prophecies concerning the day of the Lord we will see that the day of the Lord is not a twenty-four-hour period. In the Bible the word day can be used to indicate different lengths of time. In this case, the term day of the Lord does not mean a normal day of twenty-four hours; rather, it means a period of time, and that period of time is going to be set apart for a specific purpose. God has set aside a time period in which to accomplish certain things. That period will be characterized or marked out by something which is specific or by a number of things which are specific.

In this particular case the day of the Lord includes a lot of things, such as the following. The day of the Lord shall be a day of judgment, which will not only be of Israel but of the nations as well. In the day of the Lord the nations of this world shall be gathered together into one place. Also, Jerusalem shall again be broken into and many Jews will be killed. Moreover, at some specific point in this time of great distress and trouble the Lord shall appear and His feet shall touch down upon the Mount of Olives, as Zechariah has prophesied (14:4). And He will come to fight against the nations in the last battle of this age, the battle of Armageddon (Zechariah 14:3a, Revelation 16:16). In addition, He will come to purify and to save His people. And at the end of this day or period of time, there shall come the hope of all the world: the longed-for golden age—even the millennial kingdom. All these many events are included in the day of the Lord.

Now in order to help us to understand all of this better, I think it will probably be best if we should simply take one prophet, concentrate on him, and learn from him what is meant by this term, the day of the Lord.

Today we divide the prophets into two groups: major prophets and minor prophets. But actually this is a man-made division, according to which, if a prophet says many words, he must be a major prophet; and if a prophet says less words he must be a minor prophet. But this may not really be the case in all instances. I am reminded here of the adage in the world which says that those who talk much learn less and those who talk less learn more.

Joel is one of the so-called minor prophets. All his prophecies which were recorded are to be found in only three chapters and which we know of today as the book of Joel. We do not know when this prophet lived but most likely he was among the early prophets of the nation of Judah. He must have prophesied quite early in the history of that nation. The burden of Joel—his prophecies—are centered upon one thing: the day of the Lord. In fact, the whole book of Joel is taken up with this theme.

At that time there was a plague which had struck the land—a plague of locusts. Heretofore, the land had looked like the garden of Eden (2:3b), but after the locusts had come it was left barren and desolate. So the nation of Judah was under a great plague. The people had lost their food, their livelihood, in fact, everything. As the prophet of God Joel saw in this plague a still sterner, more severe judgment of God to come. He therefore rose up to warn the people: he called the people to repent, by which he meant a repentance of the heart. It was no use, warned Joel, to continue offering sacrifices on the altar of God's temple if the heart was not right. If the people would only repent from their heart, then the coming judgment might be averted. That was the burden of the prophet Joel (1:13-14, 2:11-14).

Now you may have different ways of dividing Joel's book of three chapters in terms of an outline. But I think the easiest way to divide it is according to its chapters. Chapter one tells us of the plague and of Joel's description of it. He describes for us what happened and how terrible it was. Then in chapter 2 he moves on to another matter. He mentions the northern army which will come to the land and destroy the people. The plague was, of course, something in the present for him, but the northern army shall be a terrible phenomenon in the future. Joel therefore warned the people of the coming of an army from the north to destroy the nation, and so he called the people to repent (2:20ff.). But he then saw illustrated, as symbolized by both the plague of the locusts and the destruction by the northern army, a still further judgment coming. In other words, these calamities to him were but a foreshadowing of the great and terrible day of the Lord. Hence, chapter 2 is devoted to warning the people about the northern army whereas in chapter 3 the prophet concentrated on even the later coming catastrophe of the great day of the Lord.

Now that is a very simple outline. But outlining this book is not quite as simple as one might think because, unfortunately, the way these few chapters are divided in our English-language Bible is not accurate. We can leave chapter 1 alone, but when we come to chapters 2 and 3, we have a problem. Actually, chapter 2 verses 28 through 33 should be connected with, and be the beginning of, chapter 3. Indeed, the Hebrew Bible arranges it that way. Why should this be the case? Well, Joel chapter 2 verse 28 says this: "And it shall come to pass afterwards ..." Now please notice that word afterwards. What does that word signify? It is signifying that after what has been described already in chapter 2 has all been fulfilled, that after all those things have happened, then something more shall happen.

Now in chapter 2 we find that following his description in chapter 1 of the plague of locusts Joel then prophesied concerning the coming devastation of the northern army; but even so, he called God's people to repent and foretold the mercy of the Lord towards His people. He told of how God would bring His people back to the land and that they would have a time of peace and prosperity. Which therefore brings us up to the time of the coming of Messiah. Surely the coming of Messiah to His people should be viewed as a day of merciful and gracious visitation, but unfortunately the Jews did not understand and rejected Him at that time. Let us carefully notice how Joel phrased his prophetic utterance, noting in particular the two words of emphasis added:

> And it shall come to pass *afterwards* that I will pour out my Spirit upon all flesh; and your sons and your daughters shall prophesy, your old men shall dream dreams, your young men shall see visions. Yea, even upon the bondmen and upon the handmaids in those days will I pour out my Spirit. And I will shew wonders in the heavens and on the earth, blood, and fire, and pillars of smoke. The sun shall be changed to darkness, and the moon to blood, *before* the great and terrible day of Jehovah come (2:28-31).

Therefore, the use by Joel of the term afterwards concludes what has preceded it, and his use of the term before demarcates the conclusion of what shall be happening prior to the coming of "the great and terrible day of Jehovah." And thus, these two terms employed by Joel mark out another specific period that shall be characterized by one thing: I will pour out my Spirit upon all flesh.

On the day of Pentecost the apostle Peter got up and explained what had happened to the 120 saints of God who had gathered in the Upper Room at Jerusalem. He concluded with the prophetic words of Joel. Said Peter: "this is that which Joel had prophesied and which has now come" (see Acts 2:16). Why did Peter select these words from Joel as the apostle's explanation for what had just occurred with the 120 believers? Because Joel prophesied that "afterwards I will pour out my Spirit upon all flesh." Notice the words, all flesh. When the Bible uses that term it signifies the inclusion not only of the Jews but also of the Gentiles. The inhabitants of the whole world are included. We thus find here a new departure in the working of God. Whereas in the past it had appeared that God was concentrating himself on His chosen people the Jews, there now comes a new departure: God is going to do a new thing—He will pour out His Spirit upon *all* flesh.

Hence, the day of Pentecost constitutes the beginning of the fulfillment of this prophecy of Joel's. This, in fact, brings in the dispensation of the Holy Spirit, the dispensation of grace, the dispensation of the church: "I will pour out my Spirit upon all flesh." Let us bear in mind, however, that the day of Pentecost was only the beginning of this fulfillment. Ever since that day this prophecy has been and is still being fulfilled. God pours out His Spirit upon all flesh, thus signifying that Salvation is for all. God's word is being preached and the promise of the gift of the Spirit is being given to all—both to those near and to those far; that is, to us and to our children. Everyone who believes in the Lord Jesus shall receive God's Spirit (Acts 2:38-39).

But this period of grace shall be concluded, prophesied Joel, with the appearance of some very certain signs:

> And I will shew wonders in the heavens and on the earth, blood, and fire, and pillars of smoke. The sun shall be changed to darkness, and the moon to blood, before the great and terrible day of Jehovah come (2:30-31).

At the beginning of this period of God's grace, there was the outpouring of the Holy Spirit, and the whole period shall continue to be marked by the pouring out of God's Spirit; but towards the end, when the time period approaches its closure, it shall conclude with such terrible phenomena as blood and fire and pillars of smoke, with the sun being darkened and the moon being turned to blood, and so on. Now where in the New Testament do we find the fulfillment of all these signs being mentioned? During these past months we have been going through the book of Revelation, and in this book we have found these various phenomena mentioned again and again and again—in chapters 6, 8, 9, and 16. We can find the details of these foretold signs in all these chapters over and over again: blood, fire, pillars of smoke, the sun darkened, the moon turned to blood, and so forth. As a matter of fact, it is in the book of Revelation that one comes to *the end* of this period of grace. And Joel 2:33 then declares this concluding word of grace: "And it shall be that whosoever shall call upon the name of Jehovah shall be saved ..."

From the coming of the Holy Spirit on the day of Pentecost until the time that this period shall conclude with blood and fire and pillars of smoke, it shall have been a span of some 2,000 years. Oh, how merciful and long-suffering has been our God! And during that entire time whoever shall have called upon the Lord shall be saved. No matter where you are, no matter who you are, no matter what you have done, no matter what you have or do not have—all who shall call upon the name of the Lord shall be saved. What immeasurable grace!

Many of us gathered here today have called on the name of the Lord and by His grace we are saved. We are delivered from the great and terrible day which is yet to come, even, delivered from the wrath of God that is yet to come. Is there anyone present who has not yet called on the name of the Lord? What does it mean when the Bible says for us to call on the name of the Lord? It means that you must call upon the name of the Lord yourself. Your father or your mother, your brother or your sister, your son or your daughter, your uncle or aunt—none of them can do it for you. You must do so yourself. Have you done this?

What does the Bible indeed mean when it says for you to call upon the Lord? It means that it must be from your heart. You call upon the Lord, praying: "Lord, have mercy on me!" Have you done this? If you have done that, you shall be saved. This is in fact the promise for this period of grace. As long as this period of grace continues, the promise holds true. Just call on the name of the Lord and you shall be saved, with nothing else required. There is no other salvation but through the Lord Jesus (Acts 4:12). Look to the Lord Jesus, for when we say "look to the Lord," we mean for you to call upon Him. If you call upon the Lord Jesus, you shall be saved.

But then will come the great and terrible day of the Lord. This age of the world shall conclude with a great and terrible day. Yet who can escape? Only those who have already called upon the Lord and anyone who shall now today call upon His name. Will you therefore call and call now?

We see in chapter 3 of Joel that the prophet has described the great and terrible day of the Lord. During that period of time God will gather all the nations of the world to the valley of Jehoshaphat. Jehoshaphat was the name of a king of Judah, and that name means God judges. And probably in the time of Joel the memory of the victory in the valley of Jehoshaphat was still quite vivid in this prophet's mind. King Jehoshaphat had won a tremendous victory on the battlefield—yet not by means of an army of flesh and blood but by the simple means of praising God and singing to Him. God did a great thing for His people (II Chronicles 20:1-30), and perhaps that victory was still very living and fresh in the mind of the prophet.

So the prophet mentioned that God will gather all the nations to the valley of Jehoshaphat. Multitudes and multitudes will be gathered in the valley of decision (Joel 3:14) and there God will judge the nations, and there shall the last battle of this age be fought. In the Bible it is called the battle of Armageddon because it will be fought in the hill, plain, and valley area of Megiddo in Israel (see Zechariah 12:11, Revelation 16:16).

How will this battle come about? First, the armies of the nations will be gathering themselves in and around the land of Palestine (Revelation 16:12-16). We do not know for what reason they find their way there, but they do. Some say probably it will be in search of wealth. For in that area it is fabulous: oil, various mineral and other resources in the Dead Sea area, as well as other riches elsewhere in the vicinity of Palestine. And the armies of the world shall therefore gather in that area of the world trying to find these forms of wealth and consequently gain further power for themselves. And in the process they shall break into Jerusalem. More of the details can be found in the book of Zechariah, for I do not have the time to discuss them today here (Zechariah chapters 12-14 provide all the details). So these foreign armies shall break into Jerusalem and many Jews will be killed. Yet, in this crisic time of Jacob's trouble the Lord Jesus himself shall come back; and when His feet touch down upon the Mount of Olives, it will be split into two, with its two sides moving away from each other, thus leaving a wide valley pathway in between by which the Jews in Jerusalem can make their escape at that critical moment (Zechariah 14:4-5).

Some of you might wonder and ask, Can this be true? Shall it really be so, or is this mere prophecy to be taken with the proverbial grain of salt? Well, it so happened that many years ago some scientists discovered that within the Mount of Olives there is a quake fault line, and that should there be an earthquake, it is very possible that the whole mountain will be split in two.

Accordingly, the Lord shall return to deliver His people the Jews, and a great battle shall be fought in the hill and plains area of Megiddo. And among many other details the Bible describes the terribleness of that battle; and it is also mentioned by the Lord and by the prophets that God has, as it were, prepared a great feast for the birds, which feast shall occur along the river Euphrates (Jeremiah 46:10; Revelation 16:12-14, 16; 19:18-19, 21).

Moreover, all the Jewish tribes shall moan and cry when they witness the Lord coming in the cloud to deliver them (Matthew 24:30b). When they shall see Jesus with their own eyes they will greatly moan and cry. The day shall come when the Jews shall discover that the One whom they had despised and rejected at His first coming is the same One who will now deliver them at the end of the age. He is their Messiah whom they had previously rejected and had crucified. Finally, they shall receive and accept Him. In Zechariah we are told that the Jewish people in the coming day will come to moan and cry: the house of David; the house of Nathan; the house of Levi; the man and the woman. They will be in different groups repenting and crying and moaning because they did not know the Lord whom they had pierced on Calvary's hill; but then there will be a fountain open for the cleansing of Jerusalem (Zechariah 12:9-13:1). Then, as Paul has written in Romans, all of the tribes of Israel shall be saved (11:26a). Then will arrive the millennial kingdom, even the age to come.

Let us proceed, now, to explain—more than before—some very important Biblical terms. As was indicated earlier, in the Bible there is the term, the day of the Lord or its several variants; but there is also another day which is called, the day of Christ Jesus. However, we must be careful not to mix up the day of the Lord with the day of Christ Jesus, for in the Bible these are two very different days in meaning and outcome. The day of the Lord is especially related to the Jews whereas the day of Christ Jesus is especially related to the church. The day of the Lord tells us of the judgment to come, and after judgment, the restoration of the Jews; the day of Christ Jesus, however, tells us of the coming of the Lord Jesus to receive His bride. There will be a judgment seat of Christ to be experienced by all believers (II Corinthians 5:10), and there will be either reward or discipline for all believers as well.

This is the day told of in I Corinthians chapter 3. That day shall declare whether we had labored with gold, silver and precious stones or had labored with wood, straw and stubble. In that day every work of ours shall be made manifest and a fire shall appear and test everything (vv.10-15). And in I Corinthians chapter 5 Paul instructs the church at Corinth to deliver to Satan the man who had grossly sinned for the destruction of his flesh so that his spirit might be saved "in the day of the Lord Jesus" (v.5). And in II Corinthians chapter 1 we read Paul's word about the fact that the Christian may boast "in the day of the Lord Jesus" (v.14). Also, in Philippians chapter 1 the apostle encourages the believers to live in a way that they shall be pure and blameless in "Christ's day" (v.10b). From these passages of Scripture we learn that there is another day besides the day of the Lord. For the sake of clarity let us call it the day of Christ. The day of Christ and the day of the Lord are very different. The day of Christ is for the church—that is, for the Lord's people. Let us consider some further relevant passages of Scripture.

> Now we beseech you, brethren, by the coming of our Lord Jesus Christ, and by our gathering together unto him, that ye be not soon shaken in mind, or be troubled, neither by spirit, nor by word, nor by letter as from us, as that the day of Christ is at hand. Let no man deceive you by any means: for that day shall not

> come, except there come a falling away [some translations read: the apostasy, e.g., Darby, NASB] first, and that man of sin be revealed, the son of perdition; who opposeth and exalteth himself above all that is called God, or that is worshipped; so that he as God sitteth in the temple of God, shewing himself that he is God (II Thessalonians 2:1-4 KJV).

The day of Christ shall come under certain conditions. In this passage Paul comforts the saints by reminding them of these conditions. It so happened that some people had disturbed them by their having said that the day of Christ had already come. He told them not to be disturbed by those people. He mentioned that the day of Christ could not come unless two things first happen: one; the apostasy; and two, the appearing of the man of sin. Before these two events occur the day of Christ will not arrive. So do not be disturbed: the day of Christ has not yet arrived.

First, then, the day of Christ must be preceded by the apostasy. Many people have understood the original Greek word *apostasia* translated as apostasy or falling away as meaning the falling away of the church—that today God's people in general have fallen away from the faith, from the knowledge, and from the experience of the Lord Jesus. They further point out that even in Christianity today people have begun to raise questions such as, Is God dead? Could this be the apostasy mentioned in the Bible?

But some commentators have pointed out that the Greek original translated in English as apostasy should not be understood this way. In the Greek-language of the Bible that word translated as a falling away in the English-language Bible actually means "departing," and refers to departing or exiting rather than a falling away from the faith. Now if that be the case, then the departing in view here in this Thessalonian passage is related to all of the overcomers.

And, second, we know that the man of sin has not yet appeared because there is that which thus far has restrained him and continues to restrain him, the overcomers.

> And now ye know that which restrains, that he should be revealed in his own time. For the mystery of lawlessness already works; only there is he who restrains now until he be gone, and then the lawless one shall be revealed, whom the Lord Jesus shall consume with the breath of his mouth, and shall annul by the appearing of his coming (II Thessalonians 2:6-8).

When that which restrains, the overcomers, shall be gone—that is, raptured—then the man of sin, the Antichrist, shall appear. If this is the actual case, then it could very well be that the "departing" is related to "that which restrains." In other words, the departure or rapture of the overcomers.

So there must first be the apostasy and then the man of sin, the Antichrist, must appear. And then the Lord shall come in His glory and destroy the man of sin with His sword—that is, with the very words of His mouth. And when that happens, we know that this is the appearing of the Lord Jesus.

> But concerning the times and the seasons, brethren, ye have no need that ye should be written to, for ye know perfectly well yourselves, that the day of [the] Lord so comes as a thief by night (I Thessalonians 5:1-2).

In this passage and in II Peter 3:10 the translated English phrase, the day of the Lord, appears; but the definite article, the, is missing in the original language (Darby's version is the only one that has noted this). So it should instead read, the day of Lord. This day of Lord phrase is quite different in meaning from the day of *the* Lord phrase; instead, the first of these two phrases is the same as the day of Christ. This is because both these instances appearing in I Thessalonians 5:2 and II Peter 3:10 reveal that the way of His coming shall be as a thief. We know most assuredly that the day of Christ shall come like a thief; but if He shall come like lightning, then His coming in that instance shall not be a coming like a thief since lightning cannot be hidden. The lightning shall shine from the east to the west and everyone shall therefore see it. That, in fact, is the description—given by the Lord himself in His Olivet Discourse—of the coming of the Son of man on *the day of the Lord*: "For as the lightning goes forth from the east and shines to the west, so shall be the coming of the Son of man" (Matthew 24:27). But when Christ shall return to receive His own people as His bride, His coming shall be like a thief. Whereas the day of the Lord is for the Jews and He shall come like lightning in the open, His coming on the day of Christ shall be hidden like a thief, and for a very good reason which I shall attempt to explain in the time remaining today.

In the day of Christ we shall all be brought before Him at the judgment seat of Christ and all our life and works shall be judged by the Lord Jesus. Some believers shall be rewarded and some shall be disciplined (see again II Corinthians 5:10 and I Corinthians 3:10-15). But in the day of the Lord the Jews as a nation shall be judged, and those who repent shall be saved. Consequently, there are these two different days for two very different purposes. Let us briefly review again what was shared several weeks ago out of the book of Revelation.

When the apostle John wrote Revelation and was given the vision of the battle of Armageddon, he put in parentheses there something spoken by the risen and ascended Lord for the church—that is, for the Christians: "Behold I come as a thief. Blessed is he that watches …" (Revelation 16:15a). So in my commentary regarding the testimony of Jesus in relation to the Jews, I must put in a sobering word for the church and for the individual believer. The day of Christ is coming and when He shall come for the church, there will be no warning. He may come on any day and at any hour. He will come as a thief and He will take to himself that which is most precious to Him. Are you members of His body? If so, are you watchful and therefore ready? Let us all live with that day ever in view.

Paul wrote to Timothy thus: "I have run the course, I have fought the battle, I have kept the faith. And now a crown of righteousness is waiting for me, and it is not only for me but for all those who wait for and love his appearing" (see II Timothy 4:7-8). Again I would say: Let us all live with that day always in mind. Let us live with the light of that day upon us. Are we walking in a way whereby we can withstand the fire of judgment at the familial judgment seat of Christ? Do we live as one who is living in the environment of that day? Do we let that day govern our life because that day shall come suddenly as a thief? Let us ever be watchful and therefore prepared. Thus this is a parenthetical word for the church as we have been considering what God shall do to and for His chosen people, the Jews: "Behold, I come as a thief. Blessed is he that watches …"

TITLES AVAILABLE
from Christian Fellowship Publishers

By Stephen Kaung

Abiding in God
"But We See Jesus"—*the Life of the Lord Jesus*
Discipled to Christ—*As Seen in the Life of Simon Peter*
God's Purpose for the Family
The Gymnasium of Christ
In the Footsteps of Christ
The Key to "Revelation" – Vol. 1
The Key to "Revelation" – Vol. 2
Men After God's Own Heart—*Eight Biographies from the Book of Genesis*
Moses, the Servant of God
New Covenant Living & Ministry
Now We See the Church—*the Life of the Church, the Body of Christ*
Shepherding
The Songs of Degrees—*Meditations on Fifteen Psalms*
The Splendor of His Ways—*Seeing the Lord's End in Job*

<u>The "God Has Spoken" Series</u>
Seeing Christ in the Old Testament, Part One
Seeing Christ in the Old Testament, Part Two
Seeing Christ in the New Testament